Five Shades *of* Shadow

River Teeth Literary Nonfiction Prize

SERIES EDITORS:

Daniel Lehman, *Ashland University*

Joe Mackall, *Ashland University*

The *River Teeth* Literary Nonfiction
Prize is awarded to the best work of
literary nonfiction submitted to the
annual contest sponsored by *River
Teeth: A Journal of Nonfiction Narrative.*

•

Five Shades
of Shadow

Tracy Daugherty

University of Nebraska Press | Lincoln and London

Acknowledgments for previously published material appear on
pages ix–xi, which constitute an extension of the copyright page.

Library of Congress Cataloging-in-Publication Data

Daugherty, Tracy.
Five shades of shadow / Tracy Daugherty.
p. cm. — (River teeth literary nonfiction prize)
ISBN 0-8032-1723-4 (cloth : alk. paper)
1. Daugherty, Tracy. 2. Novelists, American—20th century—Biography.
3. Steinbeck, John, 1902–1968. Grapes of wrath. 4. Migrant agricultural
laborers in literature. 5. Rural families in literature. 6. Oklahoma
—In literature. 7. Oklahoma—History. I. Title. II. River teeth
literary nonfiction prize (Series)
PS3554.A85 Z464 2003
813'.54—dc21
[B]   2002029132

"N,"

For Margie and
Ehud, who pulled
me through; and for
Anne Daugherty
and Paul Heath

CONTENTS

ACKNOWLEDGMENTS

A Literary Fellowship from the National Endowment for the Arts aided the completion of this project.

For their extraordinary friendship in a time of need, I am deeply indebted to Jerry and Joyce Bryan, Betty Campbell, Jeff and Pam Mull, Molly Brown, Kris and Rich Daniels, Bill Potts, Chris Anderson, and Gregg Kleiner.

I am grateful to the editorial board of *River Teeth: A Journal of Nonfiction Narrative* and to the University of Nebraska Press, Dan Lehman, Shana Harrington, and most especially Joe Mackall for support, encouragement, and shrewd editorial advice. My appreciation to Kathryn Lang for her help, advice, and longstanding support of this project.

Thanks also to Gene, JoAnne, and Debra Daugherty, George Manner, Marshall Terry, Martha Grace Low, and my colleagues at Oregon State University. Finally, my thanks to Ted Leeson, a model of good sense and style.

Permission has been received to quote from the following:

"Pastures of Plenty," words and music by Woody Guthrie. TRO— Copyright © 1960 (Renewed) 1963 (Renewed) Ludlow Music, Inc., New York NY. Used by permission.

"Pretty Boy Floyd," by Woody Guthrie. Copyright © 1958 (Renewed) by Sanga Music, Inc. All rights reserved. Used by permission.

"So Long It's Been Good to Know Yuh (Dusty Old Dust)," words and music by Woody Guthrie. TRO—Copyright © 1940 (Renewed) 1950 (Renewed) 1963 (Renewed) Folkways Music Publishers, Inc., New York NY. Used by permission.

Songs by Merle Haggard: "The Bottle Let Me Down," Copyright 1966 (Renewed) Sony/ATV Songs LLC; "The Fightin' Side of Me," Copyright 1970 (Renewed) Sony/ATV Songs LLC; "Hungry Eyes," Copyright 1969 (Renewed) Sony/ATV Songs LLC; "I Take a Lot of Pride in What I Am," Copyright 1968 (Renewed) Sony/ATV Songs LLC; "Okie from Muskogee," Copyright 1969 (Renewed) Sony/ATV Songs LLC. "Winds of Change," Copyright 1996 Sony/ATV Songs LLC and Sierra Mountain Music. All rights administered by Sony/ATV Music Publishing, 8 Music Square West, Nashville TN 37203. All rights reserved. Used by permission.

"Sleepless City," by Federico Garcia Lorca, in *Poet in New York*, translated by Greg Simon. Translation copyright © 1988 by The Estate of Federico Garcia Lorca, and Greg Simon and Steven F. White. Reprinted by permission of Farrar, Straus, and Giroux, LLC., and by Penguin Books Ltd.

"Big Wind," by Theodore Roethke. Copyright 1947 by the United Chapters of Phi Beta Kappa, from *The Collected Poems of Theodore Roethke*. Used by permission of Doubleday, a division of Random House, Inc., and by Faber and Faber.

I am grateful to the editors of the following publications, in which these pieces first appeared:
Crab Orchard Review: "Ooby Dooby"

Gulf Coast: "Oratory"

The Corvallis Gazette-Times: portions of "Exiled in Lents" and "The Day of the Dead"

The Writer's Chronicle: "Riley"

The Daily Barometer: portions of "Hostile Territory"

The Georgia Review: "Restitution," in different form, entitled "Old Haunts"

Southwest Review: "After Murrah"

Clackamas Literary Review: "Amarillo"

Southern Review: "Superman," "Weedpatch"

River Teeth: A Journal of Nonfiction Narrative: "Bakersfield"

Five Shades of Shadow

Five Shades *of* Shadow

PROLOGUE **Light**

Neon horses appeared one night in the misty fields of Oregon's Willamette Valley, where I've lived now for fifteen years. Electric yellow haunches, tails, manes; blue eyes, stalky ears. Fetlocks and legs glimmered, thin as lipstick in the dark, drizzly air. Through them, in the moonlight, you could see the mist, the foothills of the Coast Range Mountains to the west, fresh mint growing, black, in the night's black soil. Driving down the highway, you weren't sure if you'd really glimpsed these figures grazing near rotting barns, the way you weren't sure if you'd seen a rabbit bound across the road just ahead of your headlights' dizzy swing. As the poet Dorianne Laux wrote of them, each horse stood calm, "bright hooves sunk in black nightgrass / head dipped like a spoon to a pool of earth / delicate spine . . . arched to the stars."

An Oregon artist, Martin Anderson, had sculpted the horses, and the state had decided to display them, for a month or so, along Interstate 5, which runs north/south through the valley, from Portland to the California border. I drove I-5 many nights, then—the mid-1990s. I was living with my wife in a town called Eugene and commuting forty miles north to Corvallis, where I taught fiction writing at Oregon State University. I hadn't heard about the horses, but one night, headsore after sitting through a meeting at which nothing was accomplished but bitterness over a slimming school budget, I saw them—odd, airy creatures poised against the foothills on one side of the road, and the snowy Cascades on the other. Suddenly, the Willamette Valley ceased being the dark, dreary expanse I had to drive through. It ceased being the gloomy labor of my commute, a blurry backdrop to my work stress. Inhabited now by unreal horses, it became *thought* as well as *place*, a dreamscape, an idea of itself, and my sensibilities, startled by stumbling across the unexpected, rose to meet it. In the following weeks, I would begin to study the Willamette Valley's history, to locate an idea of myself within an idea of it, the only way I could continue to live in this place I had, until then, resisted. I'd been raised in West Texas and southern Oklahoma: the Dust Bowl. The Willamette Valley was lovely, fertile, lush, but it wasn't home. I had come here in the mid-eighties for a job; early on, the job wasn't as rewarding as I'd hoped it would be, and so, spewing my discontent in all directions, I viewed the valley as disappointing too. No: I didn't view it at all. It was, as I say, backdrop for my inner uneasiness. Then the horses seduced me.

I didn't know it, then, but in those days I was a man whose marriage would fail just as his siftings through history took an urgent, disturbing turn; whose heart was weak enough to soon need surgery; and who was faltering, as fragile as an animal made of burning light.

Back then, I was working on a novel set in Oklahoma and based on my late grandfather's youth: an old-fashioned, unironic story about the economic hope socialism gave Oklahoma's farmers just before the First World War. In the mid-1990s, not only was socialism long gone from American life (along with most family farmers), so was the straightforward, unironic storytelling I'd first discovered reading *The Grapes of Wrath* as a child in my grandfather's house. A writer-friend assured me I was committing career suicide trying such a book in the age of hypertext, in the wake of postmodernism, blockbuster entertainments, and the ten-second attention span. I knew he was probably right. But at his death, my grandfather had left me boxes of handwritten notes and cassette tapes on which he'd recorded his personal history. He'd known I had literary aspirations as a boy, and he'd graciously encouraged me. I owed him his story. I'd always meant to set it down—straightforwardly, the only way he would have liked—and now, before his memory faded any further, I decided to do it. To hell with cultural, literary, and academic taste.

One morning I was sketching a scene set in Oklahoma City, where my grandfather had taken me, as a kid, to see the state capitol and other government buildings. The night before tackling this section of the book I had driven down the valley in clear moonlight. I don't remember if the horses were on display, but traveling the highway now I always saw them in my mind: reminders of the valley's mysteries, its history of migrants—for I'd discovered that hundreds of Texans and Oklahomans had fled failing farms in the Dust Bowl and wound up here, decades before I'd made a similar journey. Visual whispers, the horses contained for me the breath of vanished laborers, recalled roadside glimpses I'd had, in the mist, of present-day Mexican fruit-pickers—hidden lives tied to the Okie legacy. Each morning, as I wrote about Heartland farmers, early in the century, pinning their futures on Oklahoma City's politicians, I hoped to burnish my prose with some of the horses' glow: a whisper, a trace, an echo or breath of workers' buried lives, both back home and here in the Promised Land so many Okies had sought.

I finished sketching the scene and stopped for an early lunch. On the television news I saw a familiar office complex, then live shots of the same place blown to rubble. Someone had bombed the Alfred P. Murrah building. All morning, I'd roamed an imaginary Oklahoma City. Now it shattered against a ruined reality. Late that afternoon, on the phone, responding to an erroneous report that the bombers had been Middle Eastern terrorists, one of my Texas friends said, "Looks like Mohammed's been busy." Maybe because I'd been reading and writing about poor farmers betrayed by the government, I replied, "No. I think Bubba may have done it."

Early next morning, driving up the valley, I squinted through fog to see the wet road. Fields, foothills, trees—all obscured in gusts as madly elusive as the smoke I'd watched pouring from Murrah's gut. This was the shadow to the neon horses' light. They'd stirred love in me. The Murrah fog, grief. I wasn't aware of it that day, but because of the bombing, I'd spend the next three years scouring this valley, its connections to the rest of the West, the routes that led out of it to Oklahoma, Texas, California, and back again. I'd comb it, over and over, for an understanding of disruption while, in my weakened heart, love and grief embraced

The Oklahoma novel had already got me plumbing my family's past, recovering as much as I could of my regional heritage. The bombing increased the urgency I felt to gather remains—of family, history, landscape—before they were lost, and to find intersections between myself and others: cusps where we could meet, perhaps, to expand one another's notions of heritage and region. In the wake of the terrorist attacks on the World Trade Center and the Pentagon on September 11, 2001, the need to gather remains would touch many more American lives, and talk of "heritage" and "region," worldwide, would gain greater importance.

The essays that follow trace a five-year period of glancing back in order to look ahead more clearly. From West Texas and childhood, and early language-play; to family roots in Oklahoma; to young adulthood, migrations, and exile in the West; finally, to national history, which inevitably dovetails with the most intimate needs and desires, these pieces reflect an evolving sensibility.

The writer Judith Kitchen has said that a "shaping sensibility" rather than plot or theme "guides our understanding and becomes what we talk about when we talk about personal nonfiction." This sense of the form not only structures these essays but voices their subject as well. How do landscape, social class, and history shape a sensibility? Millions of people come from America's heartland. They don't all think alike, yet when they proudly call themselves "Texans" or "Oklahomans," what qualities do they think they share? What makes them proud to be Americans? More pertinent to the following pieces, what do my cotton-picking Oklahoma ancestors have to do with other American fieldworkers, now and in the past? What do Timothy McVeigh, the Oklahoma City bomber, and I—white men raised in America at the same moment—share?

Whether mentioned directly or not, the Oklahoma City bombing informs each sentence here. As though I were unmoored by an aftershock, the blast sent me whirling back to my childhood, to uprootings and personal disruptions, my earliest experiences with language, politics, art. The bombing's reverberations returned me to my own stories, some of them nearly forgotten, and introduced me to others. At one end of the route mapped here lies the Murrah building, broken and burning; at the other, migrant camps, fruit fields, sites of other displaced Oklahomans.

Finally, I hope, too, that those captured breaths are here, traces of vanished people we rarely glimpse in the mist. Nadine Gordimer has said writers should write as though they were already dead, watching life unfold as it has—as it will—without us. Maybe Oklahomans understand this perspective better than most. The Murrah survivors know our enduring community lies among the missing. We are all becoming ghosts.

1 | Hard Ground

Ooby Dooby

When I was a kid in West Texas, four or five years old, I'd sit in front of my family's black-and-white TV watching Roy Orbison and the Teen Kings. They did a local show each Saturday night, crooning rockabilly tunes from an echoey broadcast studio in Odessa, Texas, an oil and cattle town. I'd plunk on a cowboy hat, pluck at a plastic toy guitar, and wail along with Roy. This was the late fifties, a few years before the song "Pretty Woman" made Orbison an international star, but even early on, he wore black glasses and topped his square face with a sheath of hair as tight and slick as a bathing cap. No one else on the planet looked like him, even remotely—he was funnier than Captain Kangaroo (my morning show) and sang better, too—and I couldn't wait to shimmy with the T Kings, as I called them, to lose myself in their distinctive southwestern sound.

One night, their show was preempted by something else, and I was so upset, I squeezed behind my mama's Frigidaire, clutching my git-box, bawling in cramped privacy, and wouldn't come out for several minutes despite my parents' pleas.

I was hooked by the simple beat of the songs, thumping like an old, flat tire; thrilled by the testimonial nature of the lyrics. Though I didn't understand the tales of squandered love, loneliness, and loss (only my divorce, thirty years later, pressed those matters fully under my skin), I caught the confessional tone. I recognized the similarity to church-talk, to whispered conversations among serious adults, and knew something important was being witnessed to.

Years would pass before I'd hear of Woody Guthrie, before I'd understand that the base of Orbison's music lay in the gumbo of gospel, folk, and blues that came to be "country," but I was a fan of Okie music before I even knew what it was.

My dad was an Okie lured to Texas by shiny new oil derricks. "Ooby Dooby" he called Orbison after a song the Teen Kings sang. "Better grab your hat," he'd tell me after Saturday supper, settling into his leather La-Z-Boy to read his natural gas reports. "Ooby Dooby's about to come on."

My parents pointed proudly to the television and the refrigerator whenever neighbors dropped by: they were signs of my father's growing success as a petroleum geologist, his escape from the stuck economy in his hometown back in Cotton County, Oklahoma. Still, he could never put the place completely behind him. We visited frequently. And even at night, while we watched TV, Oklahoma seemed ever before us. The rough and rugged behavior of characters in all the shoot-'em-up shows came straight off the plains.

Other programs I remember latching onto as a child also mirrored my surroundings. There was *Highway Patrol*—Broderick Crawford quaking whenever he barked "10-4!" into his dispatch mike—and *Death Valley Days*, sponsored by Borax and hosted by a handsome young cowboy named Ronald Reagan.

I liked *Highway Patrol* not for the action or the cop plots, which were old hat even in television's infancy, but for the safety Broderick Crawford made me feel—he was a granite block of justice—and the shots of open roads, open skies. I couldn't even ride a bike yet, but like a ramblin' man in a country tune, I was restless already with the American passion for heading out—somewhere, anywhere.

I asked my mother what Borax was. She said she thought it was some kind of salt. I don't remember the stories on *Death Valley Days*; I was drawn to the vistas of deserts, skies, snaking roads. Death Valley looked an awful lot like West Texas to me, level, bleached by sun.

And in many ways beyond my childhood knowing, it *was* home—a cradle for the excesses that had shaped our national past and would shape the decades to come. The Wild West, tamed by the mythic cowboy (personified by Reagan, even then an icon of rough charm and individual resolve). The fecund earth, bursting with mineral riches, begging to be drilled, plowed, dug for the common good.

In the sixties Charlie Manson camped in Death Valley, in an old school bus with a smattering of his followers, brooding, tripping to the Beatles' "Helter Skelter," summoning the twisted energy that would, in part, sculpt those turbulent years—the years that first formed my awareness of the world beyond the barbed wire cattle fences of West Texas.

In the eighties Ronald Reagan would spend much of his presidency trying to snuff forces released in the Summer of Love. But in 1959, dancing to the T Kings, I hadn't the faintest idea of America's past or future. It was the twentieth anniversary of *The Grapes of Wrath*; descendants of the first waves of Okies struggled, still, in California's fields, alongside Latino families, but I didn't know that. The United States government had already blundered, significantly, in Southeast Asia, setting in motion a train wreck of events that would soon rip the nation's conscience; had already ignored the blight in its inner cities so consistently that racial violence was inevitable, but I didn't know any of that.

Though I couldn't see it then, Roy Orbison's music was a link both to the Dust Bowl (built on the swing beat that carried many Okies halfway across a continent) and to the coming Beatlemania, the psychedelic rhythms that fed a social revolution, swelling like a flood in the sixties. But I hadn't yet learned my country's history or learned to spot ripples of cultural change.

All I knew was the beat. The confessional pleading. The strange pleasure that came from wrapping private pain—"My baby, she left me this mornin' "—in a powerful public groove that made your body want to move.

I sawed on my plastic guitar. "Ooby Dooby," I sang. "Ooby Dooby."

When I became a teen myself—king of pimples, angst, and gloom—when the world began to feel larger, shakier than it had before (and I could no longer hide behind the fridge), my allegiance switched from Orbison to the much darker music of Merle Haggard. It seemed to me that Merle faced things squarely, and I was starting to see the value in that.

In his early tunes, he could sound almost as cantankerous as Timothy McVeigh would sound, thirty years later. Like McVeigh—though without, of course, the murderous violence—he offered an uncompromising vision of our nation. In the mid-sixties, while the wars on poverty and in Vietnam surged ahead, Merle sang defiantly his refusal to accept government handouts. At the same time, he insisted on saluting the flag; anyone who questioned America's values, he said, would end up on his "fightin' side"—"let this song be a warning."

Tougher than Roy Orbison's music, Merle's testimony scraped and twanged with echoes of beer cans pinging, trucks shifting gears, screen doors banging in sweltering midnight winds: small lives exploding in the TV glows of cramped, rented rooms. His people drove twisted old Mercurys or Pontiacs, just as Timothy McVeigh would back from Desert Storm, cruising the interstate between Kansas, Arizona, and Oklahoma, crossing the old Route 66, dreaming of blowing up buildings.

Born in the thirties in a refinery town called Oildale, just north of Bakersfield, California, Merle embodied the blue-collar life. He wrote about his mama's "hungry eyes," a "canvas-covered cabin / in a crowded labor camp" that stoked her misery. He wrote about a "class of people" that put his Okie family "somewhere just below" the top of the social heap, one more reason for his mother's sadness.

If faith and fidelity defined the Dust Bowlers, so, often, did hard drinking, honky-tonking, roaring violence, all of which Merle's music eloquently witnessed. Good and bad, the roots of his raising made him proud, he said. One newspaper dubbed him the "poet laureate of the hard hats," acknowledging the country's class divisions, the rigid cultural categories that, for better or worse, helped different economic groups find meaning in their attitudes and habits.

In 1969, President Richard Nixon sent Merle a note of congratulations for his swipes at draft dodgers, campus radicals, and hippies in his most famous song, "Okie from Muskogee."

Donald Hart, a former mayor of Bakersfield, once said, "I think Merle Haggard summed up our philosophy here. We respect and love America, its flags and its symbols. We believe in paternalism, a strong family . . . and the merits of good old hard work. That's all— nothin' very sophisticated about it."

Thirty years later, a year after Timothy McVeigh destroyed the Murrah building, Merle released a CD entitled, simply, *1996*, like a diary heading. Most of its songs were reflective, highly personal, uncertain—much more tentative than his, or the nation's, sixties swagger. He lamented the death of his father, his losses of love, his helplessness in the face of tragedies on the nightly news. Hard work was no longer exalted as an American philosophy; it served, instead, as a desperate means to ward off painful thoughts. He ached nostalgically for the privacies of childhood, "before there was a [public] Merle."

If Timothy McVeigh, like a hard-hatted hard-liner, was now insisting on a new American symbol—let this blast be a warning—Merle was no longer defiant. As he sang about "bombs aflying and people dying," his mellow voice cracked like a log on a grate.

By 1996, what had once seemed unsophisticated about America—cultural categories, class behaviors, work, music, *meanings*—had become a perplexing social mess. "At many of Merle's concerts in Oklahoma now," the historian Roxanne Dunbar-Ortiz told me recently, "thousands of folks light joints whenever he sings, 'We don't smoke marijuana in Muskogee.'"

Nowadays, the world feels larger and shakier to most American baby boomers than ever before; mindful of tragedies, present and past, nostalgic for the innocence of the Teen Kings, I listen most often to this doubtful Merle, fretting about Mother Nature—her dwindling forests and factory-brown streams. He sounds less like a working stiff than like an old granola-head. All around us, he says, salmon, eagles, and bears are vanishing like runaway kids. Weary, sad, he pleads for us all to "stop the wrong we're doing."

"Amen," I say, cranking up the volume. "Ooby Dooby."

Oratory

I fell in love with language listening to country music. The lyrics didn't mean much to me when I was six or seven, but the rhymes were fun and made me strain to listen through the static on the transistor radio my father gave me. He worked for the Sinclair Oil and Gas Company. He'd gotten the radio at his office, part of an ad campaign. It was shaped like a gas pump, with Dino the Dinosaur stamped on the front. At night I held it to my ear, laughing at singers crooning "moon/June," "boot/suit." In time, the song's narrators made me long for fertile farms, pickup trucks, horses swift as light.

As I learned to read, I kept the radio near. *The Cat in the Hat, Little House on the Prairie, The Martian Chronicles* unfolded against Roy Orbison's laments. KOMA out of Oklahoma City was the only station strong enough to speak through my gas pump at night. Every few minutes the DJs played drag-racing ads—"*Be* there! *Be* there! *Be* there!"

Song lyrics, Dr. Seuss, and sci-fi immersed me in words, but

I trace my true literary impulses to my grandfather Harry Tracy Daugherty, named after a populist rabble-rouser. My great-grandfather was a populist—later a socialist—farmer in southern Oklahoma. One day, at a revival meeting in 1898, he heard Harry Tracy inveigh against capitalism and racism. He was so impressed, he appropriated the man's name for his son (he named his second boy after Fred Warren, who published the great socialist paper *Appeal to Reason* until the government shut it down during the First World War).

As a child, my grandfather displayed a precocious talent for public speaking. His dad taught him the socialist gospel, toured him by horse and buggy through Oklahoma and northern Texas, and set him up on street-corner soapboxes to spread the Word. He became known as "The Boy Orator," and the first time I saw my name in print, it was on a yellowed flier in his scrapbook proclaiming Tracy Daugherty a "GOOD LOUD SPEAKER" and "Oklahoma's finest young lecturer."

He went on to a distinguished political career, serving twice in the Oklahoma House of Representatives. Throughout my childhood, I thrilled to see his name—*my* name—on campaign posters, emery boards, and buttons, and in newspaper ads. Willa Cather once said her impulse to write came from seeing her name in print, in a newspaper piece. I know the feeling.

I don't come from a family of readers. Novels and poems were scarce in our home. Each night after supper my mother skimmed the paper, and my father pored over natural gas reports on letterhead embossed with the same green dinosaur imprinted on my radio. Not until my grandfather gave me *The Grapes of Wrath* did I understand language's power to evoke the world, to illuminate the daily struggles of women and men. Once I'd met the Joads, sci-fi seemed silly. Steinbeck's novel was a country song writ large, with passion, tragedy, and humor. It was a cry of rage and sympathy for the poor, like my grandfather's speeches—and sent me *back* to his talks, studying each metaphor, every nuance and pause.

My relationship to crafted language, then, is rooted in the tradition of American oratory. The sermon. The soapbox speech. The call to arms. I'm also compelled by the fact that my first name can be traced to a muckraker.

Soon after writing my first short stories, I discovered literary critics who insisted that politics and art don't mix. Of *Grapes*, Edmund Wilson said, "Human sentiments and speeches [have] been assigned [here] to a flock of lemmings"—the Joads—who simply mouth their author's opinions. But because my grandfather was a speechwriter and a politician, someone who delighted in turns of phrase as much as turns of fortune, I believed aesthetics and social ethics were inseparable. When he told a crowd, in October 1933, after witnessing an electrocution at the state prison in McAlester (where Tom Joad served time), "To watch men die and call it Justice, a man must be imbibing very freely on Oklahoma's Mountain Dew," no one could tell me the *zizzle* of art wasn't traipsing through his language.

American oratory is now in decline, in both our public life and our literature. Among other factors, television's (and now the Internet's) love of the instantaneous has reduced our national vocabulary to byte-sized bits of rubble. Even country lyrics are watered down, lately, with fewer and fewer narratives. But the epic effort to *speak* hasn't fully been silenced. Recently, Ralph Ellison's unfinished novel, *Juneteenth*, appeared posthumously. Ellison grew up in Oklahoma and shared my grandfather's linguistic tradition; his book attests to the power of oratory and—to my mind—leads us back to the wellsprings of American literary art. *Juneteenth* thunders and rolls like a summer storm, its heat lightning pulsing to the beat of Cotton Mather, Abraham Lincoln, Gene Debs, Kate O'Hare, Mother Jones, Martin Luther King; to the cotton-picking agony of field-hollers and the spontaneous release of hoedowns.

Listen: "History erupts and boils with its age-old contentions. But ours is the freedom and decision of the New, the Uncluttered, and we embrace the anguish of our predicament, we accept the penalties of our hopefulness."

That Ellison worked nearly forty years on this visionary American portrait and was unable to complete it tells us in part how vast and shifting our democratic ideals remain. Art and democracy converge, he wrote, "with the development of conscious, articulate citizens [reflected in] the creation of conscious, articulate characters," particularly characters who can speak for the perennially disenfranchised, as well as for the broader population.

As a boy in Oklahoma City, he spent time in the capitol building, absorbing not only the senators' oratorical flourishes but the basement talk of the maintenance men. For Ellison, as well as my grandfather, Oklahoma was the Territory Huck Finn, the quintessential American, sought; a prairie of possibility; a "chaos" of freedom and "frontier attitudes" that encouraged the "individual's imagination . . . to range widely and sometimes even to soar." It was a place where utopian dreams met religious rhetoric and collided with political speech—a "mammy-made" mix of black and white rhythms, jokes, talk. Reading *Juneteenth*, I heard my grandfather's high-plains populism and realized his syntax came indirectly from Oklahoma's black churches.

"On the level of *conscious* culture the Negro community [in Oklahoma City] was biased in the direction of music," Ellison said. Jazz, not country, formed the pulse behind his prose—though Okie music, like Okie speech, is a stylistic collage. Jazz variations are readily apparent in the swing beat that accompanied black and white farmers from Oklahoma to California's fruit fields in the "dirty thirties."

In his speeches, through long years of public service, my grandfather railed against the economic power of corporate giants, opposed the Vietnam War, defended civil rights. Now, many of his utopian dreams seem naive. Socialism has gone the way of the dinosaurs. Cynicism rules public speech.

In 1888, Edward Bellamy foresaw that most twentieth-century

Americans would quit fighting for social equities, having "accustom[ed] themselves" to luxuries that seemed "to leave nothing to be desired."

But *Juneteenth* reminds us that the Territory is still there to be shaped for the good of all, and that oratory, at its best, transcends the value judgments, catch phrases, and slogans that dominate our communal debates. It recognizes the link between individual and group identity. Ellison once said the "search for identity" is "*the* American theme." As he learned in Oklahoma by listening to music, street-corner jokes, swelling speeches, on some level all Americans dance to the same beat.

Reviewing *Juneteenth* in the *Indianapolis Star* in June 2001, Dan Carpenter said, "To be [truly] of this land is to have jazz and the blues and . . . back-and-forth wordplay . . . in your DNA, if not on your tongue. If you honor forbearance and forgiveness as national virtues, you are the actual or spiritual descendant of slaves." This strikes me, grandson of an orator, as a profound, and struggle-worthy, identity for any American writer.

Nothing

Growing up in West Texas's blasted terrain, trying to picture the future, my friends and I wondered, Where are we headed? What's out there? We were surrounded by land that supported little life, trapped in a petroleum economy that lined the bosses' pockets but sentenced most of us—poorly educated in mediocre schools, bathed in TV light, thrumming to the beat of country music—to a life of dangerous labor in the oil fields unless we were somehow lucky enough to stumble out of there.

The ground was flat as a map, only blank. The sky was relentless, switching unpredictably from spooky silence to howls whenever a sandstorm approached. It pressed loneliness into the skin of anyone who lived there. In my loneliness I discovered words—listening to song lyrics and my grandfather's speeches, reading books whenever I ducked into the public library to get out of the wind. Singers used words to get on the radio; my grandfather used them to reach Oklahoma's halls of power. Maybe words could be my way out, too.

Sometimes, after school, I'd visit my father downtown, in his office at Sinclair Oil and Gas, passing on the way a Church of Christ with its big yellow sign: "Have You Been Redeemed?" His walls were covered with floor-to-ceiling maps: guides to oil and gas underground. Tracing red and blue lines with my fingers, remembering the church's question, I saw them as "Roads Out," "Paths to Redemption."

But how could I find my way clear? What stories did I have to tell? Whenever I kicked around for material I uncovered desiccation, dusty, brown space.

Cartographers, like storytellers, speak of "point of view." I began to comprehend this, listening to my father and his colleagues poring over maps. For a storyteller, "point of view" means who's relating the story and to whom. For cartographers, it means "orientation." To map a place you need a center from which to begin, some distinguishing landmark—a boulder, a crater.

But in West Texas, it's tough to find distinctive landmarks. When I looked around I saw nothing. In time, keeping an eye on my father's work, I understood that the only way to become oriented in a disorienting world is to move into *whatever*'s out there, however harsh and unpromising it may seem. I discovered . . . slowly, as you'd unroll a delicate chart . . . I had to head into the wilderness, a place without givens, to find my words. From the mappers, hunting subduction zones and hairline faults, I learned to follow details. Beer bottles, trailer homes, daily trips to the store: "nothings" that most of us take for granted. But they can be starting points.

One day, in the library, I came upon Wallace Stevens's poem "Anecdote of a Jar": "It made the slovenly wilderness / Surround that hill."

An ordinary jar, *ordering the world!* Fired by the notion, I strolled through downtown Midland noting every scrap of paper, every tumbleweed and tossed-away tobacco tin. I came to the Church of Christ sign. Beneath it, on the sidewalk, an empty soft drink bottle. On it, "This bottle can be redeemed for 5 cents." A discarded barbecued beef sandwich lay beside it.

I kept walking, looking: a scrap of cloud across the sun, a poker chip wedged into sand, a rock 'n' roll record, broken and left in the street, an old fruit jar, the value of which both Wallace Stevens and Chuck Berry knew. For the first time in my life I felt centered. I believed I could pull the land and sky around me, a long, starry quilt—a quilt that looked like a map. There's nothing out there, I thought, and it's all so rich. Trudging through it, we find our stories. We learn to orient ourselves. We stumble to redemption. I wandered all afternoon, and well into the evening.

Okies on Mars

In 1968, I saw *2001: A Space Odyssey* eight times in two weeks. I was thirteen, and like most of my friends, fascinated by NASA, the moon race, rockets in general. After all, we were space-age kids, born along with Sputnik. By '68 I'd set aside the science fiction novels I'd been hooked on for years in favor of John Steinbeck's social realism (the Joads were family), but I followed the Apollo program closely and worshiped the astronauts. *2001*'s soft-voiced computer, HAL, and its lush special effects—like nothing I'd seen before, like reports of LSD trips—made me yearn again for the stars.

Or made me just yearn. Ray Bradbury had been my favorite sci-fi writer; even as a youngster, I understood that a large part of his appeal was his ability to evoke the American high plains. His stories were set in the future, but many of his heroes were average boys longing to escape the Midwest and follow their dreams to the edge of the universe:

One minute it was . . . winter, with doors closed, windows locked, the panes blind with frost, icicles fringing every roof . . . housewives lumbering like great black bears in their furs along the icy streets.

And then a long wave of warmth crossed the small town. A flooding sea of hot air; it seemed as if someone had left a bakery door open. The heat pulsed among the cottages and bushes and children. The icicles dropped, shattering to melt. The doors flew open. The windows flew up. The children worked off their wool clothes.

The housewives shed their bear disguises. The snow dissolved and showed last summer's ancient green lawns.

Rocket summer. The words passed among the people in the open, airing houses. *Rocket summer.* The warm desert air changing the frost patterns on the windows, erasing the art work . . . The snow, falling from the cold sky upon the town, turned to a hot rain before it touched the ground.

His stories were less about aliens, wormholes, and time warps than American restlessness. His stories were about social strictures, social class, and the daring it took to imagine your way out of poverty. As the writer Mike Davis puts it, "Bradbury's *Martian Chronicles* (1950) revolves around contradictions between the . . . 'westering' quest for new frontiers and poignant nostalgia for small-town America. In a sense, Bradbury took the angst of the dislocated Midwesterner in Los Angeles and projected it as extraterrestrial destiny."

In my development as a reader, it was a natural progression, then, from *The Martian Chronicles* to *The Grapes of Wrath*. Read a certain way, they told the same tale of contemporary American history. During and after the war, Dust Bowl Okies were lured west by the burgeoning aerospace and military industries to work in defense plants, nuclear reactors, rocket labs—sold the dream of the future and encouraged to link their lives to it. At the end of *The Martian Chronicles*, when a boy, along with his migrant family, looks into a Martian canal, sees his reflection in the water, and recognizes *he* is the new Martian, he is a literary descendant of a rootless Joad. As both books foresaw, indirectly, in the fifties and sixties, massive Okie energy went into fashioning gadgets that would propel America into its future.

I spent the first grade in Roswell, New Mexico. My father had been transferred there to develop new oil fields. Rumors ran through school that a flying saucer had crashed near Roswell in 1947, and that alien bodies were still being studied, in secret, in an airplane hangar on the edge of town. I believed these stories and didn't. Even to my impressionable mind, they sounded like fairy tales. On the other hand, every day brought the future crashing into our lives, and anything seemed possible. "Duck and cover!" our teacher told us, hustling us under our desks during nuclear safety drills. "If an atomic bomb falls, put your hands over your heads, like this!" The oil tanks my father took me to see in the desert (where the warehoused aliens lay?) looked like spaceships hovering against the horizon.

A year later, when we moved back to West Texas, I heard stories about "mystery lights" in the skies over Marfa, a town not far away (by Texas standards) where Elizabeth Taylor and James Dean had filmed the oil epic *Giant*. Already, that movie's Texas looked old-fashioned and innocent. It seemed to me *rocket summer* was upon us, and it frightened me. The world was full of phenomena I didn't understand and couldn't control. I waited for a swift, hot rain.

Now that the twentieth century is over, it's a fashionable journalistic exercise to revisit *A Space Odyssey* and snicker at the lousy job it did predicting the future. In the real 2001, there were no orbiting Hiltons, moon bases, or computers remotely as intelligent as HAL (or as *large* as HAL—the filmmakers failed to foresee computer chips and micro-miniaturization). The technology existed for television-phones, but they were not affordable for common use, and Pan Am, bankrupted twice since the sixties, could barely make Bangor from Portsmouth, Maine, on a weekend special, much less the moon.

But all of this misses the point. In 1968, Martin Luther King Jr. and Bobby Kennedy were shot to death. Street riots engulfed Chicago's Democratic national convention. College campuses were paralyzed by Vietnam War protesters. I saw it in my parents' faces: the world was coming apart and they were scared. For them, *rocket summer* meant, just possibly, losing their American dream, losing their children to senseless violence. In the midst of all this, *2001* showed filmgoers new possibilities—a future chilly and uncertain, yes, but also graceful (a space station spinning to "The Blue Danube" waltz!). It showed us dazzling colors and a splendid vision of rebirth, a vision we sorely needed that year.

Much more important than counting the film's errors is to try to understand *why* it missed the mark. After all, Neil Armstrong walked on the moon a year after the movie's release; it wasn't so far-fetched to imagine that, thirty-two years later, people would make regular trips to the Sea of Tranquillity. What went wrong?

Michael Prowse, a columnist for London's *Financial Times*, offers an explanation. He suggests that the "greatest shortcoming of futurologists . . . [and] sci fi writers lies in the economic field. None of them [in the fifties and sixties] had any inkling of the way that markets would come to dominate our lives. Nobody expected the revival of a largely unregulated global capitalism involving . . . the loss of job security for all but an elite. Nobody expected that politicians would wage war on . . . education, health care, and the civil service."

A misplaced faith in technology's ability to improve our lives, a blind eye toward partisan politics, economic power plays, laborers who generate capital—is there any better summary of the Cold War mind-set? For wasn't it the Cold War that seduced us into loving the power of rockets? Racing for the moon? Excusing economic exploitation for the sake of "national security"? Looking back, I wonder: Didn't HAL speak with the paternal voices of Johnson and Nixon when he told his human companions, "I can't allow you to jeopardize this mission. It's too important"? Wasn't it the Cold War we feared in HAL, in UFO reports? Wasn't it the Cold War that failed the future, with flawed visions of resources, money, and people, sparking useless wars, costly technological fiascos, environmental destruction? And isn't it the persistence of competitive Cold War thinking that fuels today's global economy? As it turns out, the year 2001 will be remembered for the collapse of the World Trade Center, not for trips to Jupiter—and many observers have noted the links between globalization and the spread of poverty and terrorism.

In *Blue Sky Dream*, David Beers, the son of a fighter pilot, writes, "[When I was a child,] Sputnik was my lucky star, its appearance in the darkness a glimmering, beeping announcement that my family would not know want." In the late 1950s, the G.I. Bill, housing loans, and government spending on computer development and aerospace created what Beers calls the "blue sky tribe," a new middle class who worshiped a "God [endorsing] progress, personal and national," and who believed they would live happily ever after in spotless, crime-free suburbs. For Okies, invited to join the tribe, these western suburbs were as weird and wonderful as Mars. Many flourished in the new economy until it failed in the 1980s, a crash no one predicted. Many others—pilots killed in Vietnam, workers exposed to radiation, farmers left behind by shifting national priorities, who'd later think of bombing buildings in their rage—could never have foreseen the consequences of what turned out to be, in so many ways, the false promise of the skies.

Superman

In 1961, when I was six, Sinclair Oil and Gas transferred my father from Midland, Texas, to Roswell, New Mexico. Eight months later, his bosses sent him back to Midland. The first move didn't upset me; it was an adventure, a chance to see snow for the first time, to hear flying saucer stories in the desert, and to meet new playmates. But returning home without *having* a home—we'd sold the house I first knew—and living on the outskirts in a rundown motel while my parents searched for a reasonable three-bedroom gave me a dislocated feeling I hadn't known before.

The Kangaroo Courts Motel sprawled next to what my father called a "greasy spoon" on Highway 20, "one of the flattest, straightest roads in America." Right away, I knew my mother was uneasy here, trying to keep my baby sister and me happy and quiet in a hot, cramped room while semis rolled in and out of the café parking lot next door, bottles broke, and people yelled at one another after-hours in the alley separating the café and the Courts.

She paced the room, dusting the faded orange curtains with cigarette smoke. At night I whisked open the drapes above the bed my sister and I shared, bounced on the mattress, and stared out the smudged window at KCRS's radio towers across the road, with their blinking red lights. Somehow, Roy Orbison's heart-breaking voice traveled up those rusted steel towers, pulsed into the lingering purple sunset, and aimed its way inside the squawky transistor radio on the nightstand next to my mother's cold cream jar. Tumbleweeds blew across I-20, snagged on the towers, and clutched the chain link fence surrounding the motel's swimming pool. The water looked muddy. A stale French fry odor seeped beneath the door; snores, laughter, weeping skittered like muffled animals inside the walls.

My mother left the Gideon Bible open on the dresser by the bathroom, to remind me to say my evening prayers. She'd prop her pillow against the wall and sit up in bed doing crosswords in the local paper, asking my father, "What's a six-letter word for—?" Sometimes she'd teach me definitions from the puzzles: *possibility, uncertainty, contradiction*. The last sound I heard each night, before drifting into dreams, was my father brushing his teeth, spitting into the sink with a force that made him seem disgusted with something. As I lay in bed, I could see through a space between the drapes. Dust obscured the stars. When I woke in the mornings Dad was gone, called upon to target oil beneath West Texas's fertile emptiness.

My dreams took the shapes of TV shows my sister and I watched all day, hanging off the unmade bed while my mother stood in the open doorway, smoking, flicking ashes into an Appaloosa-colored ashtray, blinking against sand in the air, and gazing nervously next door at transients, truckers, squabbling couples. Jets thundered low, on maneuvers out of a nearby Air Force base, rattling the windows, frightening birds. In the doorway's buttery light, Mama looked mousy, thin as a telephone pole.

Crimes, mysteries, romances—erratic, shifting, and as swiftly vanishing as soap bubbles—filled my mind while I dozed. My waking dreams, too, were shaped by the screen on the set that was bolted to the green pine wall. I wanted to fly the way Superman did—longed to soar toward the towers, snatch Orbison's warble, tuck it under my cape, and sprinkle it bit by bit over Earth's remotest areas, refreshing them with the peaceful sadness that, even as a kid, I felt only a lone balladeer could voice.

My father had taught me the word "balladeer" one night as we listened to the radio, and though I didn't have language, then, for my deepest feelings, I saw myself, based on my family role, as a quiet observer of the world's disharmonies: a highway's comings and goings, a mother's unhappiness. But I didn't have a real guitar, and more and more, I wanted to be a muscle-bound hero.

I watched, rapt, as Superman ripped open flying saucers—the kinds of spacecraft my classmates in Roswell said had crashed into the desert. I cheered as he punched aliens into oblivion. In New Mexico, my father had been summoned daily into the middle of nowhere, to check on oil rigs and roughnecking crews. I always feared he'd run into extraterrestrials and be spirited away to Mars.

One afternoon, while my sister napped and I watched TV, my mother spoke on the phone to her brother Bill in Oklahoma: ". . . wouldn't even negotiate a moving fee," she said. "Refuses to move us to a nicer motel. I swear, you'd think we were *poor*. I mean, I know we'll never be Rockefellers, but . . . he says we've got to save all we can for a down payment. Says I've got to be patient."

In the parking lot next door a woman started screaming, "No no no!" I leaped up on the bed and made for the window. A T-shirted man in oily brown overalls held a brunette by the arm. She wore a sleeveless blue dress, no shoes. They swung long-necked beer bottles at each other's blowing hair. On the highway beyond, cars hurtled into a low wall of sand.

"Bill," my mother sighed, the way Lois cooed to Superman whenever he plucked her from danger.

In years to come, at college parties with theater-major friends, I heard that George Reeves, who played Superman on television, came to believe he really did possess super powers and killed himself trying to fly off a building. In fact, he shot himself in the head, despondent over being typecast as the Man of Steel, trapped in a dead-end job.

It was George Reeves we watched in the afternoons at the Kangaroo Courts. His arms and chest were doughy. He had a soft middle. But I believed he was the strongest man on the planet. He had (I see now) a working-class face, with a massive jaw and hair so greased you knew it was too restless to lie flat for long. He had the high cheekbones of my Uncle Bill, who, more than anyone else in the family, showed the Kiowa blood in our ancestry—a great-great-great-grandmother somewhere. Because he looked like Bill, I thought of him as an oil field worker: the toughest guys I'd ever seen. Bill could lift the back end of a car off the ground—I'd watched him do it, once, while helping my mother change a flat tire on a dirt road in southern Oklahoma. What else could Superman be but a roughneck? Forget that Clark Kent stuff.

"I wish you could come take me home," my mother said to her brother. Glass shattered outside, and she closed her eyes tightly.

We were getting cheeseburgers one day at the greasy spoon. My mother stood at the counter, holding my sister in one arm, pulling quarters from her purse with her free hand. I sat on a metal stool bolted to the floor. Everything around here was nailed down, I realized, as if the wind might carry it all away. In the booths, men and women in checkered shirts and dresses nodded, half-asleep, over coffee. The place smelled rancid. An upbeat female singer chirped from the flashing yellow jukebox. The March of Dimes gumball machine was as red as Superman's cape.

"How you figger *that*, huh?" a dry voice croaked behind me. "How you figger you're worth one good crap a day without *me*? Huh?"

I turned to see the man in brown overalls, the one I'd witnessed in the parking lot before, addressing the same woman in the same blue dress. In the whole joint, only my mother, my sister, and I paid any attention to them. "What the hell *you* looking at, lady?" the man said to my mother. She stumbled back, against the counter. My sister started to cry. "This ain't the damn Barnum and Bailey!" I tensed my knees, ready to leap on him, make him apologize, but my limbs wouldn't move. The couple left. Tersely, my mother told me to grab our food sacks, and we returned to the motel in a fierce breeze that blew her tears into the dirt.

The rest of that afternoon she smoked more than usual, one after the other, while my sister wailed on a scratchy pillow and I changed channels compulsively, unable to concentrate or relax. I sneaked glances at my mother, who paced between the phone and the door, blowing her nose into a ratty pink Kleenex. She tried Bill three times. No answer. I suggested, "He's probably out on a derrick." She glared at me the way the man had stared down the woman. "Every man in my family winds up in an oil field," she said softly, as though this were my fault. "What's so damned attractive about an old *oil field*?" She lit another Lucky Strike. Her fingers shook.

"Is Uncle Bill going to take you away?"

"Your sister's hungry." Then she went to stand in the doorway again, brushing back her hair like the smiling women on highway billboards.

I tugged some beef out of a burger, held it to my sister's mouth. She sniffed, giggled, still with tears on her face, and slapped it to the gritty gray carpet.

I'd failed to be a hero in the greasy spoon. Now, as though guilt were a spring inside me, I leaped off the bed, threw myself on the meat—it was a tiny ticking bomb!—and hurled it across the room, away from the baby. It bounced off the TV, then the closet door, and hit my mother's shoulder. She stood there, looking my way but not flinching.

My father pulled up in his Olds, a company rental, just as the sky was starting to purple. His tie hung loose around his neck. Yellow circles darkened his shirt beneath his arms. "Dinner!" he called heartily and held up three sacks of burgers and fries. My mother, on her bed, turned away, rubbing cold cream into her hands. She wore a sleeveless orange blouse. A black bra strap slid down one of her arms. A crossword lay open before her; nestled in an uneven fold of the paper, a chewed-on pencil.

"Lookee here." My father waved me over. From his pants pocket he pulled a brand-new transistor radio shaped like a gas pump. "And see, it's got Dino the Dinosaur stamped on the front!" He slipped it into my hands. "Company's giving them away as promotional gimmicks," he told Mama. No response. He turned back to me. "You and me and ol' Roy, eh? Together we're the desert balladeers! Ooby Dooby!" He whirled, picked up my sister, tossed her gently into the air, caught her, and tossed her again. She laughed, drooling on his tie. My mother wouldn't watch.

I waited for her to tell him what had happened today in the café, waited for her to say she'd had enough of this place, waited to hear that Bill was on his way.

All she said was, "We've already had these," tapping one of the sacks.

"Oh. Well, then. I'll just take them back." He rubbed his chin. How could he not see the trouble around him? What kind of balladeer was he? "How about I take us to the Blue Star Inn for some chicken chow mein?"

My mother capped her jar.

After dinner, during which Mama sat silent, my father said he had another treat for us. We tooled down 20, past the towers, past a sign for "Handgun Safety Training"; next to it, a small red fox lay strung across a barbed wire fence. In our headlights, its pelt shone like a sheet of scorched aluminum foil. "The whole time I was getting my degree up in Norman, I heard about West Texas's most striking geological feature," my father said. "You know what it is?" I shook my head. My mother was stewing in the back seat, with my sister asleep in her lap, so I knew he was speaking only to me. "Well, in about ten minutes you'll see."

We passed a drive-in movie screen: a woman's parted lips, wide as a canyon. A few miles farther, Pinkie's Liquor's buzzing sign, a green cactus, illuminated a dirt parking lot. A plaster cow skull, taller than my father, framed the wooden door of a boot shop.

Finally, we turned onto a stony road that seemed to lead nowhere, and my father stopped the car. Dust rained on the windshield. "Do you know what meteors are?"

"Falling stars?"

"Right! Follow me!"

He left the headlights on; he and I brushed past brittle, grasping tumbleweeds until we came to a giant hole in the ground. "Isn't that something?" he said.

"More like *nothing*."

He laughed. "Right. Thousands of years ago, before this was desert, it used to be something—probably a feeding ground for mastodons. Or Dino. Then a falling star landed here."

"Where?"

"Right where we're standing. Iron, nickel, cobalt—"

"Maybe it was a flying saucer?"

"Nope. Just a big old rock."

I reached for his hand. "You're not going to be taken away by a saucer, are you?" I tried it like a joke. "There *aren't* any saucers, right?"

He squeezed my fingers lightly.

"Mama may leave with Uncle Bill."

He glanced at me. "She's going to be all right," he said. "No one's going anywhere." His voice was calm, and I realized he knew all along what Mama had been feeling. I watched his features closely in the dark. Adults seemed to know things without talking. How did they do this? I wondered, looking away, staring out at nothing. Where did they get their powers?

"What do you say? Think you'll study the land someday, like your ol' dad?"

I searched for something, anything, out there. "There's an awful lot of it."

"That there is."

"It's pretty empty, isn't it?"

He laughed. "A desert rat wouldn't have it any other way, eh?"

A dust devil scurried across the crater's lip. Something rustled behind us. I turned to see Mama with a bottle of formula, cradling my sister in her arms. "We need to get her to bed."

My father grinned. "Don't you want to see where the falling star hit?"

She looked up, into the dust that always seemed to sandpaper the sky. "Any stars left up there for me to *wish* on? Or have they all come down?"

My father rubbed the back of his neck. "All right," he said. "I'll get you home."

Her eyebrows pulled together, but she didn't say anything.

Back at the motel, he brushed his teeth and she tucked my sister in. I felt ashamed, sitting there, knowing my presence kept them from candor and intimacy with each other—Mama hadn't taught me these words yet, but looking back, I can still breathe the tension in the room.

A pickup circled the parking lot just outside our window, blaring Buddy Holly. My father spat into the sink and wiped his face with a towel. My mother walked around him pointedly, reaching for the ashtray and a cigarette. She tapped the Bible on the dresser, closing it, leaving a cold cream dab on its cracked leather cover. "Yes ma'am," I said, pulling the sheet to my chin.

I stared at the closet door beside the television set. "God," I began in my head. My father settled into the next bed, beside my mother, making the box springs shriek. Smoke curled from her mouth like a rope. My sister mumbled and kicked in her sleep.

Everyone knew what everyone else was feeling, but no one was doing anything about it: my resolve strengthened. "Lord, in the morning when I wake up, I want a Superman suit in that closet." Or maybe a guitar? Which would be easier for God? A costume or a musical instrument? I imagined myself sailing, shattering the sound barrier. "A Superman suit, pressed and neat on a hanger. If it's not there, I won't believe in you anymore. Thank you for your blessings. Amen." My father switched off the light. I heard the smack of his lips on my mother's creamy cheek, heard her turn away from him. All night, laughter next door. Diesels on the highway.

It was just past noon. My sister took two tottering steps toward a dead bird in the gravel lot. My mother had dropped her cigarette lighter and wasn't watching. I stood gripping the burger bags we'd picked up. The bird's eyes had been pecked out. My sister bent her pudgy knees and extended a wet finger toward a stiff black wing. I had time to stop her or call for my mother. But I remembered my father leaving this morning, and hearing, as he reached into the closet for his suit coat (damp circles already under his arms), hangers *tink tink tink*. I looked at the Bible. We'd never get away from this room.

So I watched my sister poke the bird, then, delighted, wiggle her fingers into her mouth. My mother turned, lighter in hand, screamed at her, then me. The lunch crowd was leaving the greasy spoon. Desert rats like me, I thought: truckers picking their teeth with matchbooks, motorcyclists revving their engines unforgivingly, drilling equipment salesmen scrabbling in their pockets for coins to phone families they hadn't seen in a while. The loud couple stumbled out the door, locked in each other's arms. Anger? Love? I hadn't noticed it before, but in the harsh midafternoon light the woman was tough and swarthy—an Okie look, to me. Bill's look.

Today the man and woman were smiling at each other, ignoring us, which heightened the disappointment I felt in myself, always letting Mama down. I drew a breath and screamed across the lot, "You're a *mean man!*" The food bags hissed like rattlers in my hands. The man laughed, played at eating the woman's ear, then disappeared with her behind the café. My sister sniffled. My mother grinned at me, eyebrows raised. "Well," she said, and that was all.

I ate my cheeseburger ravenously and congratulated myself for being quiet and still the rest of the afternoon, watching my sister, making sure we weren't any trouble. My mother smoked in the doorway, the way she had each day, but I remember her as more relaxed than before, languorous and loose-limbed, a soft shadow against a burning rectangle of light. Jets shrieked, followed by thunder, as though the sky were a glacier cracking apart. Birds fluttered in the motel eaves. I wished Dad would stay away, just today, so things wouldn't get troubled again. It wasn't the last time in my life I'd wish him gone. Or home. Or safe from the disappointments of his job. I hoped the sun wouldn't set, that Mama would go on standing there. My gas pump sputtered: a dislocated lament begging someone not to leave. I lay back in bed, in a puddle left by my sister, and closed my eyes, happy, drifting, weak.

High Skies

As a child, I couldn't have predicted I'd one day lose my hometown in a storm of media distortions and myths. But the nation knows Midland, Texas, now as George W. Bush's boyhood home, and the rest of its citizens are background to the story of his success. In the elementary and junior high schools I attended, W. learned his earliest, most abiding values. The classroom desks are filled with shadows, now, behind his smiling face.

In 1998, at the annual Texas Book Festival sponsored by Laura Bush, another Midlander, I met W. in the governor's mansion in Austin. We shook hands, and I told him I'd gone to Sam Houston Elementary and San Jacinto Junior High, where he'd been educated (I'm a few years younger than he is). He gripped my arm as though together he and I, two good ol' boys with our feet on the ground, could knock some sense into the rest of this crazy country. I believed it, too, momentarily, as he offered me a cocky grin and said, "All right, partner." Like most public figures, W. has the ability to convince you he's interested only in you even as he's slipping past you to shake somebody else's hand. Celebrity doesn't require achievement or character. It's a quality unto itself, a physical energy, and W.'s got it the way the West Texas wind's got dust.

This makes him a more formidable figure than his father, who was standing across the room shaking hands with *my* father as I spoke to W. People often mistake my dad for George Bush Sr.— their features are strikingly parallel, though my dad's a little heavier. The similarity doesn't end there. Like George Bush, my father was an oil man in Midland, a migrant to the desert in the 1950s. He put his kids through public schools—and the Bushes did for a while, at least. But confusion was already needling me, as my father stood with the Father and I with the Son: the sense that my feet *weren't* on the ground at all, because the ground I'd walked as a boy and the package now being *sold* as my home didn't bear the slightest resemblance to each other. When George Bush Sr. was president, Texas claimed him uneasily. Where the hell *was* Kennebunkport? And what was that garble coming out of his mouth—it warn't how Mama taught her little cowboys to talk. Then he said he hated broccoli, and that made us more likely to want to kick off our boots and sit with him awhile. But with W.'s presidential campaign, Texas in general, and Midland in particular, became so weirdly unrecognizable, I began to think one of us, W. or I, had spent our childhood in a crazy computer simulation.

In article after article exploring W.'s past, the *New York Times* and other papers called Midland "rattlesnake country," a place of "beer-bellied baseball fans" and anti-intellectuals, where most schoolkids were delinquents. In a long personal profile on May 21, 2000, the *Times* said W.'s "values" grew in West Texas's "conservative soil." "It is in the soil of Midland that Mr. Bush has said he would like to be buried when he dies, and it was to Midland that he returned in the 1970's to marry and raise a family," wrote Nicholas D. Kristof. "[Midland] gave him an anchor in real America."

The profile began with an anecdote about W.'s schoolboy prankishness, and his punishment at the hands of Sam Houston's princi-pal. "When I hit him, he cried," the former principal, Mr. Bizilio, recalled. "Oh, did he cry! He yelled just as if he'd been shot. But he learned his lesson." From that moment on, W.'s conservative values and good behavior locked firmly into place—thanks to Sam Houston Elementary School! (Never mind his later years of heavy drinking and aimlessness.)

Midland "rests on an expanse of flat, baked nothingness," the piece went on to say, noting the rough natural rigors W. had to overcome to survive. "Even its residents, searching for a kind anal-ogy, fumble a bit before coming up with 'moonscape.' The sur-rounding land, home to tumbleweeds and rattlesnakes, would de-press even a camel." As for education, "books were not a major portion of a boy's childhood in Midland." The reporter didn't talk to *this* boy—and if he had, I would have asked him how he came to be so familiar with camel psychology.

In *First Son: George W. Bush and the Bush Family Dynasty,* Texas journalist Bill Minutaglio, exploring W.'s religious faith, wrote that on Sunday mornings the "desert stillness [around Midland] was underscored by the fact that the entire town was in church." The *entire town?* 'Scuse me, sir, I'm just a poor boy who never saw a book, but I learned enough to know that sweeping generalizations have no place in so-called objective journalism.

Late in the campaign, Susan Orlean wrote in the *New Yorker,* "Midland struck me as weird . . . People [there] take in huge amounts of money, they lose huge amounts of money—then they move on to the next day. It's a manic-depressive city, spending lavishly and then desperately suffering." She was smarter than most journalists assigned to Midland but afflicted with magazine-speak, in which the point is not to write accurately but to make a place sound exotic.

As W.'s image as an affable guy from a hard-edged, down-to-earth spot began to solidify, and he posed a clear threat to Al Gore, Texas morphed again. In attacks on W.'s record as governor, Gore all but labeled Texas a third-world country, a place you wouldn't want to drink the water. To hear him talk, the only lessons Midland's kids ever learned were what a classroom wall sounds like, crumbling, and how it feels when flies dance across your face.

In his crowning moment at the Republican National Convention in Philadelphia, accepting the party's nomination on August 3, 2000, W. invoked Midland as the core of his character (Andover, Yale, and Harvard apparently didn't take—sorry, Dad, you wasted all that money) and implied that the rest of the nation should aspire to its baked nothingness. "In Midland, Texas, where I grew up, the town motto was 'the sky is the limit' and we believed it," W. said. He went on:

> There was a restless energy, a basic conviction that, with hard work, anybody could succeed, and everybody deserved a chance. Our sense of community was just as strong as that sense of promise. Neighbors helped each other. There were dry wells and sandstorms to keep you humble, and lifelong friends to take your side, and churches to remind us that every soul is equal in value and equal in need.
>
> This background leaves more than an accent, it leaves an outlook. Optimistic, impatient with pretense. Confident that people can chart their own course.

Finally, the real Midland had completely vanished. For months it had been local color, a clichéd postcard of the provinces, a metaphor for conservative values or backwardness: an element in the George W. Bush myth. In W.'s speech, it had dried up entirely, its traces occasions for code-speak. In the convention's political context, when he spoke of Midland's churches, he didn't mean real buildings with steeples and pews; he meant he would support what his campaign called "faith-based initiatives"—volunteer efforts to aid the needy—rather than federally funded programs. When he mentioned his "confidence" in people charting "their own course," the "conviction that, with hard work, everybody could succeed," he wasn't recalling childhood incidents, lessons actually taught in a schoolroom or an oil field; he was signaling his backers his support of free market forces. Midland had truly become a "nothingness," boarded over by the Republican party's platform planks.

"The Land of the High Sky" folks called Midland when I was a kid, and the phrase more accurately captures the region than the language W. or recent journalists have used. It's not that rattlesnakes and beer bellies—and churches and promise—don't exist in West Texas, but to spotlight them exclusively forms laughable distortions. The land is dry and flat, and the sky dwarfs it: this is the only generalization one can safely make about the place.

Contrary to the *Times*'s assertion that near-illiteracy is the norm there, a number of fine writers have come from the area, among them Larry L. King, A. C. Greene, Elmer Kelton. Others have been drawn to examine its complexities. In his book of Texas essays, *In a Narrow Grave*, Larry McMurtry, the state's most famous scribe, writes that Midland is a community of "nervous" oil men whose "unpleasantness quotient is very high." In a more recent book, *Roads*, he insists that there is never any reason to travel through West Texas's ugliness. Well. Even famous writers can fall prey to stereotyping and oversimplification. More accurate and evocative is Abilene native A. C. Greene. He writes in *A Personal Country* that the West Texas desert is a "billowy ocean of land [with] so few ornaments that each plane, each shadow and broken feature of the land, must play an intense part in the composition, subtly forcing the eye out to the horizon and up to the sky." He adds: "What lies on the surface is a dim but powerful prediction of what rolls along below. According to geological description, West Texas writhes in ancient, frozen agony. Listen to the violent rhythm one scientist unconsciously achieves as he tells of the subsurface 'folds, faults, intrusions, slips, slabs, and slides.' "

In *Friday Night Lights*, his book about Texas high school football, Buzz Bissinger occasionally falls into broad abstractions—"this gaping land . . . filled the heart with far more sorrow than it ever did encouragement"—but notes more acutely than Orlean the "schizophrenia" of boom-and-bust oil towns: "The highs of the boom years [were] like a drug-induced euphoria followed by the lows of the bust and the realization that everything you had made during the boom had just been lost, followed again by the euphoria of boom years, followed again by the depression of another bust, followed by another boom and yet another bust, followed by a special prayer to the Lord, which eventually showed up on bumper stickers of pickups in the eighties, for one more boom with a vow 'not to piss this one away.'"

He also provides a fair description of a West Texas sandstorm: "a torrent . . . looking like a rain cloud, that . . . turned the place so dark in the afternoon light that the streetlamps suddenly started glowing. Nothing escaped the hideousness of that sand. It crept in everywhere, underneath the rafters, inside the walls, like an endless army of tiny ants."

The most reliable history of Midland, *Land of the High Sky*, was written by John Howard Griffin, famous for temporarily darkening his skin through a series of oral medications and ultraviolet rays and passing as a black man in the South for six weeks in the late 1950s. He reported his bitter experiences in the book *Black Like Me*.

The West Texas landscape "throws a man face to face with nature stripped of all distracting elements," Griffin writes in *Land of the High Sky*. "[N]o mountains, no trees, no beautiful views, though its very simplicity is more than beauty. It overwhelms. To stay here, a man must face himself and the realities of life and death." Few people have read *Land of the High Sky*'s thorough accounts of Anglo-Indian conflicts and wars with Mexico, struggles with and on the land that led to Midland's shaping as a cattle center and later as an oil empire. The book was commissioned in the late fifties as a promotional gimmick by Midland's now-defunct First National Bank, though it far exceeds its commercial origins; Griffin was a unique and thoughtful man, a patient, careful writer. Whatever lessons or values he may have taken from Texas, they led him not to easy optimism or platitudes about neighbors helping one another, but to restless honesty, a search for concrete truths in the difficult seams, the folds and faults, of America's social strata.

W. and I talked about inheriting a political legacy, about being named after men who served in public office and wanted us to follow in their footsteps. A quieter temperament steered me toward a different relationship to language, contrasting notions of public service, than the paths chosen by my granddad and George W. Bush. But if I ever ran for elective office, what could I say of my Texas background?

I could say I got my first glimpse of politics in Dr. Dorothy Wyvell's office, just a few blocks from Sam Houston Elementary. Dr. Wyvell was our family physician. I was asthmatic as a kid, so her office became quite familiar to me. I had no idea how unusual it was for a single woman to be practicing medicine in West Texas in the 1950s. Nor did I understand the words printed on the top of her prescription pad, even after my parents tried explaining them to me. *Government big enough to supply everything is big enough to take it away*—Thomas Jefferson. My mom called Dr. Wyvell a "John Bircher," one of several in Midland; I thought the phrase had something to do with trees, and forgot about it. I was far more impressed with the cartoon map of "Fairy Land" on her office wall and her claim that she didn't own a television—how could anybody live without TV?—than I was with her politics.

I could tell anecdotes about my own schoolboy pranks at Sam Houston, and how I learned my lessons, but when a friend and I secretly smeared Elmer's Glue all over the jungle gym and the swing sets on the playground, ruining our classmates' clothes, we got away with it.

Few of us knew, at the time, that we lived just down the road from Amarillo's Pantex plant, which put the finishing touches on all of America's nuclear weapons.

In an interview in the August 7, 2000, issue of *Time* magazine, W. claims that his experiences at San Jacinto Junior High instilled in him many of his basic social beliefs and adds that there were no class divisions in Midland. In fact, the city's poorest people lived on the south end of town, separated by railroad tracks from most well-off families. The social scene was further divided among the "goatropers"—the ranchers' kids—and the "hippies," middle-class kids like me, children of oil men, who caught the country/western rhythms in early Beatles tunes (to my ear, they came right out of "Ooby Dooby") and embraced the mop-tops. At a second-hand store one day my mother bought cotton berets, glued strips of thick brown yarn on them, and made Beatles wigs for my sister and me. We slipped them on, strummed tennis-racket guitars, and lip-synched "I Want to Hold Your Hand" for our pals, charging five cents apiece for the performance. Mark Chapman, who in 1980 would assassinate John Lennon, was growing up in Texas at the same time I was. According to one of his classmates, "Mark charged neighborhood kids a small fee to watch him lip-synch 'She Loves You' in the garage." The classmate, Jim Auchmutey, writing in the *Atlanta Journal and Constitution*, adds, "From the vantage point of middle age, I know that Mark and I were no more alike than any of those other dewy faces" in the kindergarten class portrait. "We had different families, different temperaments, different brain chemistries . . . Yet . . . the surface similarities haunt me."

In 1995, Timothy McVeigh's bombing of the Murrah building provoked similar comments from people who had known him as a kid. How could this nice, normal boy from an average American community commit such violence? Yet perhaps our insistence on "surface similarities"—like W.'s claim that class divisions didn't exist in Midland—is what blinds us to the unthinkable, slouching there in the third row behind the "girls in bangs and puffy-sleeved dresses, the boys in crew cuts and horizontal-patterned shirts" like Charlie Brown's in the sweet kindergarten portraits.

In Midland, most of the goatropers wore cowboy hats and big silver belt buckles, while hippies grew their sideburns. Some took drugs. I remember driving with my father one night and seeing a boy my age, trudging through freezing rain without a shirt. We slowed beside him, asked if he was okay. He didn't even know we were there. "Where's a damn cop when you need one?" my father muttered.

Of course, race was a predictor of class. Sam Houston was strictly segregated, and at San Jacinto, all the blacks sat in one corner of the cafeteria, the Chicanos in another, and whites in still another, reflecting the town's fragmentation.

In seventh grade, at San Jacinto, I played snare drum in the school band (trying to master the Okie swing beat I'd heard all my life, trying to be Ringo); I was the only white kid in a group of Chicano drummers. During practice they'd laugh and point at me, speaking Spanish. One day, fed up, I snapped back at them, and the biggest guy challenged me to a fistfight after school. We agreed on a time and place—right outside the shop class—but never encountered each other. I remember waiting for him; he claimed, later, he waited for me.

Not long afterward, I witnessed a fistfight in an alley a block or so from school. One boy got the advantage of the other and sat on him, smashing his face. The beaten boy's eyes turned glassy, blood spilled thickly from his lips, turning black in the dirt. Those of us watching were too stunned to move or stop the fight—this wasn't like TV, where people always bounced back up, unharmed, from the cruelest blows.

In ninth grade I was bused across town, with other whites, to a previously all-black school. If there were no class or race divisions in Midland, you wouldn't have known it from the grousing our parents did that year. Throughout my schooling I only had one black teacher, Mr. Scott, a band director, who closed his eyes, patiently, whenever I flubbed a riff, and gave me records by Chicago and Blood, Sweat, and Tears. "Listen to these drummers," he urged me. "Learn from them."

In history classes I never heard the names Sojourner Truth, Marcus Garvey, or Martin Luther King Jr. I only heard myths about Sam Houston and the battle of San Jacinto.

Only once did I ever cross the tracks on my own. I had my parents' car one day; after a high school band practice I ran home a black friend of mine. He'd missed his bus. He directed me to a tiny, unpainted house on a dirt lot. Its windows were broken. The porch sagged. He thanked me for the ride. "You better not come in," he said. "You better get on out of here." We both nodded. We'd learned Midland's social codes.

Now, the value of these experiences lies in their strict particularity, their refusal to be abstracted into vague lessons or prescriptive platform planks. To turn them into code-speak or character-metaphors would be not only to diminish them but to lose them altogether.

When she was in high school in Midland, Laura Bush ran an obscured stop sign on a farm road one night, hitting another car and killing the driver. The police filed no charges. Wisely, Ms. Bush rarely speaks of the incident now, rarely talks about lessons learned from the trauma or how it formed her character. Our backgrounds help shape who we are, but who we are also forms the way we view our backgrounds—the way we carry them within us. In her quiet dignity, Ms. Bush seems to understand that experiences are singular, private, usually untranslatable from one context to another. One man's "conservative soil" is another man's bloody dirt is a young woman's poorly marked intersection.

Somehow, Laura scrounged a few books growing up in Midland and has remained an avid reader, a supporter of libraries and literary activities in Texas. Recently, she told a reporter her favorite passage is "The Grand Inquisitor" section of Dostoyevsky's *The*

Brothers Karamazov. Peter Brooks, a Yale humanities professor writing in the *New York Times*, pointed out that "The Grand Inquisitor" is a cautionary tale, warning against rigid ideologies. In the novel, a character imagines Jesus returning to Earth at the height of the Spanish Inquisition. Jesus's presence interferes with the church's bloated bureaucracy, its political activities, so He is taken prisoner and condemned to be burned at the stake.

Unhappy bedtime fare. But I hope—especially since the World Trade Center attack—that the White House echoes with Laura's voice each night, reading aloud, right before W.'s head hits the pillow. In battling global terrorism, this typical Midlander will need all the cautionary tales, all the warnings against rigid ideologies, he can get.

"Midland, impatient with ideas and introspection, was a world of clear rights and wrongs, long on absolutes and devoid of ethical gray shades," says the *New York Times*. W. promotes this crude view of the town and its effect on his character; his vision colors reporters' remarks, cementing the myths of man and place.

The fact that I, and thousands of others, emerged from Midland literate, introspective, lovers of books and ideas, is hardly enough to correct W.'s myths. For him, the sky is the limit. For me, the sky is simply high. But I submit that Midland, like any place, is full of surprises. I remember one afternoon, while I was sitting in a classroom at San Jacinto, the dry desert suddenly became, without warning, an ocean. A flash flood hit the town, rivering its streets, sweeping cars away. Later, baseball-sized hail pounded the town's buildings. I could say I learned from this storm the fearlessness and resolve of Midlanders, and I wouldn't be lying. All over the city, men like my father made heroic efforts to leave their downtown oil offices and rescue their stranded children. I could say I learned the value of motherly love, and that would be true. Dry clothes and warm food never felt better than they did that evening, when my sister and I were safely home. But it's truer to say I think of no lessons when I recall that day. I think of the water itself, the roiling clouds, the fear, the chill. "I would say people, if they want to understand me, need to understand Midland," W. has said. Me, too. But I don't want to *lose* it, so I won't speak of values. Instead— quietly—a swirl of dust, blood in the dirt, a railroad track too hot to touch.

Exiled in Lents

No one marries expecting a shipwreck. But Martha and I exchanged our vows on the bow of a restored sailing vessel on a chilly New Year's Eve and, looking back, I think we may have anticipated rough seas.

The *Elissa* was a three-masted, iron-hulled barque built in Aberdeen, Scotland, in 1877. The name came from *The Aeneid*—Elissa was the Phoenician name of Dido, queen of Carthage. The ship hauled a variety of cargoes from port to port during her ninety-year commercial history, then was abandoned for salvage in Piraeus Harbor, Greece. There she was rescued by preservationists, who brought her to Galveston, Texas, and restored her to sailing capacity. Visiting the ship, Martha and I adored her textured wood, loved saying "mizzenmast" and "jibboom." Her symbols seemed right for celebrating a lifelong commitment to each other: years of service; restoration and redemption; world travel. New Year's Eve was a time of reflection as well as planning ahead.

At midnight, all the tugs in the harbor blew their horns, welcoming 1986. Martha and I kissed beneath the trembling sails.

A few months later, we said good-bye to the high plains and traveled west for work the way Woody Guthrie and so many other Okies had. Martha was seven years older than I was, more certain of her needs and skills. I barely felt grown, barely knew what I wanted from life. John Lennon once said, "We were all on this ship . . . our generation . . . a ship going to discover the New World. [We'd say] 'It's raining up here!' or, 'There's land!' or, 'There's sun!' or, 'We can see a seagull!' We were just reporting what was happening to us." Beyond a love of words, and a desire to report everything I saw, I didn't have a clue.

The day we reached the Pastures of Plenty, I couldn't see the horizon line in any direction. Pine trees and mountains obscured the planes I'd always counted on for balance. And though the sun shone, the light lacked intensity and heat. Like countless migrants before me (like my parents, longing for Oklahoma), I felt exiled. Exhausted. Disoriented. "What the hell are we doing here?" I asked Martha.

Oregon State University, a former ag college, had hired me to teach writing. Shortly after settling into a rental home and getting down to work, I began to collect migrant tales from students and colleagues, so I wouldn't feel so lonely. For example: On Memorial Day, 1948, at 4:17 P.M., a railroad fill crumbled in Vanport, Oregon, then the largest housing project in the United States, located on the flood plain of the Columbia River between Portland and Vancouver, Washington, ninety miles north of Corvallis, my new hometown (later, Martha and I moved to Eugene). A bale of water ten feet high rumbled through the project, snatching houses and office buildings, ramming them together like a child's game of pick-up sticks. Cars went careening; the Willamette River bloated and surged in all directions, snuffing electrical power; telephone poles jogged crazily in the currents. Officially, fifteen people drowned, though survivors believe scores more vanished. Over two hundred families lost their homes. Most of them were black. Many were Okies.

They'd come to Portland in the early forties. By '42, a brilliant entrepreneur named Henry Kaiser had built or was building three massive shipyards, one near the St. John's Bridge over the placid Willamette River, another a short distance above the I-5 Columbia River Bridge, and a third at Swan Island, upstream near downtown Portland.

When the United States entered World War II, military demand for tankers and Liberty ships burgeoned, and Okies, fresh from the fruit fields, provided a huge part of the work force.

Before the war, Portland had been a slow town of light industry, with a population of about 340,000. When the shipyards opened, over 160,000 new workers flocked to the area. The laborers were reviled by established Portlanders, just as they had been hated when they worked the fields. "Inadequate housing has turned Portland into a large dormitory for shipyard workers," one newspaper said.

So Henry Kaiser purchased 650 acres of slough, pasture, and muddy farmland on the Oregon side of the Columbia and created Vanport City, a $26 million construction job funded partially by the Federal Public Housing Administration. The small homes, made of wood, were set on timber foundations in the soft land— which, fortunately, enabled them to float like wine corks, later, during the flooding.

In all, 703 apartment buildings and 17 multiple dwelling units—a total of 9,942 homes—were squeezed together in Vanport: a step up from squatters' camps in chilly orchards, but hardly Shangri-La.

From the start, heavy rains and flood risks menaced the place. No safety measures were ever taken. The *Oregon Journal* called the city's opening a "muddy miracle."

After long winter rains, dust descended on the roads—a familiar plague to the Okies. They must have wondered, What the hell are we doing here? How do we build a life out of this?

Marcelle Holmes, a former Vanport resident, recalled, "The houses looked like crate boxes with little pipes sticking out of some of the tin roofs."

"It was pretty hard to get to [work at] the shipyards," Ing Borg said. He had been living in Fargo, North Dakota, when Kaiser men passed through, recruiting labor. "The bus was always filled and standing room was nil. The bus driver would say, 'Take a breath and get someone else on.'

"Base [pay in the yards] was a dollar and twenty cents an hour when I came out," he added. "In those days, that was big money. The first night [in Vanport] I looked out of my window and saw all those houses so close . . . I thought, 'This is like living in a concentration camp.' There were a lot [of folks] from Oklahoma. People called them Okies, but really, they were wonderful people. Of course, you had your neighbors' kids in and out of your house and everything because there were no definite yards. Things just all ran together."

Most of the units contained no heat; raw sewage lingered in the river; rats seethed in the walls. No one said, "Good night, don't let the bedbugs bite." It would have been a cruel joke.

Shopping was exceedingly difficult. "Boy, anybody says they're getting pepper in down at Safeway's, there'd be hundreds of people there within the hour," Borg recalled.

In Portland, middle-class children taunted the shipbuilders' kids at school. Rumors spread that Communists had overrun Vanport, encouraging white girls to dance with "colored men." In fact, most residents were too pooped at night to say hi to one another, much less to jitterbug.

In the Kaiser yards, native Oregonians labeled the urinals "Okie Drinking Fountains." Graffiti in one workroom boldly declared, "Why don't you Okies take Japan, you took Oregon without the loss of a single man!"

In the city proper, few people mourned when torrents swept Vanport off the map.

In the summer of '95, our ship foundered, in part because I had never adjusted comfortably to life in the Northwest. Martha had the good, calm soul of a settler. I was, to the core, a migrant—restless—even when I wasn't going anywhere.

She had developed a network of friends, discovered outdoor activities she loved to pursue on her own, while I sat in my study scribbling, or reading about exiles and migrants. We had ceased making room for each other. We were leeing in different directions.

One night, after I had moved out of the house and into a small apartment, I had a dream: all the furniture Martha and I had owned together—a chicken crate sanded and varnished to make a coffee table, a white couch, bamboo kitchen chairs—and our dishes, including our Texas margarita glasses, shaped like cacti, swirled boisterously in foamy running water, bumping over rocks and fallen logs like salmon failing to make it back home. I woke alone in my dark apartment, unbalanced, wondering how I got there.

At its peak, the yard at Swan Island launched a Liberty ship per day; many of the carpenters had been trained at Bonneville Dam, building hull-shaped draft tubes in electric generators.

In 1933, Congress had allocated $20 million for construction of the dam. The Portland *Oregonian* said this "marked the moment when the U.S. government caught the Vision of the West and began to make the dreams of its great personalities come true. Began, too, to plant the seeds of those regenerative activities and influences that help keep government virile and civilizations strong."

Shortly afterwards, the *Atlantic* spoke of "100,000 migrants from the dust bowl into the Northwest . . . [who] look to these new [dam-building] projects as the Israelites looked to Canaan."

"Roll on, Columbia, roll on!" Woody Guthrie sang, impressed by the dam and the cheap electricity it promised poor farmers. He wrote dozens of songs about the Bonneville and about the Grand Coulee. At night, he'd take his pay from the Bonneville Power Administration ($226 a month, about twice as much as unskilled Okies earned, scrambling over scaffolding at the dams) and hit the skid row bars in Portland, near Burnside Street, where I shop for books now at Powell's, one of the country's last great independent bookstores.

Arguably, Woody did his best work in the Northwest, intoxicated by the place names: Shelillo Falls, Umatilla Rapids, the Cascades, and the Priest. His Oregon tunes are like miniature histories of the world, full of "wheels, whistles, steam, boilers, shafts, cranks, operators, tuggers, pulleys, [and] engines."

Recent American history notes an odd Oregon fact: the only bombs to strike the mainland during World War II fell near Bonneville Dam. Japanese submarines released several explosive balloons intended to start forest fires, to confuse and distract the U.S. military. Okie workers helped camouflage the dam, spray-painting its locks blue-gray so they'd be hard to spot from the air.

After the war, hundreds of Bonneville veterans drifted north to Washington, hoping to hire on with a new "mystery project" at Hanford. "We [had] a lot of people from Arkansas, Texas, Oklahoma, people that today we call Arkies and Okies," said Harry Petcher, a former construction worker at Hanford's plutonium manufacturing plant. "They came with mattresses on top of their cars and trucks. Really, I thought it was *The Grapes of Wrath*, to be honest with you."

F. J. McHale added, "I remember a big percentage [of the workers] were Okies and Arkies. They came here because they had nothing at home. They were damn good workers." That's what General Groves, who was in charge of the manufacturing project, said. "It was the Okies and Arkies who built this job. The ideas may have come from the scientists, but these people built it."

They earned a dollar an hour, working twelve-hour shifts six days a week, filling holes, fifty and seventy-five feet deep, with concrete. Each of the holes had a drain and a lid six feet long. The workers didn't know what the shafts were for, and their bosses told them not to ask. "The professors and engineers" knew what to do, once construction was complete.

In its first thirty years, Hanford kept such poor operating records, authorities today don't know what happened to nearly half of the plutonium brewed there—enough for at least ninety nuclear warheads. No one knows how many laborers were contaminated.

On their days off, workers swam in the nearby Columbia, though the Army had previously evacuated Indian families who had lived there for years. Millions of gallons of river water cycled in and out of the Hanford complex through a series of intake valves near the workers' swimming holes.

Day and night, wind and dust scoured the scrubby land. The Okies felt perfectly at home.

Leaving a marriage is like heading into exile.

"When something like this happens," Martha said to me one night, "it's not a question of fault or blame or even willpower." I can't remember when she told me this—maybe as we loaded my car with boxes, as we had leaving Texas. Maybe the night I drove away from our house. "We tried and we tried and we didn't make it. That's all. Right?"

"Right," I said.

"I'm sorry."

"Me, too."

She shivered and slipped her hands into her pockets. "I guess it shows you how little control you really have over your life."

"I guess," I said.

Today, her words, or the spirit of them, stir in me as I poke around Lents, a southeast Portland neighborhood, a dumping ground for exiles and migrants. After Vanport vanished under layers of mud and water, scores of Oklahomans settled here. Many more trickled down from the Hanford Reservation, once their jobs were done.

The district was named for Oliver P. Lent, who came to Oregon from Ohio in 1852 and built a sawmill here. For decades, the neighborhood prospered and was largely self-sufficient, with its own banks, markets, barbershops, and taverns. Poor people—Okies, blue-collar Mexicans and African Americans—congregated here. They took good care of the place. Then, in the early seventies, city planners ran Interstate 205 through its heart, slicing it in half, blocking several of its old narrow streets with ugly concrete pillars. Now Lents, fragmented, noisy, divided against itself, is a poverty zone, deteriorating rapidly. Portland police refer to it as "Felony Flats."

Ron Craft, a longtime Lentsian, says, "Back in 1973, the residents said there were too many gas stations here. Then they were upset at how many taverns there were. Then it was junk [stores]. Now it's sex shops."

Colin Kerr-Morse, principal of Marshall High School, tags another problem: "Here [in Lents], we have one of the lowest education levels of parents of any [area in Portland]. College is not a reality to the parents, much less to the kids. When parents don't expect much of kids, and kids don't expect much of themselves, after a while, the teachers don't expect much, either."

Drug needles glint in high grass at the edges of the high school's baseball fields. Recently, two fifteen-year-olds were shot in the school cafeteria by a nineteen-year-old boy with ties to the Crips gang in Los Angeles.

From my tape player Woody sings, "Roll on, Columbia, roll on!" I edge the car slowly down 82nd Avenue, past Powell and Holgate, and the Eastgate Shopping Center, a dull mall sitting quiet and empty as an airplane hangar. The *Oregonian* says most houses here are valued at less than $7,000. Originally, there were no zoning or sewer codes in Lents. People threw up structures any way they could. Initially, many of the area's homes were intended to be temporary dwellings, but they've housed families now for fifty or sixty years.

A modern-day Little Oklahoma, first cousin to Weedpatch, the migrant labor camp immortalized in *The Grapes of Wrath*.

At Knapp and 61st, I notice a sky blue house, small as a one-car garage. A single wall leans over the concrete foundation. The rest of the place has toppled into grass. The house I shared with Martha, just before we split, was almost this color.

My hands tremble on the steering wheel. I have to pull over. No curbs. My tires flatten the rim of a dried yellow lawn.

Rusty eighteen-wheelers, adorned with naked-lady mud flaps, block whole streets, most of them unpaved. Heavy iron Dumpsters dead-end other roads. On sagging wooden porches, dogs and cats chase each other around washers and dryers, mildewed couches, chairs.

Inching forward again, I lose control of the car and swerve to miss a trash can rolling in the road. I nearly hit a guy in a black Ford pickup. "Motherfucker!" he yells. His brown hair is matted and long. He wears a sleeveless T-shirt, stained yellow, and a leather vest. A blue tattoo spreads like a puddle on his arm.

For a nervous instant, I'm reminded of John Doe Two, the unidentified suspect eyewitnesses saw with Timothy McVeigh just before the Oklahoma City bombing. Recently, various sketches of Doe, none of which resemble one another, have cropped up in the nation's newspapers. He has never been caught.

Was he an Okie, I wonder, if he exists? Does that explain why the Murrah building was targeted? Could he have murdered his own people? If so, what better place to hide than a wasteland of drifters like himself?

The pickup spits brown exhaust, then skids around a corner.

"Roll on . . ."

Syringes in the streets. Teenage girls carrying infants, shuffling past boarded, vacant stores. "Plaza 9000 Adult Video." In stickery weeds, a rusty Safeway shopping cart.

"We come with the dust and we go with the wind . . ."

Loss of control? You bet. Like most old Okies, Woody knew all about it. Listen to his lyrics. His father drank. His mother was committed to a mental institution. In a fit of uncontrollable anger one day, his teenage sister Clara poured coal oil over her dress and set herself on fire. Woody spent much of his Oklahoma childhood as far as he could get from his family's house, roaming the streets with vagrants, singing songs and strumming guitar.

But then the dust began to blow, and he was forced to move on.

Years later, his own baby daughter, Cathy, died in an accidental fire. Later still, Woody was badly burned while cooking breakfast on a barbecue pit. Eventually, Huntington's chorea, a degenerative nerve disease, stilled his hands and voice.

When he died in '67, the BPA named a substation for him at a lovely little spot on the Columbia, near Hood River, Oregon. The *Hood River News* called the honor a "sick joke" and referred to Woody, derisively, as a "1930s beatnik." "What did this Mr. Guthrie ever do for our valley?" asked the president of the local chamber of commerce.

"Roll on, Columbia, roll on . . ."

I stop the music and swing into a 7-Eleven parking lot. Woody's dusty ballads have left me sad and parched. The store's windows are cracked, like ice beginning to thaw. I buy a Pepsi. The paper says local police found a claymore mine, primed to blow, in the back seat of an abandoned car here in Lents.

Illegal firearms. Repossessions. Drugs.

In the obits, by coincidence, I glimpse the following line: "A long-time resident of southeast Portland, he was born in Oklahoma . . ."

It may seem that I have not said enough about my marriage here, that I've hidden painful personal truths behind old stories and obscure historical details. The fact is, the Okie exodus during the "dirty thirties" was just the beginning of a massive westward migration in America in the latter half of the twentieth century. Much of what we now take for granted in the American landscape, which profoundly shapes the way we all come together and part, formed as a result of this movement: interstate highways, suburbs, fast food outlets, industrialized farms built to serve a restless population. As D. J. Waldie writes in *Holy Land: A Suburban Memoir*, postwar economics and the suburban grid "limited our choices . . . compelled a conviviality that people got used to and made into a substitute for choices, including not choosing at all." Growing up among Okies in a southern California "grid," he said, "you occasionally hear[d] the sounds of anger. You almost never hear[d] the sounds of love. You hear[d], always at night," from houses identical to yours, "the shifting of the uprights, the sagging of ceiling joists, and the unpredictable ticking of the gas heater."

To the contrary, all I've been doing is talking about my marriage.

I hadn't wanted to sail away from my family and my home, any more than the Dust Bowlers had wished to "go with the wind." But there's precious little a storyteller can do to make money. As a grad student, I'd discovered in myself a small talent for teaching, but in Texas in the 1980s, when I needed a job, the market was tight. I could cobble together a paltry monthly wage, instructing part-time at a couple of junior colleges, with no security or benefits. Or I could accept economic exile and look beyond the borders of my region.

Some people feel that folks who leave their homes are traitors. I understand that. At one time, most families in Texas and Oklahoma made their living off the land and took their values from it. Roots. The word itself indicates what the land had to teach, mostly. You dug in. You didn't let go. You drew sustenance from the dirt at your feet.

Nowadays, land provides a living for fewer and fewer Americans. But in the Dust Bowl the ancient lessons linger. You don't forsake home (a counsel all the more powerful and bitter because so many have *had* to leave). You stick by your family. You stay married.

If you don't, for whatever reasons—drought, debt, doubt—then shame follows you, like an evil John Doe, all the rest of your days. Well. I'm resigned to that. But I've also seen how little it takes, sometimes, to blow control right out of someone's grasp.

Like this: One bag of ammonium nitrate fertilizer costs about ten dollars. The bags are available at any agricultural supply store. Only a few minutes are required to make an explosive device using the substance.

Nearly a year after the Murrah bombing, Corvallis police discovered what the local paper described as a "stash of bomb-making material identical to the type used in the Oklahoma City federal building explosion" in a barn on Highway 34, just outside of town. The paper provided a map, pinpointing the barn. It was right where I'd turned to Martha, a decade ago, and said, "What the hell are we doing here?"

The police arrested three men and one woman at the barn. They had robbed a local tire store to fund their scheme. What, or who, they planned to destroy was a mystery. These people only "had to . . . mix the parts [they had]," said a Corvallis detective.

Stan Starr, owner of a local agricultural products shop, told reporters he'd once seen a farmer spend a few minutes mixing a bag of fertilizer with heating oil. He blew a tree stump fifty feet into the air.

Whole lives have changed course with less power than that. A new port to reach, a whisper of dust, rising rains, the rumor of work . . . and you find yourself exiled, with only a narrow claim to being who you are, with a need to retrace your steps, find the old roads, and know your home again in ways you couldn't have known it before.

The Novel's Sight

Despite a lingering romanticism about the literary life that appears occasionally in Hollywood movies, novelists enjoy little power or prestige in America now. In many academic circles, they are targets of enormous criticism.

Look at John Steinbeck. My university colleagues generally scorn *The Grapes of Wrath* because it's "propaganda." Often, literary critics frown at the marriage of art and politics. Political agendas pollute the purity of aesthetics, or so they say.

I've never fully accepted this view. Perhaps because my grandfather was a politician, and a man who cared immensely about language, I've forever held my peace whenever art and politics get together.

In an old accounts ledger, whose binding is cracked and brittle, I've kept many of my grandfather's speeches, dating back to the thirties: meditations on war, poverty, progress, Oklahoma history, and the desperation of poor farmers. These talks are marvels of clarity and social conscience, proof to me that art and politics *can* survive their romantic flirtation and produce a fruitful union.

The pages are yellowed now, crusty and perfumed with mildew. For a long time, then, the alliance of aesthetics and persuasion has held for me a physical, sensual component, redolent of cozy basements, earthen walls, old air and dust—wistful, joyous, and sad, like the scent of sex in an empty room.

The Grapes of Wrath dares to declare its origins in advocacy, and I admire its passion, its roots in reportage. It began as a series of newspaper articles for the *San Francisco News*. The pieces ran October 5–12, 1936. Steinbeck had toured California's migrant camps, the "Hoovervilles" and "Little Oklahomas," with Tom Collins, manager of the Weedpatch Camp. Together, they traveled in an old bakery truck, a "pie wagon," from place to sorry place. Shocked that the Okies, like the Japanese, Chinese, Filipino, and Latin American fieldworkers before them, had no political clout (they weren't covered by Social Security, minimum wage laws, or unemployment insurance), Steinbeck intended his articles to "do some good." Additionally, he urged California to establish an Agricultural Labor Relations Board to address the migrants' grievances. It wasn't until 1975 that the state actually formed one.

"The migrants are needed and they are hated," Steinbeck wrote. "City dumps are the sources for the material" of their shelters. They live in homes of "corrupted paper" and tents "the color of the ground." Hookworm ravages most of their children.

Against the state's business elite, the Okies are helpless to better their lives. "Such organizations as the Associated Farmers Inc. have as members and board members officials of banks, publishers of newspapers, and politicians." They work closely with the "state Chamber of Commerce [and] they have interlocking [partnerships] with ship owners' associations, public utilities corporations, and transportation companies."

These groups control the media with their money and are able to "impose their policies on a great number of the small farms." Their industrialized farming methods sever the migrant worker from the "ground cycle" of the land.

But worst of all, Steinbeck says, Big Business keeps the Okies docile through a "system of terrorism that would be unusual in the Fascist nations of the world."

Irate, he concludes, "[American] agriculture (as it's currently practiced) is economically unsound under a democracy."

Sometimes I quote Steinbeck to my writing students. Journalism embodies "the greatest virtue and the greatest evil," he said. "It is the first thing the dictator controls. It is the mother of literature and the perpetrator of crap. In many cases it is the only history we have and yet it is the tool of the worst men. But over a long period of time, and because it is the product of so many men, it is perhaps the purest thing we have. Honesty has a way of creeping in, even when it is not intended."

I've often wondered if a scribbler's lonely labors can really produce communal results. James Agee, who, like Steinbeck, once journeyed into hidden America, witnessing the degradations of tenant farmers and sharecroppers, said, "Words . . . are the most inevitably inaccurate of all mediums of record and communication." He didn't hesitate to marry art and politics, but he fully expected his work to fail, both as aesthetic pleasure and as a call to action—and he was largely right, though I would argue, against the grain of most literary criticism, that, in spite of its flaws, *Let Us Now Praise Famous Men*, like *The Grapes of Wrath*, is one of the great books in American literature.

Nowadays I think: perhaps the question is, What makes failure great?

As he was about to begin his newspaper articles on the lives of the Okies, Steinbeck told his agent, "I'm trying to write history while it is happening and I don't want it to be wrong." Elsewhere, he said, "I'm going to try to break the story [of the migrant camps] hard enough so that food and drugs can get moving" to the workers.

Art as propaganda. But then, when are words ever *not* assertive? The artist's one true obligation is to "come devotedly into the depths of a subject, your respect for it increasing in every step," Agee suggests. "To know at length . . . your unworthiness" of the topic at hand.

In his working journal, kept while writing *Grapes*, Steinbeck confessed, "Can't tell" if it's worth anything. "Can't tell. Just have to plod for 90,000 words. Plod as the people are plodding. They aren't rushing."

The Joads measured their ghastly journey down Route 66 in money, miles, and gas; Steinbeck accompanied them, marking his trip in words.

"We're the people—we go on," says Ma Joad, and *just going on* is how Steinbeck wrote his book. "Set one day's work in front of the last day's," he urged himself, advice I often give my students.

"Got to get [the Joads] out of Hooverville," he said at one point, as though it were a moral imperative, as well as a narrative one.

Later: "This is the important part of the book. This little strike" by the migrants against the landowners. "Must win it. Must be full of movement, and it must have the fierceness of the strike. And it must be won." A struggle for artistic integrity. A struggle for social justice. A victory on the page. A victory in the fields. At this moment in the writing, the two were inseparable in Steinbeck's mind. The writer's lonely task was fully integrated with his community's needs.

"[I]n our agricultural valleys I've seen a family that was hungry give all its food to a family that was starving . . . that is inspiration" for art, he said.

In the end, writing the novel filled him with "plain terror." He knew it could never be powerful enough to effect as much "good" as he wanted. "I am sure of one thing," he scrawled in his journal. "It isn't the great book I had hoped it would be. It's just a run-of-the-mill book. And the awful thing is that it is absolutely the best I can do."

In such admissions of failure lie the possibilities for greatness.

Rereading its chapters now, I realize that few young novelists pursue their craft with as much zeal, commitment, and energy as Steinbeck did. These days, most fiction writers spend their energy trying to find tenured teaching positions—where their colleagues will tell them the novel is dead. (In 1939, the *Partisan Review* asked a number of writers, "Have you found it possible to make a living by writing . . . without the aid of such crutches as teaching?" No one would ask the question today—the answer is too obvious.)

Now, novelists shape their books with one eye on Hollywood. And who can blame them? In 1996, the screenplay for *Twister* was worth more money than the combined sales of hundreds of tenderly crafted American novels.

And Steinbeck's commitment wore him out. In crucial ways, writing *The Grapes of Wrath* ruined him. His marriage crumbled. Personally at sea, he never again felt connected to any permanent home. His subsequent work didn't flare with the same intensity.

As he journeyed deeper into *Grapes*, he insisted, "I see [the story] better" every day. It's "getting clearer all the time."

But eventually, it seems, he lost his capacity to see what needs to be seen.

Today, given the corporate ownership of most major American publishers, and the narrowness of academic careerism, I wonder if a book like *The Grapes of Wrath* is even possible?

Can the novel—can journalism, its poor, tainted mother—still *see*?

Recent examples suggest the answer may soon be no. Immediately after the Oklahoma City bombing, most newspapers reported, based on no evidence, that "foreigners"—specifically, Middle Easterners—were probably responsible. Even after McVeigh's arrest, few apologies, or admissions of bias, were issued. Racial profiling only worsened in some media outlets, on talk radio, and on cable TV news networks following the September 11, 2001, attacks on the World Trade Center and the Pentagon.

It's easy to see the filth and squalor of a squatter's camp in Weedpatch, California.

It's much harder to see a drug network reaching from Bogota, Colombia, to Mena, Arkansas, to the streets of Los Angeles.

Harder to see, and to make *others* see, the links between, say, a civil war in the Nicaraguan countryside and a drug blight in urban America.

Today, as I chart lesson plans for my students, I know that the serious novelist who wishes to see without blinders faces far tougher challenges than Steinbeck did, and finds far less professional support.

If Steinbeck's editor, Pascal Covici, had conducted the kind of market research that today's publishers turn to, more and more, to determine what's bankable enough to print, *The Grapes of Wrath* might never have surfaced. It would have been labeled, in advance, "too controversial" by the editors, reviewers, and academics who later panned it.

Of course, market forces have always threatened great literature (remember Steinbeck's complaints). But now there may be more to fear, for those of us who truly love words. Post-9/11, patriotic jingoism increasingly fills the print media, selling war along with new toasters, cars, and homes. Slimmer and slimmer ideological outlooks drive many publishers and sellers of books. The real America may have vanished from the novel's sight.

Riley

As a teacher of writing for fifteen years now, I've done my share of emotional counseling off the cuff, though I always tell my classes, "Writing isn't therapy—if you weren't mentally stressed *before* trying to write a short story, you certainly will be afterwards."

Still, students occasionally type pleas for help disguised as works of fiction. "Watch your verb tenses," I tell them. "Avoid passive voice." In class, I keep everyone focused on grammar, form, characterization. That's my job. In private, in my office, I'll listen to anyone who needs to talk. The worst sufferers—the ones who write about their rapes, or the abuses they absorbed as kids—I refer to psychological services.

One story, once, I couldn't refuse to hear. It came from a surprising source.

In 1988, I was still a newcomer to Oregon State University, homesick every night for Texas and Oklahoma. I didn't know what stories I'd find, or create, for myself in the West.

In the spring of that year, in addition to my fiction writing classes, I was assigned to teach a course on Vietnam in American Literature. By the late eighties, most college students thought Vietnam was just an Oliver Stone film. Michael Herr, Tim O'Brien, Philip Caputo lined my office shelves: bold and beautiful writers who'd illuminated salient moments of the war. My students rarely came to talk to me about our readings—they only wanted to know the next assignment, and how to pass it with minimum effort— but one morning I found a scribbled note on my desk: "Professor Daugherty, I noticed you have a bookshelf devoted to Vietnam. I am curious about your interest in the subject. Did you do time in the 'Nam? Are you worried about a similar conflict in the future? The Janitor."

The handwriting belonged to a man. A vet? At the end of the day, I left him a note saying I'd been too young to be drafted. I was teaching a course on the war. I invited him to borrow any of my books.

For the next week, we traded slips of paper. He *was* a vet, he wrote. He might like to read some of the books, but he didn't know where to begin. Finally, I suggested he come see me during my regular office hours.

Since moving out West, I'd had few satisfying conversations with anyone about books. Nowadays, in university English departments—as in the culture at large—books don't matter as much as they used to. The study of literature is being steadily replaced by specialized studies in composition and rhetoric; video and film; advertising, rock music, and other cultural "signifiers"; identity politics; theory. Especially theory. Theory *about* theory. Once, a visiting scholar came to Oregon to give a lecture on Thomas Hardy's *Jude the Obscure*. She talked about deconstruction and gender; she referred to Freud and the literary critics Derrida, Kristeva, Bakhtin. Finally, I asked her about Thomas Hardy, whom she'd not mentioned once. She paused, startled, as if I'd leaped at her from a tree. "I haven't yet decided what my position on Hardy will be," she said in a firm, scholarly tone, then she admitted she hadn't finished reading the novel.

Oregon State's English Department is more old-fashioned than most—the *idea* of literature still appeals to my associates, even if we don't agree on who belongs in the literary canon. But one day a colleague said to me, "How can you waste your time writing novels? Don't you know the novel is dead? Any dope can see it's lost its cultural significance." Politely (though shaken) I paraphrased the writer John Barth, "The novel has been happily dying for thousands of years, and it will continue to die happily for thousands more."

John Steinbeck, my first youthful reading passion, is to most current academics a joke—a hack whose Nobel Prize was a travesty of judgment and taste. He's naive, sentimental, quaint, simplistic in his politics, stereotypical in his treatment of people. Our students need exposure to subtlety and irony, the relativity of truth—or so goes the new wisdom.

Well, maybe so. Still, I confess that much contemporary writing seems pinched to me, cold and cynical in its irony, and I long for the humanity—naive and sentimental though it may be—of a Steinbeck, and I suspect my students do, too.

Books certainly seemed to matter to the janitor.

One sunny afternoon, a short, hunched man in his late forties knocked faintly on my door. His hair was close-cropped and fuzzy, like thistle. He wore dirty jeans and a heavy wool jacket, though the day was quite warm. He blinked rapidly. The light seemed to nag at him.

"Hi," he said. "I'm the janitor." His name was Riley. In '69, he'd served in the 101st Airborne Division in the A Shau Valley, just east of Laos. I learned this after a long silence in which he simply stared at me. Finally, I told him I'd never been in combat, but I *had* heard mortar shells once, in Nicaragua, in the summer of '86. I'd gone there with a teachers' tour, I explained, taking pencils and paper to poor schools in the chaos of that country's civil war.

"Vietnam all over again," Riley mumbled.

"I hope not."

"We got no business getting involved."

"I agree."

"The shells come close?"

"What did I know?" I said. "Close enough."

So. In his eyes, I'd earned my stripes, and he told me about the A Shau Valley. In 1968, the Viet Cong had used it as a staging area for their attack on the city of Hue during the Tet Offensive. The valley was a major terminus of the Ho Chi Minh Trail—a "definite hot zone," Riley said.

"So you saw a lot of action?" I asked.

"Yeah." He couldn't keep his hands calm. He rearranged loose pencils on my desk, straightened papers, lining up their corners just so. No surprises. No sudden moves. I got the feeling I'd scare him if I talked too much, so I sat still and waited. "I like to work at night," he volunteered, "when no one's around."

A bell rang. Classes let out throughout the building. Students' voices and laughter unnerved him terribly. He whitened. He stood. "Take a book," I said.

His hands were trembling now. "Not today."

"Come back whenever you'd like."

"Okay."

Over the course of the next few weeks, he kept showing up at no set time. He talked abstractly about the "lies of our leaders"; about Dow Chemical, the makers of napalm—the obscenity of their "war-profiteering."

I recalled a line from an old political speech of my grandfather's, a yellowed copy of which he'd given me: "If, as our leaders often tell us, the right way to get ready for peace is to prepare for war, then I suppose the surest way to get to Heaven is to prepare for Hell."

Riley's voice rose and his body shook whenever he talked about such things. "It'll happen again," he said, "war, that is, if guys like you, guys who care about language, don't force the government to stop misusing words."

"What do you mean?"

"I mean tricking people into battle, making them think it's moral when it's not."

I nodded, more powerless than he imagined. After several minutes, he'd always leave abruptly, with much more to say, I could tell, but apparently no way of saying it. I sensed he was working up to something, and it might take him months to arrive.

One afternoon, he asked me what kind of stories I liked best. I told him John Steinbeck was the first novelist I'd read with relish, the first writer who made me want to *be* a writer.

"*The Grapes of Wrath.*"

"Right."

"Pretty depressing stuff."

I thought for a moment: Do I follow this up with him or let it drop? "There's a guy named Lewis Hyde who wrote a book called *The Gift,*" I said carefully, embarrassed by the teacherly sound of my voice. But maybe Riley had *come* to me, in part, because I was a teacher. "In it, he says, it's 'when the world flames a bit in our peripheral vision that it brings us jubilation and not depression.'"

Riley stared at me.

I shrugged. "I think one of the things he means by that—anyway, what *I* take from it—is that you've got to recognize the harsh things. The flames. Even if they're depressing, there's a kind of joy in the honesty of acknowledging them."

I watched him closely, to see if the quote had put him off. He nodded slowly. "If you acknowledge them, maybe you can do something about them," he said.

"Exactly." I reached for the bookshelf behind me and found *The Gift.* I searched for a passage I'd marked. "'[The gift] . . . seeks the barren, the arid, the stuck, and the poor.' Stories are a kind of gift," I said, classroom mode. I wanted to draw him out, but I couldn't risk pushing too hard. He might run. "My favorite storytellers are the ones who tackle painful subjects, bring them to light so—as you say—maybe we can do something about them, or at least understand them better. That's the gift."

"I like that," Riley said. "That's good."

I told him about the Hero Cycle then—a common structure of fairy tales and myths, graphed by Joseph Campbell and others. When there's a disruption in the community, the hero (or artist or storyteller) must go on a journey, very often to the Underworld, facing the worst life has to offer in order to understand it fully. Finally, the hero returns to the shattered homeland, bringing the gift—the new understanding, a shape for what has happened—so the community can start to heal.

Riley nodded again.

"That's the kind of thing Steinbeck did in *The Grapes of Wrath*, I think. So in the end, it's not depressing to me."

He was silent.

"What about you?" I asked. "What are your favorite stories?"

"Simple, straightforward things."

"Where the words aren't misused?"

Shyly, he grinned.

Finally one day, with no prompting from me, Riley started talking about a mountain in the A Shau Valley called Dong Ap Bia— "Hamburger Hill, we came to call it," he said, "'cause so many of our guys . . . well, they were ground into meat there. Absolute meat."

In the spring of '69, the U.S. High Command decided it was time to clean out the valley. Dong Ap Bia (officially, on maps, "Hill 937") belonged to the enemy. It was targeted for attack.

"Its peak was completely covered in mist," Riley told me. "We couldn't see what we were after—which was pretty much the whole lousy war, as far as I'm concerned. Anyway, we landed in early May and began our assault." While he talked, he arranged the pencils on my desk. A shiver went through his hands. "The point man led our column with his best buddy behind him. I was next in line. My rucksack snagged on a tree vine. While I was trying to untangle myself, another soldier passed me. He disappeared around a bend in this little trail we were on. When I got myself loose, I started after him, then I felt a huge concussion. Rocket-propelled grenades. Then there was automatic weapons fire. Bullets and shrapnel ricocheted off bamboo above my head, and everywhere around me. I crawled through some underbrush and saw my three buddies blown away. If I hadn't gotten stuck, I'd have been one of them."

He picked up a loose paper clip and placed it, precisely, near the corner of my desk. "Charlie broke contact then and vanished, leaving the trail dead quiet. The man who'd walked into the ambush in my place—I hoisted him onto my shoulders and carried him back down the trail. He bled all over me. The rest of the platoon moved up the hill a ways and recovered the other dead soldiers. When it got dark, the platoon sergeant told me to stay with the bodies. So I sat in the mud, alone with these corpses, these people I'd shared food and water with, marched with through awful heat and rain . . ."

The university's bell rang, but this time Riley didn't move. He rubbed his palms together, compulsively. "At one point, I tore open an accessory pack from my C-rations. I didn't really know what I was looking for, gum or something, something to keep me occupied. I found a book of matches and a salt packet." Riley reached into the right pocket of his big wool coat. In front of me he set an olive green matchbook and a paper container of iodized salt. The matchbook said, "These matches are designed especially for damp climates but they will not light when wet, or after long exposure (several weeks) to very damp air."

"That's what I found," Riley said. "I remembered some words, then, that a chaplain had said to our platoon while we were preparing for our mission. Something like, 'Anyone who believes in Jesus Christ is the salt of the earth and the light of this world.' All night, I sat there on the hill, holding this stuff, repeating the chaplain's words to myself."

Riley insisted I keep the matches and the salt. He gave me several photographs of himself in the forests near Laos. "Maybe someday you'll write about this," he said.

"It's not my story to tell," I said. "*You* should set it down."

"No. Writing's not my thing. You can do it. To let others know what it was like. To warn them."

"What about?"

"Never fall for government lies."

By coincidence, a week later in the university bookstore, I noticed a book called *Hamburger Hill* by Samuel Zaffiri, a former mortarman with the First Infantry Division in Vietnam. In 1969, while he was recovering from wounds in an Army hospital somewhere in Japan, he listened to soldiers describe their experiences in the A Shau Valley. Years later, back in the States, he found a few veterans of the battle of Dong Ap Bia and put their stories in the book.

I bought it for Riley and gave it to him the next time he came to my office. "Are you in touch with anyone from your old platoon?" I asked.

"No, I don't know where to find them," he said.

"Why don't you write this fellow, Zaffiri, care of the publisher? He interviewed some of these men. He could probably steer you their way."

Riley took the book. I didn't see him for nearly a month. When he returned, he was smiling—not the wan grin I'd seen when he'd talked about lies, but a broad smile of relief. He showed me a letter he'd received from Samuel Zaffiri:

Dear Riley,

I really appreciate it when a veteran like yourself likes the book because you know—really know—if what I've put on paper is authentic or not. I started writing about Vietnam because 80 percent of the stuff I was reading about the war was just plain bull. The average reader, however, doesn't know what's authentic and what isn't and that's why the bookshelves are filled with idiotic books about Vietnam.

Writing this really took it out of me. If I'd known how hard it would be when I started, I likely would have given up.

Anyway, I've included a B Company roster and a Xerox copy of the addresses of men in Bravo that I've been in contact with.

Riley told me he'd written most of the men on the roster, and they were beginning to put him in touch with some of his old war buddies. He'd thought he'd never hear from them again. Now they were sharing their stories.

He returned Zaffiri's book. He'd dog-eared several pages, marked events he'd experienced, including the account of his initial landing on the hill in the heat of the assault. The chopper he'd ridden backed into a tree with its tail rotor—the pilot had been rattled by all the sniper fire—and crashed into the woods.

On the book's flyleaf, Riley had written his name, along with

2nd Platoon, Bravo Company
3rd Battalion, 187th Infantry
101st Airborne Division

And these lines:

Theirs not to reason why,
Theirs but to do and die;
Into the Valley of Death
Rode the six hundred.
TENNYSON

And he shall judge among the nations, and shall rebuke many people; and they shall beat their swords into plowshares, and their spears into pruninghooks; nation shall not lift up sword against nation, neither shall they learn war anymore.
ISAIAH 2, 4

I looked at him. Simple? Straightforward? "Keep the book, Riley," I said.

"No, it's for you." And he left.

Now, *Hamburger Hill* sits next to *The Grapes of Wrath* on my bookshelf.

It's unpredictable, I think, the way we come to certain stories, yet sometimes in retrospect, we can see how much we needed them at the time, how ready we were to receive them. The narrative of our lives snaps into place like a lid on a box, if imperfectly, and only briefly.

I wanted to tell Riley some of this, though it probably wouldn't have mattered to him. I wanted to tell him how I believe the landscapes and encounters of our lives incline us to think and read and love and grieve the way we do. I wanted to tell him how I'd come to my own stories, how they'd steered me to teaching, prepared me, perhaps, to hear his losses (though maybe he knew these things already—in the last few weeks, he'd taught me more than I'd taught him), how they'd started a chain reaction that led to today, to my sitting with him now.

I wanted to explain to him how, when I first bumped into them as a boy, I was more than ready for the Joads. My family shared their Okie roots. Their scorched terrain, patched with oil wells, cotton, and cattle, was a place I well understood. Their journey, simple, straightforward, was *the* story for me and has remained so in spite of academic fashion.

It was the Joads who, many years later, made me want to study English (and later still, to understand the continuing struggles of agricultural laborers in Nicaragua). One day, when I was twenty, I met with the chair of the department at Southern Methodist University in Dallas, a man named Pascal Covici Jr. He had long gray sideburns, thick as cotton balls, and big glasses that made his eyes look like nervous fish. He told me he'd be delighted to have me on board, though he also warned me very kindly about the tight teaching market. "Your chances of getting a job once you graduate are very slim, I'm afraid, and I want you to know that up front," he said.

I said I did.

"May I ask you, then, why you want a degree in English?"

"I love stories," I said. "And books."

He nodded and smiled. Then he outlined the program of study. "We're rather old-fashioned here at SMU," he told me. "We still prize literature."

Of course, I thought: a man named after a philosopher of moral truth would naturally be old-fashioned about literature. Only much later did I learn that he was the son of John Steinbeck's editor. Steinbeck had dedicated the novel *East of Eden* to Dr. Covici's dad. He had asked Steinbeck, a skilled woodworker, to make him a box. Steinbeck delivered the *East of Eden* manuscript in a carved box along with the following words:

> Nearly everything I have is in [this box, this book], and it is not full. Pain and excitement are in it, and feeling good or bad or evil thoughts . . . the pleasure of design and the indescribable joy of creation.
>
> And on top of these are all the gratitude and love I have for you. And still the box is not full.

Looking back now, I'm pleased that this gentle, caring man, Pascal, stands at the beginning of my teaching career, a man connected to *The Grapes of Wrath* and to a love of books, just as I'm pleased that the books on my shelves pulled Riley out of his nighttime hallways. However disinterested my students may be in reading, however arcane academic taste may become, whenever I think of Pascal and Riley, I solace myself that a life spent with literature has not been a life misspent.

One afternoon, a jittery man in a red baseball cap blew into my office just as I was leaving to teach a class. He introduced himself as a friend of Riley's. "I won't keep you, man, I know you're in a hurry," he said.

"That's all right. Sit down."

He was pale, blinking, unused to daylight. "I just wanted to tell you, Riley's never talked about the war with anyone before, and the change in him . . . it's stellar. He's relaxed, he's opened up. You're saving his life, man. Thank you. Keep it up."

"I'm not really doing anything," I said. "I'm just listening to him."

"It's plenty. It's a lot."

"I'm glad."

Now, I suspect Riley learned his friend had come to see me, and felt embarrassed, somehow, or self-conscious, because I didn't meet him anymore after that. Most days, I'd wait for his shuffle, leave my office and gaze down the hall, even when the building was silent. No Riley. I lingered after 10:00 one night, hoping to catch him on his shift, but he didn't show up. I could have asked the other janitors about him, but I knew he'd track me down if he really wanted to. For weeks, I left *Hamburger Hill* sitting prominently in the middle of my desk, next to a pad of blank paper and a pencil. An invitation never taken. I figured, sadly, this was one story whose end I could only imagine.

11 | Cleared Ground

Hostile Territory

The landscapes of hatred are unremarkable. I've seen them.

In the Idaho woods, near the Ruby Creek bridge, protesters gathered days after Vicki Weaver was shot to death in the doorway of her cabin by an FBI sniper with a .308-caliber assault rifle. Her husband, Randy, had allegedly violated federal firearms laws; he'd refused to surrender to authorities—in fact, he refused to *recognize* the authority of the United States government. He had holed up in his cabin with his wife, Vicki, their children (one of whom, Samuel, thirteen, would be killed by a U.S. marshal), and a friend, resisting arrest. Agents from the FBI and the Bureau of Alcohol, Tobacco, and Firearms surrounded the place.

The sniper's bullet tore off Vicki's jaw, spraying two of her children with blood and bone fragments. She was holding her newborn infant when she died. Shortly afterwards, Randy Weaver surrendered. He served fourteen months in jail, convicted only of refusing to appear in court. The firearms charges didn't stick. Eventually, the United States government paid \$3.1 million to the Weaver family as compensation for the losses of Vicki and Samuel.

Near the Ruby Creek bridge, a swelling crowd, shocked by the Weaver murders, shouted at FBI agents, "Your house is next!", waved placards—"Baby Killer!" and "FBI, Rot in Hell!" From news broadcasts, it was clear that the demonstrators weren't all fringe-types—skinheads, Identity Christians (who believe Jews descended from Satan and that white "Aryans" are the true heirs of the tribes of ancient Israel), Klansmen. Proud Vietnam vets also turned out. I understood, for the first time, how prevalent mistrust of the federal government was, slicing across class and ideological lines through-out the nation.

Soon after the shootings, I attended an academic conference in Coeur d'Alene, Idaho, a meeting of writers, literary scholars, and historians. Hayden Lake, near Coeur d'Alene, is an Aryan Nations stronghold. Over the years, several white separatists have proposed an all-Caucasian country to be located in the Great Northwest—so the conference organizers had decided on a theme, something like "Racism Reconsidered" or "Deconstructing Hate Crimes." The or-ganizers wanted to "make a statement," as befitting learned per-sons who found themselves in America's heart of darkness.

Half an hour into our first session, five or six skinheads in fa-tigues and scuffed brown combat boots marched into the meeting hall. They stood, arms folded, at the rear of the auditorium. Some-one sneaked away to call the cops; nothing happened. Eventually, the skinheads left. But I'd learned my lesson for the day: "state-ments" from the Ivory Tower wither when the Big Bad World comes clomping into the room.

As a college student in the mid-seventies I'd seen Waco, Texas, many times, driving from SMU to visit friends in Austin, San An-tonio, Wimberley. Waco was nothing special. To me, it meant Bay-lor University, a kind of Southern Baptist prison where dancing was seen as a sin. Waco also meant McDonald's. I'd stop there for fries—a treat not always available in small East Texas towns. The Seventh-Day Adventist Church has many followers in the region—extremists, even by the church's normal standards—who spurn "unclean" products such as caffeine, white flour, milk, and sugar. In Keene, north of Waco near I-35, there are no McDonald's or Dairy Queens, no burgers, Cokes, or fries.

Orthodox Adventists share with Branch Davidians the belief that God picks individuals to visit from time to time. David Koresh—born Vernon Howell in Houston, a lover of raunchy rock music and guns—was an unlikely gossip partner for the Lord. In 1987, armed with five .223-caliber semiautomatic assault rifles, two .22-caliber rifles, two 12-gauge shotguns, and nearly 400 rounds of ammunition, Howell and a band of men seized control of the Branch Davidian compound at Mt. Carmel, just outside of Waco. Ben Roden, the sect's longtime spiritual leader, was killed in the gun battle. Previously, he'd challenged Howell to a contest: whoever was able to revive a corpse—Roden or Howell—would be the group's chief. Howell's ordnance settled the question much quicker. Eventually, his murder case ended in a mistrial. He became the Top Davidian. His followers claimed he could "harmonize" the Bible like no one they'd ever heard.

On April 19, 1993, when Howell and over seventy of his devotees died in Mt. Carmel, even observers who'd branded him a murderer and a zealot were horrified by the fleet of M60A1 tanks punching holes in the Davidians' building. In the ensuing fire, twenty-five children died.

Today, while debates escalate about who and what started the fatal sparks, everyone agrees that the feds botched their final assault. Even former attorney general Janet Reno said, in retrospect, "I would not make the decision [to attack the compound] again."

White crosses now fill an open field where Mt. Carmel once stood, near stacks of rubble by the concrete foundations of the old chapel and two burned-out school buses. Someone has staked a wooden sign in the soil: "World's Most Persecuted Church."

One Saturday afternoon, in October 1995, I went to a gun show at the Lane County Fairgrounds in Eugene, Oregon. I'd never been to such a thing, and I wanted to see what Timothy McVeigh had seen. I wanted to witness the American passion for weaponry that had played such a big role in the catastrophes of Ruby Ridge and Waco.

Armed guards stopped everyone at the door, checking to see that none of the men toting pieces into the hall (the majority) carried live ammo in their chambers. I waited for several minutes while a man with a badge emptied the pistol of a fellow in front of me.

"Here you go, young man," a salesman shouted as soon as I entered the hall. From behind a table he raised a sheathed knife. "The perfect backup in case you're separated from your primary weapon. Price includes a leg strap."

I shook my head.

Another man waved at me a sleek brown rifle with an infrared scope.

Friends greeted one another—"Say, stud, keepin' your powder dry?" Old men in red-checked hunting jackets, smelling of Old Spice and tobacco, spoke with thin, hungry-looking fellows in dirty Army fatigues. Others—loners, spooked old Vietnam vets, or so they appeared to me—kept close to the rifle displays and didn't say a word.

Full-color posters of Jesus, George Washington, and John Wayne hung on the walls.

On a series of ratty folding tables in the center of the room, books were offered for sale: *The Ultimate Sniper* ("How to Dust Your Enemy"), *Crimsoned Prairie*, *Unrepentant Sinner*, *The Turner Diaries*. Free pamphlets from the National Rifle Association, urging citizens to "oppose those who govern."

I knew about *The Turner Diaries*. It had been in the news. Timothy McVeigh claimed it was one of his favorite books—he'd sold it himself at gun shows and may have passed it out to onlookers during the standoff at Mt. Carmel. A novel written and published by an American neo-Nazi leader, *The Turner Diaries* advocated ethnically cleansing all fifty states and overthrowing the United States government.

I picked up a copy and read: "There is no way we can destroy the system without hurting . . . innocent people."

A few feet from me, two men playfully aimed shotguns at each other, and laughed.

My throat tightened. If I stay here any longer, I thought, I'll surely be stripped of Reason: my primary weapon.

I dropped the book and left.

On my way home from the fairgrounds, I remembered a simmering August afternoon in 1986 in Estalí, Nicaragua, when forty or fifty people, dressed in black or in olive green military fatigues, filed from a bullet-pocked church lifting a pine casket. Rain spattered the wood. An old woman from whom I'd just bought a fried tortilla told me the deceased was a Sandinista soldier, seventeen years old. He'd been shot in a Contra attack in the red dirt of the coffee fields near Matagalpa.

A young woman in the funeral cortege glanced my way. Her hair was short and black. An AK-47 hung on her shoulder. Respectfully, I backed against the tortilla factory so the crowd could pass. The young woman sized me up again, wondering, I suppose, what this damned gringo was doing here. As she stared, the grief on her face collapsed into hardened contempt; after all, my government had probably supplied the materiel that murdered her compatriot (two months later, a U.S. citizen named Eugene Hasenfus would be shot from the sky in a c-130 cargo plane full of rifles; documents found with him tied him indirectly to then–vice president George Bush). Her thin lips quivered. Her eyes closed.

Over the years, I'd thought often about her face, usually when I thumbed through the "help the poor farmers" speeches in my grandfather's political papers—the mix of mourning and anger in the set of her mouth, the private sorrow and the burden of public sacrifice. I could see it now, as I fled the gun dealers, so vividly the image almost made a sound—a cold, blue sound, a drum thump, a weary cotton chop—just behind my eyes.

In the next few weeks, the press was full of militia reports, and I discovered that the placid college where I teach may have had an indirect link to the tragedy in Oklahoma.

It turns out that William L. Pierce, the author of *The Turner Diaries*, was an assistant professor of physics from 1962 to 1964 at Oregon State University.

I'd always assumed that the most important novelist who'd ever taught at osu was Bernard Malamud, the Pulitzer Prize–winning author of *The Natural*. Critics widely credit Malamud, along with Saul Bellow, Isaac Singer, and Philip Roth, with establishing a powerful tradition of postwar Jewish American literature. As a writer, I would always be working, here, in Malamud's shadow.

He left osu in '61, right as he published *A New Life*, a novel that scandalized folks in Corvallis. It depicted a (barely disguised) college community, sluggish and dull, and a mediocre school mired in oppressive academic politics. For years I've kidded my colleagues, threatening a sequel called *The Same Old Life*.

Malamud's sins, however, pale next to those of his near-colleague Dr. Pierce—and apparently his success dims in contrast as well.

If a novel is to be judged on its ability to influence people, to touch their emotions and thoughts, then Pierce may have far outstripped his more literary fellow alum. *The Turner Diaries*, narrated by a white supremacist during a U.S. race war, includes a chapter on the annihilation of a federal building. The weapon of choice is a truck bomb made of ammonium nitrate fertilizer. Timothy McVeigh ate it up.

Malamud's words earned him accolades, prizes, and the respect of other writers; Pierce's may have helped murder over 160 people in Oklahoma. Until his recent death he lived in West Virginia, where he headed the National Alliance, an organization that Klan-watchers at the Southern Poverty Law Center call the "most dangerous hate group operating in North America."

Pierce interviewed for his job at Oregon State just as Malamud was leaving. By all accounts, they wouldn't have spoken anyway. Already, in '61, the young scientist hated Jews.

The OSU archives shed little light on Pierce's time at the school. Born in Atlanta, educated at Rice University and the University of Colorado, he came to Oregon highly recommended. The archives do contain a copy of a letter he wrote to W. H. Tantilla, a former teacher of his in Boulder, describing his adjustment to Corvallis: "I haven't had a chance to do more than get domestically settled here and start preparing for courses," he writes. "I'll be teaching classical mechanics and relativity . . . and in about a month, when I have gotten an oscilloscope, a counter, some power supplies, etc., I'll have a shiny new lab all to myself."

His relativity course quickly became the subject of rumors around the Physics Department. Students reported he never mentioned Einstein's name in class, because Einstein was Jewish.

I learned this from Dr. Clifford Fairchild, who was hired by the Physics Department the same year Pierce was and who still works at OSU. He met with me in his office one day—a tall, friendly man surrounded by piles of papers and books.

"How can you teach relativity without Einstein?" I asked. Dr. Fairchild shrugged. "I don't know, but that's what I heard. There was another rumor about him. People said that, in Colorado, he grew a meat-eating tropical plant in his home, one of those plants like a Venus flytrap that lives off of animal protein? The rumor was, he wanted to cultivate this plant till it could eat a mouse."

I wondered if there was anything in the man's demeanor, even then, that would fuel such florid speculations. "Not really," said Dr. Fairchild. "He was careful in what he said. He certainly wasn't a blatant racist. He kept his hatreds under wraps . . . most of the time. I suspected he was too radical for any regular political party, though."

"Why?"

He rocked back in his creaky swivel chair. "The '64 election came down to Johnson versus Goldwater. One day I was walking in the hall with Bill and I asked him what he thought of the candidates. He answered, 'I'd give two hundred dollars apiece to see both those sons of bitches kicking at the end of a rope.' Later, after he'd left town, I heard he'd studied *Mein Kampf* while he lived here in Corvallis, sitting at night in the osu library, and he'd joined the John Birch Society. His wife at the time, Pat, very likeable, thought it was all just a phase he was going through. Later, he divorced her."

Weniger Hall, which houses the Physics Department, looks much the same now as it did in '62—*the same old life*: scratched waxy floors and a cobwebby ceiling. A framed sketch of Galileo greets visitors at the entrance. I'd never been inside the building until the day I met Dr. Fairchild there. Heavy wooden lab doors bore signs saying "CAUTION." "Safety Glasses Required." "Strong Magnetic Field." "Radioactive Material." "Cancer Suspect Agent." I'd stepped into a strange and lethal world, it seemed, leaving behind my own safe haven. The scariest piece of equipment in the English Department is a fire extinguisher.

Of course, in and of itself, Weniger's a benign and decent place; students are trained to use volatile materials with care. Looking back, I'm sure I felt wary that day because I expected to find the residue of Pierce's hatred smudging the walls: some faint foul smell, some off-color stain. But hatred's not that easy to track. "He did his job. He worked hard," Dr. Fairchild told me. "He was one of the first solid state physicists here, trying to build a superconducting magnet . . . a pioneering effort back then. He was a good guy to talk shop with."

Nothing in physics, or science in general, could have tilted Pierce toward his racial/political views.

What about the listless community Malamud had lampooned so

fiercely in *A New Life*? "In the sixties, the police in Corvallis regarded any non-Caucasian as unusual," Dr. Fairchild said. "The Elks Club was segregated." But that was Anywhere, America, in those days—and still is, in some corners: near Hayden Lake, Idaho, and in the ashes of several southern black churches.

"I saw him on television the other night," Dr. Fairchild told me (Pierce had appeared on *60 Minutes*, denying any connection with Timothy McVeigh). "He looked just the same, except he never used to wear glasses." No camo clothes, guns, or tattoos. Just a middle-aged former physics professor. Dr. Fairchild scratched his silver hair. "Makes you wonder, where in his life did the seed get planted for that degree of hate?"

Science, he added sadly, can explain to us the innermost workings of atoms, can measure heat in the cauldrons of stars, but it offers only shallow glimpses of our very own hearts of darkness.

Restitution

On January 6, 2000, Michael Sager, a property manager in Tulsa, was checking buildings downtown in anticipation of a cold snap. He wanted to make sure that the pipes weren't leaking, that they were properly protected in case of a freeze. In particular, he was concerned about a building that had once housed an upscale restaurant, Finales, on East First Street. The restaurant had been closed for a week, and the building was sitting empty, unsupervised. In an alley beside the property, by the former restaurant's kitchen door, Sager noticed liquid pooling and spilling down the street. It was peculiarly thick and crimson in color. He assumed a pipe had broken somewhere and that the red-brick pavement, as well as the late afternoon light, had created the strange hue.

Following the stream to its source, he saw it seeping from underneath the doors of the Francisco Ray Embalming Service, directly behind the old restaurant. The blood—for that's what it was, he understood clearly now—was filling potholes in the alley three to four inches deep and rushing to a storm sewer on the southeast corner of Detroit and First Streets, which drained into the Arkansas River.

Immediately, Sager contacted the Tulsa City–County Health Department, and an inspection by a storm water management team found the blood flowing from a sewage backup in the mortuary. Subsequent investigations determined it was legal for embalmers to dispose of blood and other bodily wastes in the municipal sewer system, although the usual practice was to pack biomedical hazards in secure containers and haul them off to incinerators.

The mortuary owner was ordered to disinfect the alley using an extra-heavy solution of 20 percent bleach and 80 percent water. Straight bleach was ordered to be poured into the potholes and then vacuumed up. "We had lots of jokes about [the mortuary] when we opened," Patrick Hobbs, Finales's owner, told a *Tulsa World* reporter. "'If you don't like this grand finale [to your meal],' we'd say, 'you can get the ultimate finale next door.'"

A novelist might use this anecdote, and its unsettling details, to convey the grittiness of urban life. I can imagine it nestling effectively inside a hard-boiled crime story, the fetid backdrop to the detective hero's unsavory profession. But I can also imagine another context, in which the gruesome imagery might transcend the merely disgusting and cause a reader moral as well as physical queasiness, perhaps even adding a fantastic air: Gabriel García Márquez instead of Raymond Chandler.

I discovered this bloody alley one day in a pair of newspaper articles while researching the Tulsa Race Riot Commission, a nine-member panel charged by the Oklahoma House of Representatives with conducting a historical study and developing a record of the May 31, 1921, riot in downtown Tulsa, in which thirty-five square blocks were destroyed and scores of African Americans killed.

The commission had been established in 1997, eight decades after the riot; by early 2000 it was ready to issue its preliminary report. The panelists concluded that "government at all levels" had failed to provide the "moral and ethical responsibility of fostering a sense of community" that could bridge "divides of ethnicity and race" in Tulsa in the early 1920s. As a result, racial hatred was "institutionalized" in the city, "tolerated by official federal, state, county, and city policy." Therefore, on the morning of May 31, 1921, armed vigilantes provoked by the false rumor of a white woman's rape by a black man felt free to enter the African American neighborhood of Greenwood, pull families from their homes, burn the properties, murder an unknown number of people—probably hundreds—and bury them later in mass graves. To date, the Tulsa riot remains the worst occasion of racial violence in American history.

The commission recommended restitution "in real and tangible form" to survivors of the riot, most of whom were children at the time and are now in their eighties and nineties. Restitution "would be good public policy and do much to repair the emotional as well as physical scars of this most terrible incident in our shared past," the panelists wrote. They suggested individual compensation, as well as educational scholarships for the city's African American community.

Right away, many of Oklahoma's politicians tried to discredit restitution. "People are going to say, 'If we do this for Tulsa, where does it stop?'" said Robert Milacek, a Republican House member from Enid. "What about the Mennonites whose homes were burned during World War I? And the American Indians. We could go on forever."

Abe Deutschendorf, a Democrat from Lawton, agreed. "Who's at fault [for tolerating racial tension]? What I'm hearing is the state. Sorry . . . you did not make that argument convincing to me," he said, despite the panel's photos of several lynchings from the time, carried out with full knowledge of public officials; a Tulsa high school yearbook featuring a page of black-hooded, Klan-style "knights"; and a popular postcard from the era, sold statewide in drugstores, of a black man's torching death in southeastern Oklahoma, captioned "Coon Cookin'."

My own interest in the Riot Commission stemmed from my grandfather's lifelong career as a politician and a proponent of civil rights in Oklahoma. His beliefs, then, provided my context for the fouled alley. Here is how I saw it: Thirty-five blocks of downtown Tulsa had once vanished in hateful violence. Bodies lay unclaimed—in fact, unknown—in the ground there. Now, a handful of folks was trying to restore the city's memory of the events and in some small way rectify the tragedy. Powerful people, backed by money and easy media access, were working hard to silence them. In the middle of all this, a building started to bleed.

In the green and gold chambers of Oklahoma's House of Representatives, my grandfather once showed me reams of thin pink paper, the record of every motion he'd ever proposed as a state rep, every bill he'd ever drafted or supported. The papers were fusty, and the chamber struck my ten-year-old mind as spooky: big and dark, imposing, austere. "The will of the people gets done here," he told me, "and it's all based on stacks of old paper like this—ancient laws, tried-and-true ideas updated to fit our time."

He died in 1978, but I'm certain, from the record he left, he would have enthusiastically welcomed the state House's formation of the Tulsa Race Riot Commission, and he would have embraced restitution as a means of stanching the blood of the past.

For me, because of his passions, the power of language has always been bound up with buildings: the creeds, oaths, mottoes, and poems etched into stone in the official institutions he taught me to revere; the names of past legislators carved into copper plaques; democracy's yellowed documents preserved under glass in hallowed halls; the sad, simple names of the dead imprinted in the faces of war memorials.

Something about thin script and the tonnage of marbled walls, the combination of the seemingly ephemeral and the old and permanent, has always impressed on me the essentially elegiac nature of words. And I have come to believe that the languages of literature work together with our nation's official languages in this manner: literature is a stylization of our individual consciences and our most intimate thoughts; laws, as public decrees, are stylizations of our awareness of others. The panelist, charged with investigating legal abuses, observes ownership deeds. The novelist observes the bleeding building. The panelist calls for restitution to heal a public rift. The novelist tells us that restitution is both necessary and yet wholly inadequate to heal our own souls—telling us this to promote not fatalism but generosity, an appreciation and forgiveness of the depths of human frailty. Both views are integral to our understanding of community, of the present and the past.

In 1996, as I sat by the chain link fence surrounding the void where the Murrah building once stood, reading scribbled poems and rain-smeared notes left by families from all over America, I realized that the bombing had felt deeply personal to me, an ambush on the physical home of the values and language my grandfather had once shown me, here in this very city. I took home a piece of the building, a small gray stone. Every day now, I keep it close when I write: a wordless reminder that my words, to say anything at all worthwhile about America, need the heft of a sorrowful stone, the pressure of the past.

In the early morning hours of May 31, 1921, just up the road from Oklahoma City in the Greenwood district of Tulsa, eight-year-old Kinney Booker ran with his six-year-old sister from their burning home, which collapsed behind them. They had been hiding in the attic, listening to rifle shots ricocheting throughout their neighborhood, overhearing intruders downstairs shouting at their father, "Nigger, do you have a gun?" and then dragging him down the street. When smoke began to curl around them, the children fled on their own. Booker recalled, for the Riot Commission, that dozens of frightened families were surging randomly out of the neighborhood. Even the telephone poles were in flames. His sister gripped his hand and asked, "Kinney, is the world on fire?"

Until the commission made a concerted effort to locate and interview riot survivors, Booker's story, despite its drama and importance, had never been told; his words had not been recorded, not added to any public accounting. "I thought I knew history. But . . . the shame has been that for decades, even in schools here in Tulsa, children can grow up and not know something like this happened in their community," says Eddie Faye Gates, a retired history teacher and commission member who interviewed over sixty children of the riot. "How can we expect them to learn from it and do better if we don't teach them?"

Many survivors told the commission their loved ones simply vanished. Otis Clark, who was eighteen when the attack began, never heard from his stepfather again after he was forced from his home. "Nobody knows what happened to him. There was no funeral, no memorial, no nothing."

In fact, prior to the commission's report, there was only one serious legal investigation of the event: in 1926, a white man who owned a theater and a hotel in the black neighborhood sued the American Central Insurance Company for refusing payment on his ruined properties. The company cited a "riot exclusion clause" in the policies and won the case; at the trial, its lawyer admitted that a "few hundred to several thousand" white folks intended the "extermination of the colored people of Tulsa and the destruction of the colored settlement, homes, and buildings, by fire."

For years, then, after the trial, another long hush fell. It was as Edgar Allan Poe had written at the end of "The Fall of the House of Usher": "There was a long tumultuous shouting sound like the voice of a thousand waters . . . [then it all] closed sullenly and silently"—only to bleed through the walls again, decades later.

Nationwide, now, our sense of our surroundings appears to be eroding. Old buildings topple; new ones seem more and more temporary. As I write, New York University plans to destroy a Greenwich Village house where Poe once lived and to construct a new law school building. "Nevermore" the spirits who once haunted those rooms and enriched American art. Recently, I heard an engineering professor extol the Internet's virtues, insisting that face-to-face encounters were overrated, that physical classrooms were more trouble than they were worth—it costs too much money and time, he said, to maintain *place*. He believes learning could occur more efficiently online, in the no-place, no-fixed-hours of cyberspace. This vision is gaining currency in education, business, and government, and will no doubt find a bigger voice in our national and international literature.

I fear that Poe's settings will come to seem quaint next to the chic prose-wastelands of the future. But real skeletons will continue to be hidden in real closets, the worst purposes will unfold in actual dungeons, truck bombs will shatter material buildings with mortal people inside, and tangible neighborhoods will fall in genuine flames. A storyteller who flees from ghosts, seduced by the illusions of freedom from time and place, flees the very source of storytelling; fails to learn how best to be a citizen both of the nation and of art; fails to see past the merely gruesome and into a subtly moral realm; fails to understand how, one morning, as small leaders continued to reject the cries of the past, a building started bleeding in Tulsa.

After Murrah

Friday, July 12, 1996: Dr. Paul Heath wants to see the getaway route. "Let's head down this alley, and see if he might've gone that way," he says. He walks briskly north and east, away from the chain link fence, draped with teddy bears, that rings the grassy spot where the Alfred P. Murrah building once stood. The bears, yellow, brown, white, some purple, some green, stare after us. A warm breeze stirs strings around the koalas' waists, the grizzlies' chests, knotted tightly to the fence. Cotton feet tap the silver posts: like kids, impatient to play.

It's a humid, full summer day, a year and three months after the morning Dr. Heath crawled from the rubble that used to be his workplace, the Veterans Administration Office on the fifth floor of the now-vanished structure. He seems dazed as we talk. So am I. We're both here for our own reasons.

Glass shards still sprinkle portions of Northwest Fifth Street, near the crumbled curbs, where Timothy McVeigh allegedly parked a Ryder rental truck containing dynamite, fuel oil, and four thousand pounds of ammonium nitrate that blew the face off the building, and collapsed all its floors, at 9:02 A.M. on April 19, 1995.

Dr. Heath leads me across Robinson Street, then behind the YMCA, which was also badly damaged in the blast. Its windows remain boarded; chunks of debris and glass pepper the grounds. I stoop and find a piece of blue plastic, about the size of a hangnail. This could be a fragment of one of the barrels that held the explosive mixture, Dr. Heath tells me. If that's the case, I'm amazed it's still lying here after a year, amazed it hasn't been tagged as evidence. Though fifty to seventy-five people an hour come to stand at the fence, even as late as 10:00 on hot summer nights, few are here to scavenge. Most are from out of state and approach the place as sacred ground. They stare quietly at the teddy bears, the photographs and poems slipped into Baggies and attached to the fence as tributes to the dead (168 total) and the survivors.

As for evidence: "The morning of the explosion, I had a briefcase sitting open on my desk, and the bomb blew material into it," says Dr. Heath. "There was some blue plastic from the barrels. Later, I showed it to the FBI, and they said, 'We'll take it if you want us to,' " not very interested. They already had plenty of it.

The south wall of the Oklahoma Water Resources Board, directly across the street from the Murrah site, is a tic-tac-toe game of Xs and Os drawn by FBI agents to mark bits of evidence in their case against McVeigh. He didn't just leave a trail; he left a spray.

But it's the trail we're searching for today. Glass as fine as spun sugar cracks beneath our shoes as we enter the alley abutting the Y. According to information that has surfaced in preliminary hearings for McVeigh's trial, and the trial of Terry Nichols, a surveillance camera on a building across the street from Murrah may have captured the fatal parking job; another camera, down the street at the Regency Tower apartment building, may give us a clue to McVeigh's movements before 9:00.

Dr. Heath, who has attended the hearings in Denver, tells me, "The Ryder truck stopped in front of the Regency Tower at one point. An occupant—which we now think was McVeigh—got out and entered a grocery store that's there on the first floor of the apartment building. He bought some cigarettes and some matches—it's said he doesn't smoke—and a couple of soft drinks, then drove around the block, came back, and parked a second time right in front of the camera." Presumably he was waiting for an opportune time, or for a parking place in front of the Murrah building. Some eyewitnesses say McVeigh was accompanied by another man, who has yet to be identified (apparently, Terry Nichols was not in the city that day).

Purportedly, shortly before 9:00, McVeigh left the truck in front of the northeastern side of Murrah, just under the America's Kids day care center. He sprinted across Fifth Street to a sun-blistered yellow Mercury Marquis, parked in an alley near the Water Resources Board and a restaurant called the Athenian, then drove with his mystery partner out of the area. The bomb had a two-minute fuse.

"There was supposed to have been a guy smoking his pipe near the intersection of the alley and Robinson Street, where there was a Dumpster," Dr. Heath tells me now. He doesn't know who this man was—a worker from a nearby building, perhaps, on a morning break. "The guy swears he saw McVeigh and one other person in that car come out this way, nearly hitting the Dumpster. I suspect they went right up here, behind the Y."

He glances back across the street at all the stuffed animals. Yellow and purple ribbons around their necks rustle softly in the breeze. "They were probably right here, directly behind the Y, when the bomb went off. They would have been showered by the glass from up above." He points at sheets of plywood on the windows. "One of the things the FBI could do, if they wanted to make sure which direction McVeigh took, is they could match some of this glass with the glass in his tires." He shoos away a pesky flying ant. "I don't know if anybody's thought of that," he says. "I'm sure they did."

We stroll farther east. The ants are getting thicker. So is the humidity. "What I'm curious to see is, does this alley extend to the next block?" he says.

It does. North of us, not far, is a raised loop of Interstate 235. "Why couldn't he have come this way?" Dr. Heath asks himself. His voice wobbles just a little; his eyes are moist. Clearly, it's vital to him to know everything that happened that day. "One of the people in my office, Martin Cash, claims a client of his who lives over here by the railroad tracks saw McVeigh that morning with the other person, later, after the bombing, changing cars near the tracks and Ninth Street. That would support the hypothesis that he came this way, and it might explain why the other person was not with him." McVeigh was alone when he was stopped by a highway patrolman an hour and fifteen minutes after the blast, seventy miles from Oklahoma City.

There's usually not much traffic here at that time of the morning, Dr. Heath says. Now, just before noon, the streets are nearly empty. This whole section of downtown has yet to recover from the attack.

He shades his eyes from the sun and looks toward the freeway. "Recently, evidence has come out in court that McVeigh and whoever was with him were here on Friday, December 16th [four months before the bombing]. McVeigh says he was just driving around, but those of us who worked in the building know they were also, at some point, *in* the building. Many of us saw them inside. So it was a premeditated, deliberate act, as far as I'm concerned."

He peels off his green sport coat (this summer, Oklahoma is experiencing a scorching drought as severe as the Dust Bowl drought in the thirties) and adjusts the wire-rimmed glasses on his face.

He's a short man in his fifties, with a smile that looks both pained and serene. He's attentive to detail, quick to smooth the wrinkles in his coat, but gently, not in a fussy or overstated way. "Some folks think the trial will bring us all closure, but I'm not sure about that," he says. "The trial gives people something to focus on, but it doesn't give you any reassurance that it won't happen again, it doesn't bring back the people that you loved. It's very easy for all of us who were there to live it over again and again."

He stops, considering how much of himself to reveal to me—or so I guess, awkward with him now. After all, we've just met. Months ago, I'd written him from Oregon, explaining that my family was originally from Oklahoma, that the bombing had unsettled me more than I'd expected it to—more than I had any *right* for it to. I didn't spell out that last part, nor did I add that my marriage had recently ended, that I was so depressed I could barely get out of bed each day, that I couldn't tell, any longer, where my private pain, and my grief over public events, finished or began. I'd simply asked him if he'd tell me his story, and he'd generously agreed.

Today, I'm relieved to find, he seems to need to talk, and to understand that I need to listen to whatever he has to say.

2

On the bombing's first anniversary in April 1996, I sat in my apartment in Corvallis, in front of my television screen, knowing I'd be swarmed by sadness. But I tuned in anyway, needing, on this day, a community for my grief, even if it was a gathering I couldn't touch, brought to me, crisply, by the latest satellite uplinks.

The morning shows featured survivors of the blast, multiple shots of children gripping teddy bears at the memorial service in Oklahoma City. Tabloid talk shows ran bloody videos. Finally, that afternoon, Oprah topped her competition, profiling not only Murrah building victims "in their shared journey toward healing" but also the victims of other American calamities. Her apocalyptic potpourri closed with the story of a cat, hurt while dragging her kittens from a burning building.

In effect, this astonishing sequence—the capper to a series of terrorist acts, murder, and accidents—told viewers, "We know how to make you cry in spite of yourself, and there's not a damn thing you can do about it."

I distrusted Oprah already. On the phone, my cousin Anne in Oklahoma City had shared with me rumors that Oprah and a camera crew had stormed through a children's wing in a city hospital shortly after the bombing. She burst into a room of bandaged kids, her cheeks glistening with pity . . . only to realize that these weren't the blast victims. She'd found, instead, the kids' cancer ward. Abruptly, and without another word to the patients, she wheeled out of the room demanding to know where the Murrah kids were. (Oklahomans were also galled by CBS news reporter Connie Chung, who arrived at the Murrah building in a limo and asked the city's assistant fire chief, "Can you handle this?" in an inflection that hit the locals as "You poor, dumb Okies.")

In spite of myself, I watched Oprah's anniversary show and cried just as hard over the cat as I had over images of Baylee Almon, the dead baby clutched by the fireman in the now famous photo. Earlier, at 7:02 A.M. Pacific Time, I had lighted a candle in my living room to coincide with the beginning of the memorial ceremony in Oklahoma City. From my closet I had pulled a teddy bear dressed in farmer's clothes—a joke gift from my mother one Christmas. I set it by the candle on my living room floor, then watched the TV kids weep behind their own stuffed animals.

I felt self-conscious and silly with my little ritual, though no one was there to make fun; I felt embarrassed to be so easily manipulated by the television networks.

But I also felt, in those moments, genuinely attached to Oklahomans, grafted again to my family's roots in that place. I felt the brief, sweet, *urgent* release of open mourning.

Now, I have to admit: I don't know how much of my experience that day was authentic, how much created by the camera. My own sorrow puzzled me, and troubles me still.

The Daughertys are Sooner-born and Sooner-bred; though I was raised in West Texas, my parents took me to Oklahoma several times every year from the summer I was born until I was a young adult.

In the 1930s, my grandfather served as a deputy sheriff in Cotton County, Oklahoma, devoting himself to keeping order in the state. In the late fifties and early sixties, he was elected, twice, to the Oklahoma House of Representatives; his picture still hangs in a hallway in the capitol. For these reasons, I cared more for the state, for its laws and public buildings, perhaps, than the average TV viewer outside of "America's heartland."

Still, I'd never set foot inside the Alfred P. Murrah complex. No one I knew was injured or killed in the explosion.

My cousin Anne worked downtown and was one of the first volunteers to feed and clothe rescue workers after the blast. But mine were circumstantial links and hardly accounted for my profound depression about the event.

Throughout the anniversary coverage, newscasters reminded viewers of the alleged sequence of actions that had led to the destruction of the building, and Americans watched helplessly as the crime unfolded all over again. Over the course of a year, and dozens of other news events, I'd forgotten a lot of details—and *I'd* been paying attention.

ITEM. In the spring of 1991, Timothy James McVeigh of Pendleton, New York, a Gulf War veteran, failed to be admitted into the U.S. Army's Special Forces. Physically, he wasn't ready for the rigorous tests required.

ITEM. Disillusioned now with the Army, McVeigh began driving cross-country, selling weapons at gun shows in Tulsa, Las Vegas, Phoenix, Grand Rapids, and elsewhere. On the gun circuit, he met various state militia members and started reading their literature. Publicly, he expressed anger at the U.S. government for allowing the United Nations to create a "new world order" under which Americans would eventually be forced to surrender their guns.

ITEM. In February 1992, the *Lockport [New York] Union Sun and Journal* published a letter to the editor from McVeigh, saying, in part, "What is it going to take to open up the eyes of our elected officials? America is in a serious decline . . . IS CIVIL WAR IMMINENT? DO WE HAVE TO SHED BLOOD TO REFORM THE CURRENT SYSTEM?"

ITEM. In August 1992, McVeigh raged to friends about federal agents who had killed the wife and son of a white separatist named Randy Weaver in Ruby Ridge, Idaho.

ITEM. In the spring of 1993, McVeigh drove to Waco, Texas, where members of the federal government's Alcohol, Tobacco, and Firearms agency had surrounded the compound of religious leader David Koresh. McVeigh protested the government's siege and expressed outrage when the compound burned, on April 19, killing Koresh and many of his followers.

ITEM. On April 19, 1995, seventy-five minutes after a truck bomb blew up the Alfred P. Murrah federal building in Oklahoma City, Timothy McVeigh was stopped by a highway patrolman, seventy miles from the city, for not having a license plate on his car. Subsequent evidence connected McVeigh to the rental truck that contained the bomb, and he was arrested for the crime.

ITEM. Terry Lynn Nichols, a farmer from Herington, Kansas, and a former Army buddy of Timothy McVeigh, was soon arrested as a coconspirator in the plot to blow up the building. Prosecutors claimed the men were seeking revenge against the federal government for Ruby Ridge and Waco.

Listening to this summary, once, twice, twice again, I felt keenly my vulnerabilities as a citizen, and I experienced a kind of narrative dread. "Life can only be understood backwards, but it must be lived forwards," the philosopher Søren Kierkegaard once said. But even in retrospect, the bombing was a story that made little sense, that needed to be erased.

There's not a damn thing you can do about it.

Among my favorite childhood memories of Oklahoma are fire-flies—cotillions of them, weaving in and out of rose bushes or sultry wisteria vines, drooping coquettishly in the heat of dusk. While playing hide-and-seek with my cousins, I'd push through swarms of glitter as if running through beaded curtains.

My hometown in Texas sits flat in the middle of a desert; often, on summer evenings there, I'd watch dry lightning stalk the skies, jacklighting the burning sand on which I lay. Oklahoma, in con-trast, was dripping with dew and sparkled wherever I looked, in the grass or in the sky. Snatching the fireflies out of the air, sealing them in jelly jars, was like storing powdered lightning.

In my teens, I grew restless with the deliberate pace of rural life and dreaded heading north to cross the Red River, but as an arid child I'd found Oklahoma to be a lush—and moistly forgiving—paradise.

I remembered all this the morning the Murrah building was bombed. I remembered hiding in a field behind my grandparents' house, holding hands with Anne. As kids, we'd promised to marry each other. Instead, a dozen years ago, she'd wedded then swiftly divorced a man who abused her. At the time, I recall thinking her husband was a lummox. At the wedding reception, I didn't want to shake his hand. My childhood crush on Anne had long since passed, but I found myself jealous nevertheless—and worried for her safety.

I thought, I don't understand her. Why would she marry such a creep? I just don't know her anymore.

When Murrah blew up, I tried to phone Oklahoma, to see if Anne and others in my family were okay, but lines into the state were jammed. For days, until I could get through, it seemed to me that the whole middle part of the continent had simply gone dark. Six years later, on 9/11, a similar conviction swept through me, as rogue planes seemed to swarm the entire East Coast— evidence of a war, wrote John Edgar Wideman, that we may "have already lost."

In the summer of '95, my own separation stunned me as much as Anne's troubles had, years ago. In our twelve years as a couple, my wife and I had always worked well together day to day, shopping, cooking, tending our garden. But back then, I was often given to depression, and that was a bigger problem for Martha than either of us knew how to solve.

We kept a cat named Jake. Martha had found her beneath a car when Jake was just a kitten. She brought her home, bathed her several times to get the grease out of her fur. Sopping wet, the poor thing wasn't much bigger than my palm. She shivered and mewed pitifully. "What's shaking, Jake?" I said, and the name stuck. One afternoon, years later, I was sitting in a chair reading a book. I looked up and noticed Jake in a square of sunlight on the living room carpet washing herself, licking her legs and rubbing the backs of her ears. She looked surpassingly happy, languid, fluid, fully at peace with herself. The warm, buttery light nestled in the cinnamon streaks of her fur. Something in me eased. For a minute or two, watching Jake luxuriate in the light, I relaxed. *Darkness, heaviness*—neither word accurately captures the drudgery of chronic depression, though they're the terms most often used. Constriction. Lack of air. In any case, Jake freed me for a moment. Life seemed perfectly calm and natural. Not a struggle. Not a bruising tug of war with every ticking second.

This is what it's like, I thought. This is what it's like not to be depressed. I was astonished, and bitter to be missing this serenity most of the time. Later, when I described my afternoon to Martha, she looked at me in shock. "That kind of calm is normal," she said. "It's what I feel every day."

A month and a half after the Oklahoma City bombing, she told me, "I don't want to be married anymore."

I'd been more depressed than usual, withdrawing from her, obsessively watching the news. "Do you want to go skiing this weekend?" she'd ask me. "Or hiking? Anything. Let's just get out of the house, okay?"

"You go," I'd tell her. "Have a good time." Then I'd watch the dust of Murrah, stir a few more memories.

I recalled, as a child, reading in my grandparents' living room: *Charlotte's Web*, *Little House on the Prairie*, and much later, Steinbeck's *In Dubious Battle*, about the hard lives of California fruit-pickers. "Where's Route 66?" I asked my grandfather one day while reading *The Grapes of Wrath*. "Is it close by?" He looked at me over the top of his newspaper. "Well, Professor"—he called me Professor, he explained, because I always had my "dirty face" in a book—"it isn't far. It isn't far at all," and I dreamed of following the mythic old escape path, living out a story the way the Joads had.

Behind me, as I read, an oak clock hugged the wall; its clackety ticking, steady as the beat of a country jug band, seemed part of my books, as natural as page numbers or margins: tales of the FBI, adventures of the G-Men. When I grew up, I decided, I'd work in the FBI lab, studying the magic of fingerprints, trapping my nation's enemies, the Dillingers, the nasty Capones.

Or I'd dash off stories of my own about people fleeing dust—the darkness, the heaviness, the terrible lack of air.

Boo Radley shuffled through my dreams, in a swirl of blowing leaves. I loved Atticus, Scout, and Jem, and all the others in Harper Lee's wonderful novel, but it was Boo I understood—not the violent part, the crazy, mute part, but the part of him that lived in the dark, worrying, worrying.

"I don't know what to do when you get like this," my wife would tell me, years later, when she'd return from a hike or a skiing trip in the Cascade Mountains to find me sitting silently in an unlighted room.

Then one day: "I feel like I'm being suffocated," Martha said. "I want you to leave, please."

So I moved into a place on my own.

At first I hunkered down, seeing no one, rarely talking to anyone on the phone. I'd go to bed early each afternoon. Finally, I managed some short steps back into the world, calling family and friends. After many months, Anne agreed to talk to me about her volunteer efforts following the Murrah attack. I didn't know why, but soon after my marriage had failed, her story came to seem vital to me, as if by knowing her again, understanding what had happened to her over the years and learning her coping skills, I could cope too. I wondered if the sands and slopes of our childhoods, which shape our geographical senses, our understandings of time and space, also frame the way we grieve. I suspected so, and I needed to see those perspectives again, to chart my mental contours.

The poet Roberta Spear once wrote, "I always knew where I came from / I just couldn't believe it."

And Dr. Paul Heath wrote to say he'd see me if I came. I'd glimpsed his name in a newspaper article on survivors of the blast—he'd been listed as a spokesperson for the victims' families. On a computer data bank in a school library, I found his address, then contacted him on impulse. It was just like writing a story, I thought, living it forwards, with no intimation of the end.

3

Oklahoma City appears to me, after many years away, to be mostly parking lots. It covers 608 square miles ("a horse pasture the size of England," Will Rogers once exaggerated). Its skyscrapers are squatty and boxlike, rising out of a baked prairie of one-way avenues. Blank walls outnumber windows (Murrah was a notable exception). Angles swallow curves.

Blurs of cars shimmer in heat waves shimmying up from the

streets. Red bricks, brown bricks, tan bricks, with few guiding signs or words of any kind.

It feels like the fifties here. Leisurely. Easy. Life neither forwards nor backwards—just marking time.

"I've decided I'm going to get through this," Dr. Heath tells me now, observing his city's scars here at the meeting of Fifth and Robinson. "I recognize I'm going to have a normal amount of depression—you've seen me cry here today. But I'm over the rage, and in all honesty, about three weeks after the bombing, I was able to say, 'Whoever did this, I personally forgive them.' I pardon them completely. Because it's in *my best interest* to do that. I can't continue to carry the anger. It'd eat me up."

In early December 1995, the Tenth Circuit Court of Appeals ruled that the defendants deserved a more objective trial judge than the one they'd been assigned—in the bombing, Wayne Alley, initially set to hear the case, suffered damage to his courtroom and chambers, located one block south of Murrah. A member of his staff was injured.

Richard A. Matsch, the new man on the bench, moved the trial to Denver, his hometown, seeking an impartial jury pool. As soon as he did so, Dr. Heath filed a lawsuit that would have forced the judge to broadcast legal proceedings back to the survivors in Oklahoma via closed-circuit television. Matsch threw the lawsuit out; he claimed it was superfluous in light of the new national antiterrorism bill, which included provisions for broadcasts.

He hinted that, though he would later make a final ruling, he was not inclined to have cameras in the courtroom.

Since Dr. Heath has already made his peace with the suspects, he's looking for the trial to "send a message" to his fellow citizens. "It'll show we're determined not to tolerate this kind of behavior," he tells me as we stroll again toward the vast absence that once was the Murrah building. "But we'll seek justice within the framework of the law. Our constitution works. Our system works."

And McVeigh's involvement? "I think he drove the truck. And I think he'll *tell* you he drove the truck. He probably believes he was trying to start a revolution. I think he allowed his anger at life to fester and fester until it grew into hate, then he got with others who cultivated that hate until it resulted in evil. That's the way I have it figured. Time will tell if that's true."

We're behind the Y again, in another cloud of ants. "There was a day care center in this building, too," Dr. Heath says. I smell dust and hear liquid dripping somewhere inside the shell of the Water Resources Board down the street. A little girl, visiting somberly with her family, reaches toward the fence around the Murrah site and grasps a teddy bear's furred hand. Nineteen children—some of them infants and toddlers—died on the second floor.

Officially, the first child ever born in Oklahoma City was a girl. Her parents, Mr. and Mrs. Jefferson W. Cunningham, originally from the little town of Taylor, Texas, named her Oklahoma Belle. She came crying into the world in a modest home at 324 Northwest Third Street, just two blocks from the spot where the first beams of the Murrah building would be erected, eighty-four years later.

Oklahoma City itself was born instantly in the midst of history's biggest horse race. The Cunninghams had joined thousands of other families on horseback, in buggies, on foot—some even leapt from moving trains—to snatch whatever acreage they could in the massive land rush that opened up the Unassigned Lands in Oklahoma Country, starting at high noon on Monday, April 22, 1889. At dawn on that day, the area now known as Oklahoma City (then called Oklahoma Station) was largely unoccupied; by nightfall, around twelve thousand people crowded onto undefined lots. There were no borders, fences, streets, or alleys; there was no municipal government. Boasts and claims proliferated. No one really knew who owned what. Only one water well existed, at what later became the corner of Main and Broadway Streets downtown, and the man who said he owned it charged five cents apiece for a pint cup.

W. L. Couch, the first elected mayor, was shot dead in a land dispute less than a year after taking office.

The city's first large-scale disaster occurred on its first Fourth of July, when a bleacher built for people to view horse races and a baseball game collapsed, injuring several spectators and killing a little boy.

Over the years, frequent flooding of the North Canadian River, which runs through town, hatched hordes of mosquitoes and periodically left many families homeless.

An April 1892 article in *Harper's* magazine assessed the place this way: "There are no Indians in this scene. They have been paid [by the U.S. government] one dollar and twenty-five cents an acre for this land, which is worth five dollars as it lies . . . [It is] prairie land with low curving hills covered with high grass and thick timber. This as far as the eye [can] see, and nothing else." The writer, plainly impatient with his subject, then concludes, "I think any man who can afford a hall bedroom and a gas stove in New York City is better off than he would be as the owner of 160 acres on the prairie."

Thus was the Heartland dismissed, and largely ignored by the rest of the country, until John Steinbeck in *The Grapes of Wrath*, Woody Guthrie in his songs, and Dorothea Lange in her stark black-and-white photos, documented the Dust Bowl migration of poor Okies.

Oklahoma Belle Cunningham married in 1912 and remained in business in the city, as a floral dealer, until her death in the 1970s—her contained, unchanging existence testament to both Oklahoma City's conservative steadiness and its relative youth.

As a young woman she may have gone downtown with her husband to listen to the symphony, featuring then a young harpist named Gail Lawton, whose fingers, in closeups, later substituted for Harpo Marx's in difficult harp solos in the Marx Brothers' movies. Or she may have driven to the Shrine Theater, a former Masonic lodge at Northwest Sixth and Robinson, to watch Will

Rogers perform his rope tricks and comedy routines. The theater was within walking distance of St. Anthony, the city's first permanent hospital, as well as the oldest churches in the area, the First Methodist (which hosted believers of many creeds until other denominations could build their own sanctuaries) and St. Joseph's Cathedral.

On April 19, 1995, St. Joseph's, just around the corner from Murrah, would suffer severe structural damage in the bombing and lose most of its stained glass windows. The First Methodist Church, also nearby, would be so badly wrecked that it is now scheduled to be completely torn down and rebuilt.

The first victims from the Murrah building, including Dianne Dooley, a young woman from the Veterans Administration Office and a colleague of Dr. Heath's, were taken to St. Anthony's Hospital. The Shrine Theater, which had become the *Journal Record* building, was devastated in the blast and now stands empty, its windows boarded. It was straight across the street from Murrah, where now only a wild kingdom of colorful bears exists. A sticker above one bear's head says, "Proud to be an Oklahoman."

"It will always be safe. It's between two churches," thought Ann Shaw, Alfred P. Murrah's oldest daughter, right after the new federal complex was built and dedicated to her father in 1977. Now, she says she has no idea why she thought that—before, she'd never considered the relative safety of buildings.

Her father, born in Indian Territory in 1904, became, at thirty-two, the youngest federal judge in American history, appointed by Franklin D. Roosevelt at the height of the Great Depression, two years before *The Grapes of Wrath* was published. My grandfather, just beginning to run for elective office at the time, would certainly have known of the man and may even have heard him speak at Democratic Party affairs around the state.

By the time Murrah retired in 1970, he'd earned a reputation as a strict, fair, demanding judge—the same terms later applied by reporters to Richard Matsch, who'd hear the Oklahoma City bombing case. Murrah, said the *Daily Oklahoman*, "could cut through drama, dogma, and doubletalk with the ease and speed of a hot knife slicing butter."

The structure erected in his honor, a steel-reinforced, poured concrete and glass rectangle, was supremely energy-efficient: tinted glass walls on its north, east, and west sides took full advantage of the prairie's abundant sunlight. The design won a national energy award, at a time when Jimmy Carter, then president, touted conservation.

Convenience was the building's other hallmark. It contained 107,000 square feet of open office space and 11,750 square feet devoted to snack shops and restrooms. The double-wide front doors were only 30 feet from a curbside parking area near the Fifth Street sidewalk. Infants in high chairs in the America's Kids day care center, on the second floor, often slapped the northside windows, laughing at the passersby below, many of whom looked up, waved, and smiled. Friendly folks, stopping to visit in the streets. The place was so safe, only one security guard was assigned to it.

"Oklahoma City on April 19, 1995, could probably best be described as typical of cities that have had desegregated school systems which resulted in a significant amount of white flight to the suburbs," Dr. Heath tells me. "We've had a tremendous outflow from the inner city"—but this trend began as long ago as the 1930s, when the parking meter was invented (right here in Oklahoma City) and downtown began to be perceived by most citizens as a crammed, impossible place to be.

In the 1980s, an oil bust, followed by several bank failures, emptied many buildings. The bombing, which harmed structures for several blocks in all directions from the cleared ground of Murrah, seemed to further dim prospects for downtown revitalization.

Clearly, though, for Dr. Heath, desegregation has been the major social development in his city—and in most other American cities—in the last thirty years. The high emotions surrounding it relate directly, in his mind, to the bombing; as he sees it, racism and intolerance for diverse viewpoints marked both events.

"I think that desegregation, in my own lifetime, has not been a bad thing either for the schools or for children," he says. "In fact, I thought that by doing it, we were avoiding a social revolution. Folks like McVeigh, I guess, had other ideas.

"We had a governor in this state, Raymond Gary, who, when the Civil Rights Act passed, went out, took a bulldozer, and bulldozed down all the small, black, separate-but-equal schools. Just tore them down. That took care of it in the rural areas, as far as he was concerned. In the metropolitan areas, we didn't do that. We took yellow school buses and moved people around." He believes that integration, in the long run, has benefited American culture, but he admits that, in the short term, it galvanized certain people's fears of racial myths, extremists like Timothy McVeigh. "I don't under-stand those attitudes." He shrugs. "It's my Okie roots, I guess. My mother didn't raise me to believe that people were all that different from one another."

Apparently, he's decided I'm okay, I think. He's going to reveal himself to me, and I'm grateful for his trust. In this terrible place, I feel us both relax. I brush away a pair of flying ants.

He tells me his mother was a riveter for the Douglas Aircraft Company during World War II. The family moved from a farm in Shawnee, Oklahoma, to Oklahoma City when his stepfather's G.I. Bill ran out. For the last twenty-eight years, Dr. Heath has been a counseling psychologist with the VA, helping mainly Korean, Viet-nam, and Gulf War veterans. He now works out of an old post office on the site where Oklahoma Belle's father once built a three-story brick building for his business.

"My mother was a problem solver, and she always wanted to do the right thing," Dr. Heath explains. He's silent for a beat, watching me; when he speaks again, his guard's back up, as though he's caught himself in a crucial mistake. I've done nothing but walk beside him, paying close attention; still, somehow, the fragile trust with me, so carefully developed, is gone.

Who can blame him? I think. Who the hell am I? Just another stranger in town.

"I think we all learn our trust in people at home, with the family, and that trust gets the most disturbed—leading, perhaps, in extreme cases, like McVeigh's, to hatred and racism—when you have an ineffective mother," he says carefully. I nod. I'm hearing now the VA doc, the smart, professional man. Precise. Impersonal. Unexposed. He's testing me again. "You can have a fairly ineffective father as long as you have a strong mother, and still produce people that function pretty well."

I'm listening. I'm with him. I smile to let him know.

He clears his throat and goes on. McVeigh's mother abandoned him when he was about fourteen. McVeigh withdrew from the world and began ordering survivalist equipment from gun magazines.

"Of course there's more to it. I believe he probably has a delusional feature to his paranoid character disorder," Dr. Heath says. "He's been deluded into thinking the government is out to kill him, and he has to kill it first. My experience with people with delusional features is that, usually, you can't reach them, no matter what you do."

His voice deepens: Diagnostic Mode, confident, clipped. "The groups that are beginning to pop up nationwide, the militia groups and so on . . . I think if you look closely, you'll see that the seeds of their discontent stem from the fact that we no longer have a common enemy outside of the United States, so they focus on a make-believe enemy within. Many of them, like McVeigh, are disillusioned because they come from broken homes. They expect the government to be that perfect mother and father they didn't have, and when they find out that people in government aren't perfect, they're unforgiving. They overreact with the hostility they feel for their own family."

He rubs his face. He's sweating lightly. The sun's become a stark white coal. "As for people who are disappointed in their society to the point of committing evil . . . " In his face, I believe I see a softening of muscles, a flicker of trust again—or the *need* to rely on someone. "One of the things I hope we can do, to prevent future pain, is *tell this story*."

4

Just before flying to the actual concrete and steel, gravel and glass, oak-lined Oklahoma City to listen to Paul Heath's story, I had found another OKC, a virtual, ever-updating, mega-bytten place, and it was exploding all over the Internet.

CLICKSITE #1: Casualties as of 4:30 A.M. EDT, April 21 [1995]. Urban Search and Rescue Task Forces reported 47 confirmed dead at the morgue.

CLICKSITE #2: If we could be [in Oklahoma City] to help, we would. Fort Worth thinks of you often. We've watched every day.

CLICKSITE #3: "Last Rescued Victim Files $4 Million Suit": Brandi Liggons, 15, had entered the federal building just before 9 a.m. to obtain social security information . . . the lawsuit [says she] . . . was injured as a "direct and proximate result of the wrongful conduct of the defendants." The injuries are said to be "permanent, painful, progressive, and disfiguring."

CLICKSITE # 4: "An Open Letter to Timothy McVeigh": Timothy, it is necessary to destroy the false illusion of moral authority that power systems, both religious and governmental, have always contrived [to create]. Be aware that the media, by any name in any age, exists to control the masses. In response to media questions . . . always attack . . .

These were just a thimbleful of over 2 million references to Oklahoma City I found on a single information server the first time I surfed the net. Some of the notices had been posted within days of the bombing; others were up to date. None came with much context. CNN, the *Daily Oklahoman,* the *Denver Post,* and Court TV all had online locations for continuous bombing coverage; the complete indictment against McVeigh and Nichols was available, as were transcripts of the pretrial hearings in Denver. Self-styled "patriots" and militia groups had their own home pages, with ever-expanding theories about what had happened to Murrah (including one suggestion that the British monarchy had ordered the attack, for reasons never made clear).

One former Navy man claimed the authorities were obscuring the truth of what had happened in Oklahoma, just as they were hiding the fact that flying saucers had been invented by the Nazis. He wrote, "'The One World Government' plans to use human-built saucers to stage a mock alien invasion, thereby drawing humanity together under the control of the secret world government."

An Internet "prophet" named Sollog claimed to have faxed a warning to the news media the day before the bombing, predicting the explosion. His fax began, magisterially, "Tomorrow night there shall be a comet. The comet called One . . . all shall see with their own eyes the star of Alpha be born. This is the sign that the One is upon the Earth." Then his diction crumbled ("Oh yeah, there is also Man and Woman"), echoing, finally, an old Top Forty hit by Three Dog Night ("One is the only number you can never divide and it is also the loneliest.")

It was as though the bomb in Oklahoma had utterly fragmented our language, scattering it in millions of different directions. The Tower of Babel looked like a playhouse next to the Web and its chat rooms.

Searching under "Okies," I found several web pages devoted to Route 66: digitized images of the photos of Dorothea Lange taken during the Depression, quotes from *The Grapes of Wrath*, U.S. maps in bright yellow colors, dust clouds swarming the screen that clicked me into yet another level of graphics, information, photos, and texts. If my computer had been powerful enough, I could even have listened to an interview with Woody Guthrie, then switched over to a simultaneous video display.

It takes little hand-to-eye coordination to turn the pages of a book, to follow lines of print, left to right. In books, words are organized neatly into sentences, paragraphs. Direction is clear.

Internet "pages," I learned, leave direction to the viewer, and the mind is engaged on many levels at once. The eye roams the screen, left to right, right to left, up and down. Pictures, words, moving graphics, sounds. CLICK. Another layer. Then another. Or return to the layer above. "Chronology" is meaningless. Events like the Oklahoma City bombing, already senseless to a rational mind, can become even more scrambled in this vast net of context-less information bytes.

That first day, I sent my mouse scurrying through the rubble of words, bookmarking several sites so I could run right to them when I logged on again.

This will end your Windows session
OK   Cancel

Absurdly, Rodgers and Hammerstein marched through my head: "Oklahoma, OK!"

I switched off the machine.

Each evening, I packed a little for my trip to the Heartland. Short-sleeved shirts (it was going to be hot). Pen and paper. Paul Heath's address. A portable tape recorder. A plastic vial with a super-tight cap for my pills.

On doctor's orders, I'd started taking an antidepressant. I was too embarrassed to mention this to friends. After all, what did I have to be depressed about? I was moving on, wasn't I, despite my separation? It seemed obscene to me to be feeling bad, when people in Oklahoma City had lost, forever, husbands, wives, parents, kids.

One of the symptoms of my depression, or maybe it was a side effect of the medication, was that I was terribly forgetful. I lost track of things. Misplaced items. For the first time in my life, I started keeping lists, just to help me through the day.

Pick up pants at cleaners.
Water the plants.
Call your doctor.

The act of packing wore me out. After spinning effortlessly through the arteries of the Internet, the prospect of actual, fuel-powered movement, of heaving my body forward, dragged on me considerably.

Shoe polish, socks, Band-aids, handkerchiefs.

Why go someplace, when you could sit in your favorite chair and access the world?

Oklahoma City had its own home page on the Web:

HELLO NEIGHBOR! CLICK here for Historic Photos of old OKC.

a) Oklahoma City's airport opened in 1932 on 640 acres purchased by city bond procedures. It was renamed Will Rogers Field in 1941 when the Army Air Corps assumed control.
b) The first uniformed band in Oklahoma City [was] organized in 1891.
c) [Belle Isle Park] was constructed in 1907 by the Oklahoma City Railway Company. Here, boats go cruising on the lake . . .

Gauzy images, the color of Milky Way candy bars, accompanied these captions. A sweetly innocent place, with few automobiles, weapons, federal agents; no one who'd ever read *The Turner Diaries*.

This, in contrast to the militiamen occupying the Internet's suburbs:

Timothy McVeigh kicked ass!
Freedom to the Terrorist
Terrorists Rule the World
Anarchy Forever

I'm glad that bombing was done.

I was told Bob Dole was inside.
you scum-sucking maggots, no one gives
a good god-damn for freedom

Blurry seismographs were available, suggesting that someone—
a murky government agent, perhaps—had planted extra bombs
inside the building.

A "patriot," convinced of Timothy McVeigh's innocence, offered
a step-by-step "How-To" on his trial defense: "I'd start with a . . .
picture of the so-called Great Seal of the United States as seen on the
back of a dollar bill," he wrote. "I would show that, over the eagle,
thirteen five-pointed (pentagonal) stars form the six-pointed Star of
David . . . [symbol for] a world Zionist government . . . then I would
relate the wars, occupations, assassinations [conducted by] America,
from Dixie to Mexico, to Panama, to Grenada, Germany twice,
Vietnam, Iraq, Waco, Ruby Ridge . . . tens of millions of people killed
and maimed in pursuit of the New World Order."

He concluded: "Since governments were first formed, Timothy,
they've created incidents like the Oklahoma City bombing to advance agendas such as wars or greater police powers."

Videos and T-shirts were for sale, commemorating the event.
Bomb-making manuals. Survival guides.

Just enough truth (*occupations, assassinations*) to almost—
almost—justify paranoia and hatred.

OK?
Cancel?
Error in the System.

Hold mail.
Pay bills.

It was agony, preparing for my trip. As I dragged my body around town, buying what I'd need, I felt as heavy as the planet. Despondency made my joints ache.

Recycle newspapers.
Allergy shots.

I wondered, also, if the Internet had spoiled me, made me lazy, atrophied everything but my clicking finger. It was so much easier—cleaner, more efficient—to travel the Web, meeting no one, than to actually get up and move.

Or perhaps all this weight I felt was the clot of confusion in my head, after hours of exposure to documents—arguments, investigations—on Oklahoma City, floating across my monitor.

I was losing my ability to focus. To really *grasp* anything.

I'd never seen a more massive body of information—but it was a body, I realized late one night, without any substance or shape; a body surprisingly *light*, flickering, easy to delete.

I sat down, to take the weight off my feet.

A body that felt no pain.

A body incapable of "permanent, progressive, and disfiguring" injuries.

A body that didn't bleed.

On the eve of my trip, it seemed likely to me, based on all known evidence, that Timothy McVeigh was operating, in Oklahoma City, on a principle similar to our country's Middle East policy (a policy McVeigh knew well, from his days in Desert Storm). Since 1991, whenever an American president has bombed Iraq, he has done so, he has said, to "send a message" to its leader, Saddam Hussein.

These "messages" have consisted of twisted metal, shattered stones and, occasionally, the mangled bodies of citizens, some of them children.

Like so many of his brothers and sisters posting notes on the Net, McVeigh wanted to "send a message" to the government of the United States.

But the Web was too light for him, its body too thin. He chose, instead, the unmistakable weight of thousands of pounds of explosives. His message, like the memos of Presidents Bush and Clinton to the ruler of Iraq, consisted of rubble and the bodies of kids.

Reminder: Don't invade Kuwait.
Don't torture your citizens.

For a human body to become a message like this, it has to shed its pounds, to be stripped of its flesh-and-blood reality; it has to be seen as a symbol.

In times of war, a soldier's body, tortured or killed by the enemy, is a warning, a clear text, meaning, "Don't mess with me. What I do to this individual, I will do to your country, to your values and your laws."

So.

Early one April morning, Timothy McVeigh sent a message to our nation.

Since then, on the Internet, "Oklahoma City" had lost its mass, notwithstanding the reams of words clinging to its surface like barnacles; it had become a series of symbols, signifying different things to different people.

A site as light as a bubble.

A city floating in air.

A weightlessness that weighed on my conscience day and night.

Mitchell Smolkin, a philosopher and medical doctor, once wrote: "One tends to persist unquestioningly on his journey until he experiences pain," an injury, a trauma, separation from someone he loves . . . "Pain immediately obliterates consciousness of all else. The previously witty and articulate traveler can now only cry and groan."

Since leaving my wife, I'd spent many late nights alone, traveling the Net, and I'd learned it was easy and fun. No need to question the statements you encountered there, since many of them were anonymous and unverifiable. No complications, as in a marriage; therefore, never any pain.

Its body, as I'd already discovered, was incorporeal (or "virtual") . . . which is finally why it couldn't tell me anything about myself or Oklahoma City.

Every Net user I'd clicked to, day after day after day, saw the bombing as a symbol for everything wrong or right in America. An example, light as paper—*lighter*, unless you printed it out— of the nation's spiraling violence. Lost innocence. Government oppression.

None of these travelers, nor I, had tasted the grit of buckled concrete in his mouth; none of them bled from her ears, struggled to free a trapped leg, or watched his own hand fly, severed and on its own, across a street.

In all our remarks, drifting, drifting back and forth across the wires, there wasn't a single tug of gravity.

No agony.

Reminder from Dr. Smolkin: "The pain that causes no inner suffering is of [little] interest."

In the days before laser-guided "messages," Oscar Wilde wrote, "God spare me . . . physical pain, and I'll take care of the moral pain myself."

But in this age of bombing as long-distance communication, physical pain gets translated instantly into moral stances, all across the planet.

Exploring the consequences of this, the literary scholar Elaine Scarry writes: "Pain engulfs the one [experiencing it], but remains unsensed by anyone else. Though indisputably real to the sufferer, it is . . . unreal to others."

The victim writhes and dies, while television crews scramble to the next big disaster, totting up their frequent flyer miles. Internet browsers turn to other topics.

All that remains is the message in the air.

A little byte out of your day. A floating tic across your screen. HELLO NEIGHBOR!

Maybe, I thought, drifting, drifting . . . maybe, all along, my depression has been a kind of airsickness. A longing for the ground.

Obsessively, now, I read about pain.

> Ramon y Cajal: "Physical pain is easily forgotten, but moral chagrin lasts indefinitely."
> Karl Marx: "There is only one antidote to mental suffering, and that is physical pain."
> Reminder: Clear out leftovers in the fridge.
> Get a sixty-watt bulb.
> Buy a new surge protector.

I didn't know what any of this meant. I didn't get the message.

OK?

Vacuum. Sweep.
Traveler's checks.

My mental suffering, the pain in the heart of the Heartland, my need to go there to that sacred place of bodies, living and dead, with their poor, dumb, lovable human weight.

Close windows.

End session.

Get well soon.

5

Early in the morning, Dr. Heath and I had walked together to the U.S. federal courthouse behind Murrah. It was here—in the same place where Karen Silkwood's family won a $10 million suit against Kerr-McGee for "detrimentally affecting" her with nuclear radiation—that the change of venue hearing was held, which ultimately shifted the bombing trial to Denver. (Gerry Spence represented the Silkwood estate; he later represented Randy Weaver, after the shootout at Ruby Ridge.)

The courtroom was large and bright. Dr. Heath pointed out to me where Timothy McVeigh sat during the hearings, where Terry Nichols sat.

Nichols, he said, is clearly remorseful over whatever role he played in the bombing plot; when the prosecution ran videos showing children's bodies being removed from the building, Nichols's throat tensed visibly, and he struggled to stay calm. McVeigh, on the other hand, smiled, laughed, joked with his lawyers: the sad kid from the busted home who pictured himself a revolutionary hero.

"This country's not going to have a revolution," Dr. Heath scoffed. "The middle class is not oppressed, and you don't have revolutions without that being the case. But McVeigh doesn't see that. He's obviously proud of what he's done. He was apparently a soldier's soldier in the Gulf War. Compulsive. Did whatever he was told."

McVeigh's hawkish nose and whippet-thin frame give him a harsh, ascetic aspect. "Apparently, he never showed much of an interest in girls," Dr. Heath said. "In fact, when you look at him in court, you see he doesn't have much facial hair, much body hair— almost as if there's not a fully matured person there." (From jail,

McVeigh confessed to a British journalist that being the primary bombing suspect was "better than being Princess Di's lover.")

Later, outside the courtroom, in the sun, Dr. Heath and I stood grimly, stunned by all the boarded windows.

"The plate glass windows in the store beside us . . . were blown to splinters," says the narrator of *The Turner Diaries*, which was found in Timothy McVeigh's car following his arrest. "A glittering and deadly rain of glass shards continued to fall into the street from the upper stories of nearby buildings for a few seconds, as a jet-black column of smoke shot straight up into the sky ahead of us.

"The whole wing . . . of the [federal] building . . . had collapsed . . . A huge, gaping hole yawned in the courtyard pavement just beyond the rubble of collapsed masonry."

"I can remember the sound of the bomb," Dr. Heath tells me. "I can recall the dynamite." He snaps his fingers. "Then the bomb itself sounded like a huge electrical short. A bomb doesn't make a *boom*; it's a grating, like a transformer blowing out. I also heard the third sound, of the building crumbling and coming apart. All within one or two, three seconds."

We're standing right where the truck was parked, on top of the dusty, filled-in crater left by the bomb. Dr. Heath believes McVeigh chose Oklahoma City, and this particular building, because of easy access, and because the building was largely glass, back and front— energy-efficient—which meant the blast could go all the way through it.

"At the time of the explosion, I was standing near the service elevator on the fifth floor," Dr. Heath says. "The bomb [debris] went right over the top of my head, blew all around me. It covered me up to about [my chest], mainly with soft material that came off the ceiling. Light fixtures and so on. But I was not physically injured. I did have shards of glass—in fact, I got some glass out of my neck just recently. It kind of hooked on my pillow at night. I got up and took the tweezers and some magnification and picked it out."

Like many others in the area that day, he has also suffered some high-frequency hearing loss.

"Approximately three feet from where I was standing that day, a steel safe came down from the ninth floor, an evidence safe [from one of the law enforcement offices], and blew in right at my feet. About eight feet from me, there had been a hallway, but it was gone.

"We had an employee, Stan Rombaun, sitting within two feet of a window when the bomb went off. His right eye was put out. Another man, Martin Cash . . . a chunk of glass blew into his left eye. He pulled it out and pulled his eye out. When I got to him, he had his left eye hanging in his left hand, and massive cuts, a hole in his head. But we were all in shock, so these guys weren't bleeding much. Just trickles of blood. Stan had two fingers severed, hanging with flesh, and he wasn't bleeding.

"The first thing I thought was, 'God, help me keep my head and get out of this alive.' I thought I was dead, or about to die. I could see little sparkles of the bomb powder or the fertilizer popping in the air. As the black smoke cleared, I could see these flares of explosive material all around me, like sparklers."

He helped his colleagues out of the building, down the south stairwell, which was still intact, then started aiding the medics, who'd arrived on the scene almost instantly. In the past, he had headed the building's Safety Committee, practicing getting people in and out during fire drills, tornado drills. "At some point, soon after getting out of the rubble, I started looking around for my Safety Committee," he says. "I discovered that I *was* the Safety Committee. I was the only one left."

He leads me through the parking garage, underneath Murrah, where he still parks his car every morning. We emerge onto what's left of the building's south patio. "We set up a triage area here," he says.

"Triage" is a rather pretty-sounding word for a state of hell, for both victims and doctors. Medics have to make instant decisions about who needs immediate care and who can wait, despite whatever pain they're in. Often doctors must decide to let people who are beyond saving die on the spot.

Sand, crumbled granite, and glass snap beneath our feet. Where we're standing, blood-soaked toys had lain scattered among children's bodies.

"The bodies came out in parts," Dr. Heath says softly, his voice faltering again. "The building literally sliced people into pieces, which caused all kinds of trauma for the Medical Examiner's Office . . . to this day, they're still just reeling from the emotional devastation of seeing that many bodies that quick."

In numerous press reports, and on the Internet, much has been made of a second bomb scare about an hour after the blast. Conspiracy theorists claim that more explosives were discovered inside the building, and have floated various suggestions as to who put them there.

I ask Dr. Heath about the "second incident." "They were just educational training bombs from [the law enforcement agencies on] the ninth floor. But the guy that found them was an amateur rescuer in there, and my understanding of what happened is, he hollered, 'I found more bombs!' The rumor rippled out all over the area."

The FBI evacuated the site, forcing rescuers to leave victims they'd been aiding trapped under massive slabs of concrete. Many of these workers, civilian volunteers rather than professionals, weren't allowed to reenter the building once the scare was over. In some cases, they never learned if the people they'd tried to help survived. Dr. Heath spent much of the rest of that day counseling these folks. "They were just *out of it*," he says, "leveled with guilt for leaving."

Late in the day, he spoke with the building's architect, James Loftis, who'd arrived to help firefighters find expedient ways in and out of the structure's remains. Loftis claimed that if the bomb truck had been parked five feet on either side of where it was left, it wouldn't have taken out the main support beam, and the building wouldn't have collapsed so completely. He called it a "lucky shot."

That night, says Dr. Heath, "I curled up to my wife's back and went to sleep. And then the next morning at 5:00 it started all over again. Our work [pulling bodies and equipment out of the building] was chaotic, but it was *purposeful* chaotic behavior. It was amazing, really. People did what they had to do. On that first day, if they had to leave, if they were too upset to stay around, they left. And people have been very forgiving about that. No one's been unkind to those that had to get out of Dodge, as we say here."

On the third day after the Murrah blast, Dr. Heath asked federal officials if he could retrieve material from his office. He'd had 1,200 veterans' files, including information on specially designed houses the va was building for ex-soldiers disabled in wars.

He tells me this as we stroll around the fence full of bears. "This big ol' tall FBI guy from the South somewhere looked at me—he had his glasses on, these half-glasses down on his nose—and he said, 'Now, boy, let me see if I understand what you're asking me.' He pointed up there at the fifth floor, and he said, 'You were in that building when it blew up?' 'Yeah.' 'And you want to go back in there? Boy, do you really know what you're asking me to let you do?'

"I was filled with energy, and I was wanting to get stuff done because it was getting ready to rain. So I pulled out a piece of paper and started writing, 'I authorize Dr. Heath to go back in the building . . .' The FBI guy said, 'What is that?' I said, 'Well, you know, I'm tying you up here, and if you'll just sign this, I'll go on.' He said, 'How long have you worked for the government, boy?' 'Twenty-eight years.' He answered, 'Well, I haven't been at it that long, but I'm smart enough to know not to sign that.' "

Finally, though, the agent made a deal with Jon Hansen, the assistant fire chief, and Dr. Heath, wearing a face mask and a hard hat, accompanied five firefighters back up over ridges of rubble to the remaining fragments of floor five. He found most of his folders, prying them out of jammed file cabinets with two-by-fours. "Stuff was still falling off the ceiling . . . one of the firemen said, 'This is the dumbest thing I've ever done.' "

No one else who'd worked in the building went back in. "To my knowledge, I'm the only one. And it was the smartest thing I ever did."

I ask him why.

He considers for a moment, then answers in a manner wholly appropriate to the city he loves. "Emotionally, it was like falling off a horse for me. And I got back on."

In a 1983 essay entitled "Terror and the Sublime," Terrence Des Pres, whose book *The Survivor* explored the psychological effects of the Holocaust on its victims, speculates that the human mind, encountering terror, may often experience, instead of dread, "astonishment, reverence, [and] wonder." Quoting Longinus, he says that brushes with horror and death can create an "elevation of mind" resulting from "vehement and inspired passion"—specifically, the passion for self-preservation (and I would add, the preservation of others).

Perhaps Des Pres's theory accounts, in part, for the combination of serenity and pain I see in Paul Heath's smile; perhaps it explains the calm, the *goodness*, I feel in the man. Or perhaps everything boils down to something simpler—like Okie roots.

"Grieving, as I see it, is like a triangle," he explains. "In one corner of the base is the emotional response to the tragedy. You have shock and disbelief, numbing, rage; alcohol, drugs, too much food and other inappropriate substances you put in your mouth. The other part of the base is the feeling that you perpetrated the event. You did something you shouldn't have done. You said something you shouldn't have said. Or you *didn't* do or say something.

"The third part of the triangle is helping others—and thereby helping yourself," he says. "Because my colleagues and I are federal employees, and the bomb was directed at the federal government, we all felt that somehow it was our fault. The truth of the matter is, I know who blew the building up. It was *not me.* So that takes care of my guilt."

We've walked back around the site and stand now on the deserted children's playground at the YMCA, which was also used as a triage area on the day of the bombing. In helping fellow survivors cope with their grief, Dr. Heath never says they'll "get over" what happened. "You can never get over this," he says. "You get to a time in your life where you've worked through it as much as you can, and now you're simply wherever you are. I call this a 'new normal.' " People are getting there. OK City may never be okay again, not completely, but "we're a tenacious bunch," he says. "We've survived the Dust Bowl, we've survived the oil bust . . . Remarkably, folks are doing as well as they can." He spreads his hands. "But then, we weren't the only ones attacked, were we?"

He watches me closely. He seems to know I've been grieving, too, for whatever reasons, public and private.

"The Murrah building, since it was a federal facility, belonged to everybody in America. The state offices across the street belonged to everybody in Oklahoma. The street in front of the building, and the utilities that ran under it, belonged to the city and the county. The Catholic church, with international affiliations, belongs to every Catholic in the world."

He stops to hold back tears. I almost put my arm around him, but then I think, I don't know him well enough to do that. All day, it's the most awkward moment between us, and later I'll regret I didn't comfort him. "After the bombing, we took people to the First Christian Church to notify them of their lost family members," he says. "I knew the pastor, Don Alexander's, father, who died in a plane crash years ago. When I was a college student, I worked at Sears to pay my tuition. I remember selling shoes to the Alexander family. We're all in this together."

It's funny, he says, but a person learns many new meanings of "community" in an ordeal like this. He shakes his head. "At the change of venue hearing, the lawyers were still fussing about the leg." A severed leg from the ruins had lain unidentified for several months. "They had grilled Dr. Jordan, the doctor in charge of the Medical Examiner's Office in Oklahoma, claimed he was incompetent, and his staff was incompetent, because they'd got this leg mixed up.

"Well, that's ridiculous. Six corpses were buried without a left leg, because people were just in pieces.

"Anyway, after he testified, and at the break, I went over to Dr. Jordan, told him who I was, put my arms around him and hugged him. He started to tear up and I just held him.

"Recently, on the phone with him, I asked, 'What else can I do for you?' He said, 'Next time I see you, give me another hug.' "

On July 15, 1996, just three days after my conversation with Dr. Heath, Judge Matsch ruled that the trial or trials (whose starting dates had yet to be set) *could* be broadcast in Oklahoma City on closed-circuit television. Outside the courthouse in Denver, Dr. Heath, speaking on behalf of all the survivors, called the ruling a major victory for the citizens of Oklahoma.

6

The day I left the city, a massive thunderhead coiled in the west, and the temperature tumbled into the sixties: a break in the drought that had crippled the wheat fields, and killed the webby cotton, for miles all around. As a kid I'd played among rows of cotton, bales of wheat, in "Native America." But now, with committee meetings to attend, students to teach, bills to pay in Oregon—with a divorce still to be finalized and faced—I didn't know when I'd ever be back here.

I'd come for relief, for comfort, for reassurance and answers to questions I didn't even know to ask. I'd come for selfish reasons. I think, now, I wanted to believe something like this: it's our selfishness, our condition of being trapped in bodies that suffer anguish, that enables us to empathize with others.

We listen to a man tell survival stories and offer him silent respect. We hear of a man pinned beneath girders in a hell of smoke and ash and feel a twinge in our own frail limbs.

We start with ourselves and wind up with the beginnings of community. With rituals and bonds.

That's what I'd hoped to find. Had I succeeded?

I didn't know, any more than I knew where truth lay on the information highway, or where my life was headed from here after the sorrowful split with my wife.

As I packed my bags, I heard squabbles of traffic beyond my motel window: impatient horns, eager squeals of tires. This morning, the city was doing just fine.

"Little picky things that might have irritated you about someone, before the blast, are meaningless now," Dr. Heath had told me, just before we'd parted. "What is meaningful is that our work family got out alive. And we tend . . ." He'd smiled and wiped his eyes. "I would use the word 'love.' There's just more love and respect for the work family than there was before, because so many people we know didn't make it."

My cousin Anne had concurred (it was the only coping lesson she could offer): "People were kinder than usual right after the bombing. If anything aggravating happened, you know, it was like, 'Well, okay.' People just stepped back." She added, "But I think tempers are flaring again now. Instead of being kind all the time, we're arguing again and blaring horns and shooting the finger if somebody changes lanes in front of you . . . sometimes I want to say, 'What happened to all that *Heartland* stuff?' "

But, presumably, renewed irritation is a healthy sign, a sign of the "new normal."

"No one in our generation—no one in *any* generation in America—has ever experienced what we've experienced," Dr. Heath had said. "So no one knows how to do this. All we can do—all of us, all across the nation—is encourage each other to talk, to tell each other *what we know,* what it is we've learned about life. All we can do is share our stories."

One last time I went to visit the bombing site. On the fence, next to a stiff metal sign saying "U.S. Property, No Trespassing," a stuffed bear in a nightdress clutched a baby bear; Barney the Dinosaur, with bright purple fur, dangled next to a lifelike doll of a human child, its smooth, bald head spackled with mud; on the grass sat a black cotton cat, like my old kitty Jake. Red and yellow roses ringed scribbled notes, poems, photographs of the dead. Thousands and thousands of toys, enough to fill hundreds of cribs, surrounded tiny American flags, stuck in holes in the mesh of the wire.

A war memorial to infants and kids.

But, in fact, I reminded myself, people of all ages died on this spot. All races, all possible persuasions, every conceivable viewpoint, were represented here—and the number would grow, six years later, in the rubble of the World Trade Center, the Pentagon, Afghan villages.

That day in Oklahoma City, the details of lost lives unspooled like ribbons loosed from around a Book of Broken Promises:

> *He worked hard to support his family in Oklahoma, and in his native Mexico.*
> *He loved baseball (he played outfield at company picnics).*
> *She was the ultimate movie buff. Her video collection included over six hundred titles.*
> *He played clarinet in the orchestra of St. John Missionary Baptist Church.*
> *She had large eyes that could look straight through you.*
> *A die-hard Beatles fan.*
> *Strong-willed, she joined the service so she could someday finance college and nursing school.*

*On sunny days, he was always outdoors—playing in the dirt, riding his
Big Wheel.
She had just started to walk and say, "Mama."*

And now, because of all these ghosts, Okies are once again looking west, as in the days of the Dust Bowl, seeking justice, the
promise of relief from loss. From a smoldering crater in Oklahoma
City to a small Denver courthouse they'll travel, like the Joads of
old, "moving, questing people . . . migrants now."

"There is a crime here that goes beyond denunciation," Steinbeck
wrote near the end of *The Grapes of Wrath*. "There is a sorrow here
that weeping cannot symbolize. There is a failure here that topples
all our success."

On the plane back to Oregon, I pass over mountains, deserts, plains,
remnants of the old Route 66, roads that survivors and families of
Murrah building victims will take to attend the trials of Nichols
and McVeigh . . . past barbecued rib joints, barns with peeling paint,
used car dealerships, fireworks stands, old Catholic cemeteries, nuclear plants.

I finger Paul Heath's business card, with its now-gone Fifth
Street address—his Murrah office—crossed out in ink and the new
address scribbled in. I think of my grandparents' basement, of
stormy nights when my grandfather, frightened by thunder and
lightning, hustled Anne and me and our brothers and sisters down
below. We huddled together in candlelight, in dank, earthy corners
next to old newspapers, empty picture frames, kindling, busted
springs, odds and ends. I think of the safety I felt, clinging to my
cousin—my cousin who'd promised to marry me, *till death do us
part*—several feet deep in the rich Oklahoma soil.

Cousins

"We get bomb threats on the job all the time," my cousin Anne told me one day in a coffee shop near her office in downtown Oklahoma City. "So far, the callers have been crackpots, but you never know. Once, a guy kept calling in—he was angry because he had to pay child support, and there was a warrant out for his arrest. But he gave his name! *You know*? Crazy."

She's a supervisor for the State Department of Human Services, specializing in adult abuse cases—"grown children beating up their parents, taking over their bank accounts, that sort of thing. It happens a lot." When she meets people for the first time, she still tells them she's a state official, though she's aware that, in certain ideological circles, hers is not a popular position. "Many people here in the city were angry when they learned that McVeigh and Nichols weren't going to be tried for the deaths of *everybody* in the Murrah building, just for the government officials."

She shrugged. I hadn't seen her much in the last ten years, and I didn't know if the changes I sensed in her—a harder shell, a greater care with her words—were a factor of time, or the recent shock of Murrah, or both.

Now she looked puzzled and sad, scratching her short, frosted hair. "Maybe, when I tell people where I work and what I do, I'm taking a chance in this day and age, with all the antigovernment feeling out there, but I'm not a *bad* state official." She spread her hands. "I'm just doing a job."

Usually, buildings aren't evacuated right away when someone phones in a threat, she said. The police are alerted; individuals in the office, who've been chosen for the task, search each floor for anything out of the ordinary. Most of the time, nothing turns up.

One day, shortly after Murrah, an anonymous caller claimed to have planted a bomb in her building. In her supervisory role, she told the people on her floor there wouldn't be a mandatory evacuation, at least not until the cops told them all to leave. "But if you feel uncomfortable about this," she said, "you can go now."

One of her employees rose nervously from her desk. "It's going to be like that other deal," she said. "We'll never know there's any real danger, then we'll all be blown sky-high. Some people, like you, all the supervisors, *you'll* be tipped beforehand—"

"Whoa," Anne said. "What are you talking about?"

The lady wouldn't look at her. "The BATF agents over there, their lives were spared. They got a warning from the government two days before the blast. They knew it was going to happen, you know, so they were gone that day. Out on the golf course."

"That's crazy," Anne said. "That's just a stupid rumor."

As it turns out, none of the Alcohol, Tobacco, and Firearms agents, whose offices were on the west side of the ninth floor, died in the Murrah blast. This fact has made many people, folks ordinarily resistant to extremist views, suspicious of the federal government. Some of them even believe Washington destroyed its own facility, then pinned the crime on Timothy McVeigh, so it could justify quashing militia movements and confiscating people's guns.

On certain Internet pages, the reasoning runs like this: the feds claim McVeigh was angry at the BATF for Ruby Ridge and Waco. He took his revenge by blowing up Murrah.

But if he knew the building's layout as well as prosecutors insist he did, why did he park the truck on the side opposite his primary target? And why *were* the BATF offices so deserted when the bomb went off—did they receive some kind of tip?

These are serious questions, and they deserve investigation, Anne thinks, but she doesn't really believe there's any mystery. The bomb went off early in the morning; not everyone was at work yet. And McVeigh parked the truck where he could, on a busy public street. The blast did, in fact, effectively destroy the whole structure.

But gaps in the story of what happened that day, and the rumors they've sparked, make Anne's daily job even harder to do than it usually is. The bizarre theories, the stress that most downtown workers still experience more than a year after the event, burden an already difficult series of duties. "Often, health agencies will call me and say that someone's neglecting themselves and they need to be in a nursing home," Anne told me, her voice forceful and clear, the voice of someone used to explaining things patiently to people who might not grasp what she's saying at first. I began to understand that what seemed to be her hard shell had been learned in the field, over time, as self-protection.

"What workers like me determine, sometimes with the help of a doctor, is whether or not a person has the capacity to take care of themselves," she said. "If someone's forgetful—doesn't remember where she puts her checkbook, say, or something like that—yet she's neat and appropriate and oriented, she can stay in her home. That's what I try to protect—the person's right to do what they need to do, whether it's stay in their home, go live with one of their children or some relative, or receive twenty-four hour care." She shook her head. That's crisis enough for any day.

The morning of the Murrah bombing, she was running late for work. Driving downtown, she noticed smoke in her rearview mirror but didn't think much of it. When she got to her office, someone told her a gas line had probably broken nearby.

By ten A.M., everyone in Anne's building had been ordered to evacuate. By then, the authorities had determined that a bomb had caused the destruction and were worried about other official institutions being targeted. There was a citywide government lockdown.

Anne's department is set up to respond to any crisis—tornadoes, floods; in emergencies, every state employee has a function. The Murrah event didn't fall under normal disaster guidelines: the Red Cross appeared almost instantly on the scene. Still, word went out over government computers that anyone willing should volunteer to help the aid agencies.

Anne went first to give blood. She stood in line all day. "I went to three different places," she says. "They kept shifting me to other locations because I'm O-Positive, and they didn't need any more O-Positive at that point. I finally wound up at the Clarion Hotel on Lincoln Boulevard, not far from the state capital complex. At 6:00, the National Guard brought in sandwiches and chips for us, and by 9:00 I was on a table, finally, with a needle in my arm."

For hours, standing in lines, she heard snatches of rumors and radio reports about what had happened downtown. In one of the locations she was directed to, a portable TV screwed into a wall showed the gaping maw of the building. "We heard foreign terrorists had done it," she says. "Immediately, that's what everybody's conclusion was—it couldn't be an *American*, you know, none of *us* would hurt children."

Periodically, ambulances whined down the streets, as if the city's health agencies were staging the kinds of practice runs Anne had witnessed many times; she had to keep reminding herself *This is real.*

In those first few hours after the event, she didn't think she knew anyone who'd been in the building at the time. She found out later she was wrong.

"By the time I got home that night—I guess it was about 10:00—I had twenty-something calls on my answering machine, because everybody thought I might have been in the bombing. It unnerved me to think of my family and friends worrying about me, and not being able to reach me," she says. "Of course, it had been even more unnerving that morning when they'd started locking all the facilities and brought in the bomb-sniffing dogs. When I got home, all the pent-up pressure of the day caught up with me. I just took a hot shower and thought about the fact that I was alive."

When Anne and I were children together, playing in our grandparents' yard in Walters, Oklahoma, just across the muddy Red River from Texas, we ran and hid from each other, held hands, and laughed.

We slept together on the same foldout couch, and learned, in our presexual way, the comfort of a nearby friend at night. We learned that, if we giggled too loudly in the dark, our grandfather would step into the room and warn us, "Hush now, or else!"

As an Oklahoma official, a state representative, he always evinced a reverence for government buildings, from the state capitol to the courthouse square in Walters, where the sheriff used to burn bootleg whiskey. From him, we learned to love "Native America," as Oklahomans call their land. He taught us that the sky blue wash of the Oklahoma flag signified devotion; its insignia meant bravery, balanced by a peace pipe crossed with an olive branch.

He used to take us to Sultan Park, on the outskirts of town, to watch the powwows of the Kiowa and Chickasaw Indians. The smells of their deer meat and stews cooking over open fires, the sight of their bright, bristly feathers both frightened and delighted Anne and me. Through our grandfather's eyes, we learned to appreciate the Indians' movements. He told us not to be scared. "They're just like us," he said.

"*Just* like us?" I mouthed off one day.

"Yep. Good folks hoping to have a fine old time."

"They *look* different."

He pulled Anne and me close, then knelt beside us. Behind him, women in jingle-dresses danced around a drum. "You know how you two have different parents, but you're part of the same family?"

We nodded. "We're *cousins!*" Anne said.

"That's right," said our grandfather. "Different, but just the same. Got it?"

"Yes," I said.

"Well, that's how it us with the Indians and us."

Anne and I laughed, then, though we didn't really understand what he meant, and ran through the park. We ate and danced. We played with the Kiowa kids. Watching their families gather, grandparents, parents, and children, we learned about communities—the importance of rituals and bonds, of approaching people different from us, who were not so different, after all. We learned what it meant to be cousins.

On the fourth day after the bombing, Anne volunteered at City Center, a post office just across Harvey Street from the crumbles of Murrah. It had been set up as a pharmacy and clothing supply for the rescue workers, who were still hoping to discover survivors in the building (none were found after the first day). The post office was shaky. The bomb had weakened its structural supports; it has since been razed.

After a full day on her regular job, Anne worked from midnight to six A.M. at City Center, unloading clothes (furnished by various local organizations), separating the sizes, arranging eye drops, bottles of aspirin, and cremes on dozens of folding tables. Advil, Aleve. Imodium AD, Gaviscon, Mylanta. Kleenex. Bausch & Lomb. Cold Comfort.

"We got our 'Volunteer' badges at the *Journal Record* building, directly across from Murrah," Anne says. "There were different colors of badges for different locations. It was real hard to get one after the second day, because so many people came by—some out of curiosity, others out of a genuine desire to help. I don't mean a *dismal* curiosity. People just wanted to know what was going on. But if you lost your badge, you were really in trouble."

Early one morning, she worked at the Myriad Convention Center, a few blocks south of Murrah at Reno and Northwest Robinson, serving breakfast to emergency personnel, squeezing oranges for juice—"A *lot* of oranges, I mean *basketfuls* of oranges. The Restaurant Association of Oklahoma brought in most of the food," she says. "They were cooking racks of bacon starting at midnight. Belgian waffles. All sorts of ungodly stuff."

When a group of New York City firefighters, just flown in, said, "What we'd really like to have is beer and pizza," Jeff Welsh, president of Magnum Foods, Oklahoma's franchisee for Little Caesar's Pizza, ordered his firm to establish a twenty-four-hour pizzeria at the Murrah site.

"A lot of the rescue people who'd also helped after the World Trade Center bombing in 1993 said that, in New York, they all had to pay megabucks to vendors for their food," Anne says. "Oklahoma City wasn't charging anything."

At the Myriad, citizens erected hundreds of cots for the workers, who'd come from New York, Florida, Colorado, California, Oregon, Washington. Some patients at Oklahoma City's Children's Hospital wrapped ribbons around teddy bears and had them delivered to the convention center. Anne says, "All of the volunteers went into these rooms with the cots, put teddy bears on the pillows. Chiropractors came in and set up little booths, to offer services for aches and pains. There was a hairstylist."

Soon, the rescue dogs began showing signs of depression. They weren't finding anybody alive inside the Murrah building. "They walked around with their tails tucked in," Anne says. "Just moping along. So the men took them outside to the Myriad Gardens and played hide-and-seek seek with them. Someone would crouch in the bushes; then another man would release the dogs. The dogs would find the person and get excited again, so they could go back in the building for two or four more hours. Then their depression returned."

Back at City Center, she could see, herself, how demoralizing it was for the men, scrabbling through rubble. Often, rain delayed the search efforts. "At one point, chaplains started coming around to talk to the rescue workers," she says. "One night, one of the workers just broke into tears. What he'd been doing—what they'd *all* been doing—was going into this building, walking to and fro, looking, you know . . .

"So anyway, one night he just stops and breaks down, because what he's done . . . he's walked by this person who's taken in the blast, and who's been imprinted in the wall. Yet, for several days, no one knew he was there.

"It was getting very tense for everyone—this was four days after the blast. The chaplains were everywhere, and they talked to this guy. They even visited with us. I guess they weren't sure what we'd hear, and how we'd react."

One night, a worker confessed to her, "We're not looking for those alive anymore." "It was the nicest way he could put it," Anne says. "I just sat there, stunned.

"The place was eerie at night. They had spotlights on what was left of the building. I don't know who put all the flags up, but there were, like, twelve of them all in a row. The United States flag and different state flags. The fog's rolling in, and the lights are on, and these flags are just waving, waving." She searched for the sky blue banner of Oklahoma. There it was, near the top. "It gave me a sense of security, in spite of everything," she says. "I thought, 'Things are not okay right now, but they will be.' "

She wasn't close to Lanny Scroggins, a staff accountant for HUD, who died on the building's eighth floor. He was a year ahead of her in high school, when they were both growing up in Holdenville, a small town southeast of Oklahoma City. "I remember him being kind of a cutup in school," she says.

And she remembers a woman from the Murrah building's Social Security Office. "She used to work in Holdenville, when I had a job there with the Human Services Department. We'd talk a lot about clients: who was receiving what benefits, that sort of thing. I found out later she was also killed."

When she heard the list of victims read aloud at the memorial service, she was "floored." "Up until then, I'd been kind of floating along, volunteering, comforting people," she says. The kinds of things she does every day. "Then it hit me: I'll never see these people again."

Briefly, she admits, she lost the professional detachment she's developed in order to manage the city's traumas. She gave in to tears—a luxury she doesn't allow herself very often. Even as a child, I'm thinking now, listening to her, watching her mild, composed face, Anne didn't cry much. After fights or broken toys, she always got on with things, trailing her cousins behind her.

These days, *getting on with things* often means keeping her head down, burying herself in statistics and reports.

"Each year, traumatic brain injury . . . is associated with 52,000 deaths and accounts for one third of all injury deaths in the United States," says the *Journal of the American Medical Association*. It adds that, in Oklahoma, in 1992–93, horseback riding was the leading cause of traumatic brain injury.

It took *JAMA* a full year to assess the medical results of the Murrah bombing, to reduce them, in its own professionally detached manner, to "risk ratios" and "preparedness mandates."

"The most frequent cause of death [from the blast] was multiple injuries," the journal reports. "Among survivors, soft tissue injuries, fractures, sprains, strains, and head injuries were most common; these injuries were . . . often caused by flying glass and other debris and collapsed ceilings."

Thirty-five percent of the survivors suffered head traumas.

Thirty-seven percent had fractures or dislocations or both.

Twenty-three percent had ocular injuries.

Overall, the Murrah results suggest that, in bombings of this nature, most of the fatalities occur instantly; those who are wounded tend to be treated and released fairly quickly. There are few in-betweens.

For doctors and city workers like Anne, this is necessary, as well as useful, information: a way of whittling down tragedy until it's just another job. Tragedy overwhelms, especially in the bustle of an urban setting, Anne explains. A job, a daily task, can be tackled and completed.

"I volunteered for four days," Anne says. "I did as much as I could—I did my civic duty—then I pulled out. I really needed to, because of all the strain. A lot of people stayed with it, and some of them have had emotional problems. One woman I work with got so wrapped up in it . . . not just from being there all the time, but also because it's all you heard on TV and radio for days and days and days . . . she's still fighting serious depression.

"Another one of our employees is on disability because he and a woman he worked with downstairs in Child Support went to the Murrah building. The woman's husband worked there, and my friend took her down there to see if he was all right, which he wasn't. They saw some pretty unpleasant sights." She closes her eyes. "I never saw any gore. I could maintain a calm . . . It was like I'd separated myself from everything that was going on. I'd look across the street from City Center, and think, 'That is *not* Oklahoma City. That has got to be Beirut.'"

Even now, she admits wanting to be "Alice in Wonderland—you know, *This didn't happen.* This year, on the morning of the first anniversary, the people in Child Support decided to go outside at 9:02 and observe a moment of silence. They had taken balloons and put the names of all the people who'd died on them. For some reason, it's very strange, but two of us stayed away from the group—they were all standing outside, holding hands. A friend of mine and I just kind of hung back. I don't know—it was like, if we got too close to these people, something would happen. Then, about that time, the jets came over in formation, in a salute to the dead, and of course I was in tears.

"The anniversary week was really tense," she says. She stiffens, just thinking about it. "We had people in from our psychological assistance programs to visit with us. We were told that if our employees started having problems, we should just say, 'You need to go home. Get out of here. Take a day of leave, whatever you need to do to make yourself feel better.' I didn't think it played that much on me, but by the time I got home at night, every night that week, I was exhausted. I was feeling things more strongly than I'd admitted to myself, even a year later."

She adds quietly, "Here in the city, even if you weren't directly affected by the bombing, what you did, all the time, in those first few months after it happened . . . you'd run into somebody who knew somebody who'd died."

When we were kids, Anne's mother used to read us poetry to lull us to sleep at night, or to calm us when we'd had too much excitement for the day.

My favorite was Emily Dickinson: "It was a Common Night/ except the Dying/this to us/Made Nature different."

One summer, when Anne and I were ten, I learned what Dickinson meant. Early one afternoon, I sneaked through a field of weeds behind my grandparents' yard to a sad, abandoned house. It was across the street from a Chevron station. Its boards had split, its shutters cracked, and the walls inside were crumbling. I stepped over rusty nails in the floor, stuck my fingers through a rip in the wallpaper, and pulled out brittle chunks of sheetrock. In that moment, I discovered I could tear a house down with my hands! Delighted, I proceeded to destroy the wall.

"Young man!" someone yelled behind me. "Stop that, you hear?"

At first I thought it was my grandfather, admonishing me the way he used to silence Anne and me at night. But when I turned, I saw an old gent in a green cap and uniform—the gas station manager. He scowled at me and threatened to call the police. I was a hoodlum, he said, a delinquent, a threat to the neighborhood.

I ran from the house, back through the weeds, until I found a blackberry bramble to shield me. I'd hidden here many times in games with my cousins. Once, I'd stolen away to this spot to hold hands with Anne.

The fellow returned to his station and, with a black garden hose, cleaned the drive by the diesel pumps. Sweat tickled my ribs; grasshoppers popped at my feet. Angry, frightened, I whispered, "I wish you'd die, old man!"

A month later, I learned from my grandfather that his good friend, the man at the filling station, had suffered a fatal heart attack out by the pumps. I could feel myself blanch. I imagined the black hose snaking around his body, gushing spray across the highway, onto the porch of the collapsed house.

"Did he suffer much?" I asked my grandfather meekly.

"I don't really know."

"I'm sorry."

"I'll miss the old coot."

I never told anyone, not even Anne, about my hateful wish. After that, games of hide-and-seek in the weeds never felt the same to me. A pall had seized the field.

Thirteen years later, when my grandfather died of emphysema, I delivered a eulogy at his funeral, as he'd asked. He'd always encouraged my writing and speaking, and he hoped I'd one day follow him into public service.

At the funeral, I recounted his distinguished career as a servant of Oklahoma and closed with those Emily Dickinson lines Anne's mother had taught us long ago.

After his passing, my attitude changed toward more than just the field adjoining his house: the whole state—all of "Native America"—felt different to me. Chilly. Empty.

And now again.

Hateful wishes.

. . . *the dying.*

In her early forties, Anne is an even more assured person than I played with as a kid, a stronger woman than the one who once married an abusive man—though she's not strong enough to talk about him, or those old days. Or the fact that she and I both, who'd long ago promised to remain faithful to each other, have seen our marriages fail. "Are you dating?" she asks, and when I tell her no, the subject's closed.

Otherwise, she's in full command of a room when she enters it—though always acutely attuned to others. She's devoted her life to Community, to the public service our grandfather so cherished. Like Paul Heath, she copes with trouble by counseling others.

Twenty-four hours a day, she's on call to aid her city.

"The first five years, this job almost ate my lunch," she admits to me now. "In fact, I quit for fourteen months, but I came back because I missed the contact with the people. It makes you feel good when you can rescue someone, and you learn when to detach yourself."

She rubs her temples. "The week of the bombing, there was a double impact. I had this one case . . . an eighty-six-year-old woman who'd already had one leg amputated from diabetes complications. She needed the other one taken off, but she wouldn't let anybody do it. Basically, she had capacity—she could hold herself together pretty well during a thirty-minute interview—so we couldn't force her. We were really having a tough time deciding what needed to be done. She was dying. She kept saying God would take care of her. Well, no. Not without help, anyway. Finally, we went in front of a judge and got a guardianship on her. Doctors removed her leg, and she's doing fine now.

"Anyway, the girl who was working with me on that particular case, her sister worked near the Murrah building. The woman was uninjured, as it turned out, but it was really tough dealing with people out here, in the city, that are being hurt every day by relatives or by their own neglect, and then dealing with the bombing. People were coming down with more headaches than usual, or becoming ill, from the stress of what had happened, whether they knew somebody in Murrah or not."

Later, driving downtown on our way to lunch, Anne glances out the window of her car. "In general, my job is probably a lot more stressful than I want to believe," she says quietly, affectionately watching her city. "I keep thinking it's okay, yet I've got blood pressure that goes up steadily, and I'm going, 'Well, I guess it *is* affecting me a little.' I see, on a daily basis, people getting injured, exploited—so, in a way, for me, the bombing was just one more tragic deal. On a higher scale, of course."

She studies the rushing bodies of pedestrians, off to face their afternoon crises. "But you know, I never felt a sense of hopelessness," she says. "I never thought we wouldn't pull through this." She smiles to herself, the way I remember her happy as a child, running through a field.

Crossed Over

Charles K. Johnson, a former airplane mechanic, was born in San Angelo, Texas, fifty miles from my hometown. All his life he insisted Earth was flat, and died believing it. As a young man he left Texas for southern California, as so many Dust Bowlers did. There he founded the International Flat Earth Research Society, based, he said, on the six-thousand-year-old Society of Zetetics in Greece, which held that the world was a horizontal disk floating on primordial waters.

San Angelo's as flat as day-old beer, as is much of desert California; it's not surprising that Johnson's impressions were strong. The tenacity of his beliefs is also a West Texas characteristic. He swore that the Apollo moon landing was a hoax, scripted by Arthur C. Clarke and staged in a southwestern warehouse like those in which flying saucers were said to be stored. Sunrises and sunsets were optical illusions. Solar eclipses . . . well, "we really don't have to go into all that," he told the *New York Times* in 1979. "The Bible tells us the Heavens are a mystery."

Johnson's Heartland stubbornness fascinates me because it's the same hardheadedness that fosters unshakable mistrust of government and other authorities; no amount of communal pressure could dislodge it. It was a defiant assertion of private feelings over public discourse.

After the Oklahoma City bombing, I fretted constantly about the lines between private and public: where they crossed or didn't. I wondered why this national tragedy, thousands of miles removed from me, affected me so personally. I wondered if I was using a large, abstract grief to distract myself from the more acute and immediate pain of my failed marriage.

I could console myself that I was a man of conscience, as in the Book of Deuteronomy, weighing "life and good, death and evil." Or was I, like Johnson and Timothy McVeigh, clinging to some private darkness in irrational disregard of forces I couldn't understand or control?

In the midst of my worries I came upon a book by Beverly Lowry called *Crossed Over*. In 1983, Lowry's son Peter was killed in a hit-and-run accident. Soon thereafter, she became inexplicably obsessed with Karla Faye Tucker, who, fueled by drugs one night in northwest Houston, helped kill a man and a woman, for no particular reason, with a pickaxe. She was on Death Row in Texas—"the personification of evil," one prosecutor had called her. Lowry began a correspondence with her and eventually met with her several times in prison. "In March, 1986, the Houston *Chronicle* published a front-page story about Karla Faye, accompanied by a color photograph of her in prison whites, cupping her chin in her hand," Lowry said. "The photograph . . . captured my attention . . . There was—I don't know how else to describe it—an old-fashioned sense of goodness about her. She was pretty, alert, warm. More than anything, she looked calm. I envied that calm."

Since receiving her death sentence, Karla Faye had embraced Jesus and renounced her old life. But it wasn't this conversion or the sense that a decent person who'd made a horrendous mistake was about to be unwisely executed that moved Lowry to contact her. "I could not stop looking at the newspaper picture of the lovely young woman with the dark rolling hair and the soft brown eyes," she said. "I knew then that death was my subject. It had become the only thing that interested me . . . I met a condemned murderer because Peter had been killed."

Her personal grief had forced—allowed?—her to cross over into a larger tragedy, and to enter other lives viscerally, with no boundaries to protect herself. In her book, she tries to reason out her obsession: was she indulging her depression, using Karla Faye as distraction, responding to similarities she noticed between Karla Faye and her son, or herself? In the end, none of these possibilities provides her with a fully satisfactory explanation. She falls back on landscape, to suggest we're all susceptible to primitive, unseen forces: "The land Houston is built on is reclaimed swamp, after all. The ooze constantly threatens to rise up and take back its rightful place." And she despairs of narrative's power to ever completely explicate complex emotions, quoting Donald Barthelme, an old writing teacher she and I shared: "Endings are elusive," he said, "middles are nowhere to be found, but worst of all is to begin, to begin, to begin."

Reading Lowry's story, I thought of the French theologian Paul Ricoeur, who attempted to trace the roots of Western culture's notions of sin, defilement, and guilt. Lowry's experience seemed to me to exemplify Ricoeur's belief that "man is . . . 'burdened' with fault; he need not be the author of the evil to feel himself burdened by its weight and the weight of its consequences."

And, thinking of Murrah, I was struck by how, in our time, buildings carry the import of our sins. Jails have always housed the guilty, but now terrorists—insisting that government sites are symbols of evil—have forced most of our official institutions to be fortified like prisons. Walking into a post office or a Social Security bureau, surrounded by barred windows or steel-reinforced doors, we *all* feel imprisoned and maybe even guilty.

The architect Beatriz Colomina suggests that "shock is what characterizes" modern life—global tragedies documented instantly—and that mass communication, by delivering these horrors into our homes every day, has eroded the boundaries between public and private, displacing our "traditional sense of an inside, an enclosed space, established in clear opposition to an outside." The windows of contemporary buildings are like camera lenses or movie screens, she says. Whether we're inside or out in public, we're all either watching or being observed. Intimacy, privacy, and protection have vanished. If her claims seem extreme, I can say, nevertheless, that I experienced, after the Murrah bombing, the collapse of more than just physical walls.

On February 3, 1998, Governor George W. Bush refused to issue a reprieve, and the state of Texas gave Karla Faye Tucker a lethal injection, despite the protests of religious leaders nationwide. Even some of the lawyers who had originally prosecuted her case felt she had changed and no longer deserved to die.

"Here she comes, baby doll, she's all yours," said Richard Thornton, husband of one of the victims, as the poison ate into Karla Faye's veins.

"May God bless Karla Faye Tucker," W. said.

"Choose life and you shall live," says Deuteronomy.

Beverly Lowry said, "I don't like talking in metaphors about death. She's gone. Cold flesh. And, after a time, dust."

"I got out of my place, that's all," Karla Faye had told her. "The Devil tempted me, and I got out of my place."

And what is *our* place, the place of those of us looking on, as people die in buildings all around us? What is our best response, our appropriate posture? Lamentation, perhaps, heads bowed, eyes fully open, hands beating the flat, flat earth.

Irreconciled

In the fall of 1996, as a new teaching year started, Timothy Mc-Veigh's trial began, and my divorce became final. I walked to the sheriff's office to pick up the papers. They'd been delivered from Lane County, Oregon, where Martha lived, to Benton County, my current residence, forty miles away. As a defense against sadness, I thought briefly of swaggering into the building and booming at the receptionist, "Okay darlin', where's the crime? I'm on the case now." But this wasn't an occasion for jokes.

IN THE MATTER OF THE MARRIAGE OF—

Irreconcilable differences between the parties
have caused the irremediable breakdown
of their marriage.

The Petitioner should be required to assume
the following obligations—

The Respondent should be required—

WHEREFORE, *Petitioner prays for a judgment:*

Dissolving the marriage of the parties.
Granting the Petitioner relief in conformance with the allegations set forth in this Petition—

I sat on the curb outside the Benton County Jail. The last twelve years of my life had been reduced to hideous sentences. A blague of neutral words, meaningful, of course, to a lawyer . . . but it struck me that nothing was more meaningless than neutral language engaged to contain passion, joy, pain, life's sloppiness. Kisses, embraces, laughter, shared dinners, tilled gardens, late-night talks had been recast into "differences," "matters," "requirements." The limits of the legal, of law and order, of civilization's strict and panicked urge to pave our bumpy human landscape, had never been more apparent to me.

"Petitioner prays for a judgment"? Strike me dead, Lord, right here by the jail. Guilty as charged. Perhaps this *was* an occasion for jokes, after all. The State of Oregon was mocking my failure to stay married. No. The state didn't care about me one way or another, as long as it collected its legal fees.

Back in my apartment, I held the divorce decree as I fixed myself a cup of coffee. I didn't know where to put the papers. Logically, I should have filed them away with my tax forms, but that seemed too efficient and final, as if divorce were a routine matter. At the same time, I didn't want them on my desk or anywhere else in the open, reminding me of my life's meager wreckage.

I paced my small rooms, sipping coffee, gripping the documents.

The desk, the bedspread, the pictures on the walls, the cup in my hand all reminded me of the life I'd—officially now—lost: I'd purchased most of these things with Martha.

I knew I had to get out of my place. I tossed the legal storm in a corner on the floor and dumped my tepid coffee.

All the rest of that day I walked, in town, in the woods, then back to town, hoping the pale fall sunlight would somehow grant me relief.

In the last few months, as McVeigh's trial had approached, the Oklahoma City bombing had been transformed from hatred, detritus, bodies, and tears into "Hearing[s] before . . . Subcommittee[s] of the Committee on Appropriations [before] the United States Senate, One Hundred Fourth Congress, Fifth Session."

"A request for resource packages and support personnel" had replaced the cry of "Why?"

McVeigh's impassioned threat to the BATF, "Die, you spineless, coward[ly] bastards!" had become, in the words of the criminal complaint against him, a desire to "damage and destroy by means of fire or an explosive, any building, vehicle, and other personal or real property in whole or in part owned, possessed, or used by the United States, any department or agency thereof, in violation of Title 18, United States Code, Section(s) 844(f)."

One hundred sixty-eight dead Oklahomans had become Criminal Action 96-CR-68 in the United States District Court for the District of Colorado.

And, as if to further strip the event of its blood and bone, one day a political consultant on CNN dismissed the long-term public impact of McVeigh's trial, saying, "If it's not on television, it barely matters."

Eventually, I tucked my divorce decree in a drawer with my cancelled checks and tried to get on with life, which meant teaching classes.

I've found that in writing courses, clarity is the hardest virtue to pass on. Most beginning writers slip into the clichés they hear on television: *My heart was bursting with happiness.* Or they fatten their prose with overwrought metaphors: *My heart was a silver clothesline strung with the sheets of my bliss.*

Passion, joy, pain, life's sloppiness are hard to render, and most young writers don't try. The task intimidates them, so they stick with more fanciful stuff. For example, in over a decade of fiction writing courses at Oregon State University, I've received dozens of stories about cows with glass stomachs.

Despite my students' attempts to explain their source, these pieces always puzzled me ("unclear metaphor," I thought) until I began taking walks after class.

West of campus, out by the married students' housing, the elegant brick architecture of most of the university's buildings gives way to peeled-paint wooden fences, hay barns, and corrugated metal pens. Philosophy, history, and literature yield to seedlings and manure, lowing and bleating.

The loveliest road in Corvallis passes cattle stalls, sheep pens, and rabbit hutches, part of Oregon State's agricultural research facilities, on its way to Irish Bend Bridge, a covered wooden walkway, milk white and slender, over the leafy trickle of Oak Creek.

This became my favorite after-class path at dusk, or even later in the evening when stars spun slowly over the Coast Range foothills and the patchy fields skirting campus. I'd stroll past the squalid family apartments, misnamed Orchard Court (another overwrought metaphor), with their clamor of squealing infants and frying foods, by a series of crystalline greenhouses, gorgeous at night, glowing with pink and purple light. Inside, long yellow stalks trembled in artificial winds from quietly humming machines. I'd press my face to the mist of the buildings' glass and watch the gauzy plants. I thought of Theodore Roethke's "Big Wind" (now *there* was a man who knew metaphors!):

Where were the greenhouses going
Lunging into the lashing
Wind driving water
So far down the river
All the faucets stopped?—

And later in the poem:

. . . she rode it out,
That old rose-house,
She hove into the teeth of it,
The core and pith of that ugly storm,
Ploughing with her stiff prow,
Bucking into the wind-waves . . .
Carrying her full cargo of roses.

Past the greenhouses, the road to Irish Bend Bridge aimed for short hills beyond the research barns with their "No Trespassing" signs. In the dark, with no one around, I'd cross fences into cattle stalls, listen to cows huff and snort lazily in mazes of sweet-smelling hay, or I'd stand beside sheep pens, eavesdropping on the infantlike cries of the lambs, as the temperature cooled, and swift clouds scoured the constellations.

The animal sounds calmed me: simple, primal, oblivious to human needs. Like the purring of a cat, the bleating, the snorting, and the long, snouty sighs set me at ease.

In the house I'd shared with Martha, my old cat Jake regularly curled in my lap while I wrote, purring, relaxing us both through rainy afternoons. I missed Jake whenever I walked to the bridge, past larger, louder creatures.

One day I took an early walk after class. The cows were out, eating grass in the fields beside the stalls. One of the animals appeared to have an object—a small saddle?—hung on its hide. Closer, I could see the thing was actually a plug shaped like a porthole, offering a view, when removed, of the cow's insides. Somehow, researchers had opened a hole in the animal and covered it with plastic or rubber, presumably to study digestive patterns. Now I knew what my students had been referring to all these years!

The cow appeared unperturbed by its transparency. It ignored me and went on cropping the grass.

In my students' stories, these see-through animals were nearly always clumsy metaphors for false appearances, physical frailties, or humanity's insensitivity to the natural world.

One girl wrote a fable, urging her readers not to judge others by their looks. We're all made of "icky stuff" inside, she argued; we're all just mammals, with fragile tummies.

In a courtroom, as in a classroom, clarity is hard to come by.

This became apparent to me the first week of Timothy Mc-Veigh's trial, as I read the daily transcripts accessed from the Internet. On the witness stand, none of the survivors could effectively describe the feeling, or the sound, of the blast. It was a "boom." It was a "thunder clap." Phrases and metaphors so familiar, they had no impact.

At times during questioning, the witnesses, sometimes even the lawyers, became flustered or confused. On the second day of testimony, during direct examination, Cynthia Lou Klaver, who worked in the Water Resources Building across the road from Murrah, tried to set the scene in the streets immediately after the explosion: "There were some people sitting on curbs cut up. It seemed very desolate and quiet and smoke everywhere and there were . . . I ran into co-worker Mike Mathis and he had a deep gash in his forehead. And he was going to drive himself in his pickup down to the south clinic, Southside Clinic in Oklahoma City. And I was aware that head gashes are probably not a good idea to drive."

Her last sentence is clear enough, and there's even a kind of melancholy charm in the misstatement. I appreciated Ms. Klaver's difficulty—we don't expect *War and Peace* from the witness stand—but the more I read the transcripts, the more fretful I became about the elusiveness of evidence, eyewitness testimony, and descriptive words.

My uneasiness soon became zealousness in the classroom. "Plain imagery," I stressed to my students, "faithful observation. Learn how to *see*." I cut their easy metaphors, the strained adjectives, the magic cows. "Be *specific*."

Most of my students' stories ended with airy morals or swelled with the sort of sentimentality I'd seen on Oprah the day she'd featured a brave mother cat who'd saved her kittens from perilous flames. "Always tell the truth," I taught. "Drop the sweetness and light, okay? Life isn't like that."

But maybe life *was* like that for these folks. Maybe I was just a hopeless depressive. My ex-wife certainly thought so, I reminded myself. I had the papers to prove it.

Late one night, I was sitting in my apartment reading trial transcripts when Martha phoned to tell me Jake was dying. She'd stopped eating and drinking. She'd developed a respiratory infection she couldn't shake. Martha wanted to take her to an all-night veterinary clinic and end her pain. Tonight. "Wait for me. I'll come," I said.

I drove slowly, crying. It took me an hour to get to Martha's place, down Highway 99, the road most Okies followed when they migrated north out of California's orchards in the forties. My headlights dusted pines by the road; a hoot owl swooped from a tree, over rows of wet mint, into the dark.

My mind ticked back and forth between the transcripts I'd been studying and my poor old cat. Tevin Garrett's mother, Helena, had been on the stand that day in Denver:

PATRICK RYAN, PROSECUTOR: *You have two children?*

HELENA GARRETT: *Yes, I do.*

Q. *What are their names?*

A. *Sharonda Garrett and Tevin Garrett.*

Q. *How old is Sharonda?*

A. *She's seven.*

Q. *How old is Garrett?*

A. *He's—he was sixteen months.*

Q. *When did Tevin Garrett die?*
A. *On April 19th . . . 1995.*

As I whisked past darkened farmhouses and an abandoned skate rink, battered by winds, I remembered living in Houston with Martha, years ago, the day Hurricane Alicia hammered the city, shattering glass in the downtown buildings, tossing trees into the bayou. In the gale, the double doors of our old garage whipped up and down like soggy matchbook covers. I pulled her to me and cradled Jake in my lap.

> A. *I tried to imagine the building like it was [before the explosion], and I said . . . that's where Tevin is, and I started climbing the debris.*
> Q. *Why did you start climbing at that spot in the rubble?*
> A. *Because if the building wasn't destroyed, Tevin would have been in that particular room of the day-care center. He would have been right there; and I just closed my eyes and tried to be where he was.*

We lost Jake once, on a camping trip in Colorado. She crept from our tent and raced off under tall ferns on a riverbank, beneath jagged cedars. I thought we'd never see her again. An owl would get her, or a bear. We searched for hours. At dusk, my failing flashlight beam swept a pair of glittering eyes in a niche beneath a rotted, sweet-smelling log.

As she aged, she stuck closer to Martha and me, rarely letting us out of her sight. I wrote a whole novel and a short story collection with her asleep in my lap. She liked my small attempts at order. She liked a happy household.

> Q. *Mrs. Garrett, there's a water pitcher . . . with some glasses there in front of you. Would you like for me to pour you a glass of water? Can you do it? Let's—tell me what—what happened [next]?*
> A. *I was crying and I was screaming. I said [to the rescuers], "You got to— please don't lay our babies on this glass." It was black glass everywhere.*

I said, "Please don't lay our babies [there]. We don't want our babies on the glass."

Martha looked exhausted and thin. We hugged.

"How are you?"

"Thanks for coming down."

Jake lay on the bed. Her lungs heaved; she sounded like a badly stripped engine. Each shallow intake shook her body. She'd stopped bathing herself. Her matted fur was firm as wax.

Martha and I didn't speak much as we bundled Jake into her carrying case, then placed her in the car.

The clinic was next to a busy freeway, on an access road. Its sign cut the night with garish blue light. Inside, in the pale white waiting room, another couple fussed over a big, bony tomcat. They hushed when we sat down with Jake; her throaty racket unnerved them. The woman told the receptionist, "We can wait if their cat is sicker than ours."

Though most of her strength was gone, Jake tried to stand and peer around the room—a flare of her old curiosity. She wobbled. Martha and I held her together.

A young man led us into an antiseptic back room. We set Jake on a cold metal table. Her eyes leaked. Each breath was a shriek. The vet, a kind young woman, produced a bright green towel and slid it under Jake's legs. It was hideously ugly. She asked us to hold Jake tight. "I'll give her a shot in her hind leg here. It'll take effect almost immediately. She won't feel any pain. It's the most humane way we've ever found of putting an animal to sleep."

I remembered running playfully around the house, chasing Jake, then turning and letting her chase me. I remembered her paws on my face in the morning, prodding me until I rose to feed her. I remembered her in afternoon sunlight, bathing herself, lifting my gloom.

A. *A lady came, a nurse, and she started tagging our babies; and right then I realized they were dead.*

If a student told me he'd written a story about the death of a cat, I'd say *Toss it*: "Too sentimental. Too Oprah."

If he confessed he'd combined the death of a cat with details of a horrible crime, I'd say, "Forget it, it's offensive to equate a dying animal with human suffering."

Yet here I was, in a bright, homely clinic, my head spinning with Helena Garrett, wracked by my cat's final minutes.

She watched my eyes, trusting. Martha cupped her head in her palm. The doctor inserted the needle.

"Good-bye, Jake," I whispered.

Martha said, "Good-bye."

I know what we both were thinking. How could we help it? Jake's death was a metaphor for our marriage. We'd embraced Jake when we'd opened our lives to each other, many years ago. We'd nurtured Jake as we'd nurtured each other. And now, our cat was dead. Our marriage was over.

Pray for a judgment.

Of all the things I felt as I lifted Jake's body to my chest, self-loathing was strongest. Why hadn't I demanded a prettier towel for her to die on?

I hated that towel. I hated it more than anything I'd ever hated in my life.

Martha and I slipped Jake into a large gray shoebox. We touched hands.

Did it help us to see this night as a ritual, a ceremony signaling, once and for all, our severance? There was a symmetry about Jake's time with us and our time with each other. A parallel.

Let this be a funeral, then; a formal acknowledgment of an ending. A quiet letting go.

But here was that hideous green towel, insisting on itself, refusing to be romanticized or turned into anything neat. Life is what it is, I thought, closing the shoebox, and it's best to see clearly. To say things, and to write things, with clarity.

A cow with a hole in its belly is not a metaphor for anything.

The Pastures of Plenty

Early June in Oregon's mid–Willamette Valley is often overcast and wet, the sky a smudgy earthen bowl, the meadows at the base of the Coast Range foothills dark and slick with snowmelt, mud, sprinkles from light and snaky mists. The rivers are full, flanked by budding blue iris, wild clematis, hawthorn, laurel. Rabbits nest in new grasses; bobwhites call at dusk in knuckly red oaks. Soon, strawberries will ripen in all the sloping fields.

These are the Pastures of Plenty Woody Guthrie sang about in the best of his Dust Bowl Ballads, tracing in simple verse the path of poor Okies west in the wastes of the Great Depression, and later, in the fever of coming war:

> I've worked in your orchards of peaches and prunes,
> Slept on the ground in the light of the moon,
> On the edge of your city you've seen us and then
> We come with the dust and we go with the wind.

California and Arizona, I make all your crops,
And it's north up to Oregon to gather your hops,
Dig the beets from your ground, cut the grapes from your vines,
To set on your table your light sparkling wines.

He penned these words in '41, living in Portland while on retainer for the Bonneville Power Administration. The BPA had told him he might appear in a documentary film praising dams and hydroelectricity. The film never got made, but while in Oregon, Woody wandered through the migrant camps of the mid–Willamette Valley, meeting fellows from home, huddling in the foggy damp. "I made a little speech in each [Okie] tent [I saw]," he wrote a friend. "I said, you folks are the best in the west, why don't you take time out and write some songs about who you are?"

Now, in early June, in that same part of the Willamette Valley, I stand on a muddy road, watching horseflies pop through rye grass, humming "Pastures of Plenty," thinking hard about who I am.

Of the warm western rain, the kind that squalls through this valley in the spring, and sometimes well into the summer, Steinbeck wrote, "The clouds came in brokenly, in puffs, in folds, in gray crags; and they piled in together and settled low . . . The rain began with gusty showers, pauses and downpours; and then gradually it settled to a single tempo, small drops and a steady beat, rain that was gray to see through, rain that cut the midday light to evening."

A mighty storm roars through the final pages of *The Grapes of Wrath*, nearly drowning what's left of the Joad family, who'd begun its western exodus when the last rains had abandoned Oklahoma, drying it to leather. Readers are left wondering whatever came of the Joads; after moving west, I learned that many of their real-life counterparts left California, tramped to Oregon, and pitched the stone-colored tents Woody stopped to visit. They worked in valley orchards, in growing city shipyards, and even, just across the state line, in Washington's brand-new nuclear weapons plant.

This afternoon, Woody, Steinbeck, and all of Oklahoma are

keenly on my mind. For three days now, Timothy McVeigh's jury has been deliberating his guilt or innocence, and the wait has been excruciating. In newspaper interviews, the bombing survivors, and families of the dead, have been airing their fears that McVeigh may go free.

"My stomach's in a couple hundred thousand knots," Don McKinney, whose wife died in the building's wreckage, told a Denver paper. "The worry is, there's something the jury didn't like [in the prosecution's presentation] that might mess things up."

The day the jurors retired to discuss the case, Dan Demoss, who was severely injured in the Social Security office on Murrah's ground floor, said, "I wasn't worried [about the verdict] until this afternoon. I don't think America is ready for this."

He wasn't alone. From the first, the press had pitched McVeigh's trial as a referendum on America's judicial system. Rodney King, the Menendez Brothers, O. J. Simpson: these were the extra burdens, symbols of miscarried justice, that weighed on the bombing trial, along with Ruby Ridge and Waco; reports that the nation's central FBI lab was tainted; tons of Heartland rubble most Americans wanted to forget because the pain was overwhelming.

"Justice" is fighting for its life in Denver, said the *New York Times* midway through McVeigh's trial. "What is clear beyond doubt . . . is that much more than Mr. McVeigh's guilt or innocence is being tested. On trial with [him] . . . is the credibility of the nation's . . . law enforcement."

Now, on this early afternoon (a rare sweltering one in Oregon), after the most massive federal investigation since the assassination of John F. Kennedy, America was waiting for twelve Coloradans to tell it if Justice could be resuscitated from the pit of a smoking crater.

In public opinion polls, most people said they thought McVeigh was guilty, the evidence against him as tall as the building he'd brought down. If he walked, the rage from coast to coast . . . well, no one wanted to face it.

"I've had dreams about [McVeigh], that I was with [him] and his father," Vicki Hamm told the *Daily Oklahoman*. She'd worked in the U.S. Army recruiting office on Murrah's third floor. "In these dreams, I was wanting him to talk to me, [to] say, 'I did it. But I didn't mean to.' And then I would have some feelings toward him besides anger."

I'd also dreamed of chatting with McVeigh, sitting with him on the plush lawn at the Murrah site in the dew of first light, asking, "Why?"

In one of these dreams, he'd laughed and shot back, "Did *you* mean to?"

I demanded to know what he was talking about; then I woke up.

Lately, I'd felt an urgency to stand again at the fence furred with teddy bears, but my teaching job kept me in Oregon. My homesickness, my anxiety over the verdict, my dreams of Oklahoma dust, made me think today of Woody, made me hum a few old ballads. "Your songs are not your songs alone," he'd said.

I'm the son of Okies, and I'm living now in the West. That's the sum total, I thought, amazed by the simple truth of it. That's who I am.

I taught my classes for the day, then headed for the fields of the valley, where lately I'd imagined the ghosts of Okies grouped in muggy tents.

In my pocket I carried a deputy sheriff's badge from Cotton County, Oklahoma. It had belonged to my grandfather in the thirties. It was dark and heavy, horned at the top, rounded below like the Route 66 signs that used to line America's "Main Street." Copper-colored, burnished like a teapot on a stove, it brought me luck, or so I hoped. Since the start of McVeigh's trial, I'd hauled it around, a kind of prayer for fairness and peace.

"Whenever he got an emergency call in the middle of the night, he'd reach for his necktie but never for his pistol," my grandmother once told my cousin Anne and me. Instead of a gun, he carried a squat leather blackjack, which I've also got. He never used it, either.

In 1934, he joined Oklahoma's manhunt for Charley Floyd, erecting roadblocks on 66 and dusty farm trails, hoping to nab the notorious gangster.

"I knowed Purty Boy," Ma Joad brags. "He wan't a bad boy. Jus' got drove in a corner" by desperation.

And in the most famous of his Dust Bowl Ballads, Woody sang:

Some will rob you with a six-gun,
Some with a fountain pen.

Then he praised Pretty Boy for aiding the poor with cash he'd stolen from the rich.

My grandfather never glimpsed Floyd. "It takes a hell of a lot of luck to catch a guy," he told me once—an observation Charlie Hanger (and later, American intelligence officers searching for Osama bin Laden) would probably affirm. Hanger was the highway patrolman who'd pulled Timothy McVeigh over after the bombing. According to the trial transcripts, if McVeigh's license plate hadn't fallen off his car, he wouldn't have caught Hanger's eye and might never have been found.

In the valley now, in dappled, dreamy light through the trees, it's easy for me to imagine my grandfather pacing a windblown road, a road buzzing with Okies heading west, robbed by bankers of their hardscrabble acres.

I see him leaning on a rickety old sawhorse, a roadblock, waiting for luck, straightening his tie . . . like Woody, but in secret, admiring the legendary outlaw, who at least had the guts to stand up to the rich sons of bitches . . .

Then the scene changes; Timothy McVeigh whizzes past. It's a whole new era, and words like "justice," "fairness," and "peace" are fighting for their lives. My grandfather scratches his head.

On my way out of town, I'd checked a television in the student union. Still no verdict. On CNN, Jannie Coverdale was crying. Her grandsons Elijah and Aaron, two and five, had died in the day care center. She said, "Everybody [from Oklahoma] is tense, tired, and confused. I smoked a whole pack of cigarettes yesterday. I'm also drinking more coffee. I just can't seem to keep still."

Martin Cash, another survivor, said, "It ain't over till the slim guy swings." He wore a patch over his missing left eye. Once, during the trial, McVeigh blew a contemptuous kiss at him across the courtroom. "My best satisfaction is that he feels . . . he wished he'd killed me," Cash said.

For weeks, newspaper and television reporters noted McVeigh's stoicism, claiming he never showed emotion in the courtroom. Only Paul Heath, perhaps because of his training as a psychologist, saw anything different in the defendant. McVeigh "was clenching his fists so hard together that the blood gathered in his hands and actually turned almost a dark gray," Dr. Heath told the *Daily Oklahoman*. "He's not sitting there without feeling. He's got a *lot* of feeling."

My grandfather's badge weights my pocket. I lower my car windows and feel the pleasing heat. The valley here wasn't always open prairie with thick, fertile soil. It didn't automatically produce the Plenty so many Okies craved. In the last century, before white settlers overran the area, the Kalapuya Indians set fires in late summer, killing the valley's brush but nurturing its wild grasses. Game thrived on the grass and made good hunting for the Indians. The fires kept trees from taking root, except in the Willamette's higher stretches, where black oaks fleshed with firm, corky bark resisted the fast-moving flames. In the damp regions nearer the valley's floor, camas, a lilylike perennial, proliferated; the Kalapuyas loved to eat its sweet bulbous roots.

If native peoples cleared the valley so small farmers, then larger landowners, could cultivate it, using Chinese, Filipino, and Okie labor, then the Okies cleared the way for Mexican fieldworkers by flocking to the Kaiser shipyards in Portland during the Second World War.

In August 1942, the federal government began its Bracero (or "Strong-Arm") Program, importing temporary employees from Mexico to make up for the labor shortage in the orchards and the fields. In Oregon, the program, known locally as the Emergency Farm Labor Supply Act, was administered by the state college in Corvallis, where I teach now and where the records of the program still exist. From 1942 to 1946, 15,136 *braceros* picked Oregon's vegetables and fruit. The farmhands were bunked together in shacks or in mobile tent camps.

Today, as I look for a quiet spot off the main roads, a place to sit in soothing sunlight both to think about the trial and then to forget it if I can, I see in the distance small wooden shelters at the edges of the fields, and I know they'll soon house workers. Strawberries are a week or two from picking. According to published reports, most Mexicans who work in the Willamette Valley speak little English and have no idea how much they're getting paid. Their wages for picking fruit average around twelve cents per pound. If they complain, they're fired. Plenty of other families are on the move down south, willing to work.

Little has changed since the old Okie days. Steinbeck wrote about white men. When white men and women left the fields, so did middle-class outrage over labor conditions.

From where I'm standing now, beside a muddy old logging path, the workers' shacks are almost hidden. Their lives are even harder to see.

I sit in cool grass. Watching the shacks, I rub my grandfather's badge—like stroking a rabbit's foot. I imagine Riley crouched on Dong Ap Bia, clutching his salt packet and his book of matches, praying to get through the night. "I've asked God that if Tim McVeigh is guilty, to have the jury *find* him guilty," Jannie Coverdale has said. Silently here, on the crest of this hill, surrounded by restless ghosts, I second that.

The people of the land have
used oppression, and exercised robbery,
and have vexed the poor and needy;
yea, they have oppressed
the stranger wrongfully.

My grandfather once quoted these lines from Ezekiel in one of his old political speeches, a rouser extolling economic justice for small farmers. I have a copy of it at home, in a collection of his papers, and I've read it many times, enough to memorize it. Today, on this hill, as I recite the words to myself, they seem to me both appropriate and eerie.

Therefore have I poured out
mine indignation upon them; I have
consumed them with the fire of my wrath;
their own way I have recompensed upon their heads,
saith the Lord GOD.

Later, at home, I turn on CNN. Apparently, the verdict is in, but I've missed it.

A reporter is showing off the Survivor Tree, across the street from Murrah. A slippery elm, nearly forty feet tall, the tree has weathered several bouts of Dutch elm disease; now it's endured the blast. Slippery elms are known for the soothing benefits of their smooth inner bark. Legend has it that George Washington's troops braved a brutal winter sipping gruel made from the limbs of a slippery elm.

The Survivor Tree is most likely a "volunteer," occurring naturally from a windblown seed that settled in the brick red soil of downtown Oklahoma City. Mark Bays, a forestry coordinator for the Oklahoma Department of Agriculture, says, "The citizens of Oklahoma are *watching* that tree."

Now, in a live TV shot, Paul Heath is standing in the shadow of the elm, addressing a big, close crowd. He's wearing a light green sport coat. I can't tell from his face whether he's happy or sad. He smiles, but his eyes are pained, as if seeing too much light. Clearly, he's not the type of person to celebrate a guilty verdict. He's a man who understands the gravity of tragedy.

"This old tree may be gnarled and ugly, but its roots run deep into the Oklahoma soil," he says. He raises a plastic container. Everybody else has one, too. "These may look like bottles of water to you and me," says Dr. Heath, "but I ask you to see them as full of memories and tears."

He bows his head. The sky grays. "We pray not for ourselves," he says, "but for our nation, a nation under God, a nation under law, a nation under order."

Then, one by one, twisting off the bottle caps, each person steps forth beneath the tree, each person with a deep, private story, as well as a story here together, and slowly refreshes the roots.

III | Grounds for Survival

Amarillo

"WHAT'S A SONIC BOOM AMONG FRIENDS?

"Well, it's somewhat startling, but very solid assurance of protection. It's an unspoken pledge that the safety of you and your family is the prime concern of the day-to-day business of the U.S. Air Force."

This ad appeared in the *Amarillo News-Globe* in 1961, on the tenth anniversary of the siting of a Strategic Air Command base in the dusty Texas panhandle.

By 1975, Amarillo's Pantex Plant had become the final assembly spot for all nuclear weapons manufactured in the United States. At its peak, Pantex produced 1,500 warheads a year—an average of at least 4 a day.

Many of the locals, hired to work on the bombing components, were fundamentalist Christians who anticipated with relish the world's end. It meant establishing the Kingdom of Heaven on Earth.

I'm passing through the panhandle today after seeing family in Oklahoma City. My ex-wife's parents live near here. Unless I call them today I'll probably never see them again.

A sign on Route 66, just across the Texas state line, says, "Rattlesnakes. Exit Now." From Clinton on west, billboards have been screaming, in blocky red letters, "The Big Texan Steak Ranch. 72-ounce steak. You'll be glad you waited."

In Amarillo, stoplights sway over wide, empty streets, clicking green to yellow to red to green to yellow to red. There is no traffic. Tumbleweeds. Caliche. TV satellite dishes. A cracked Dairy Queen sign says, "Amarillo. We Like Where We Are."

This part of the world—my big, gusty backyard where the bomb came to sit one day—has always filled me with loneliness. These days, in the Cold War's wake, it seems more desolate than ever.

For the casual traveler, with nothing personal at stake (but who would come *here* casually?), *Fodor's* sums the place up well: "As the last echoes of the Civil War cannon died, and men turned their thoughts westward, they aimed at nearly every corner of the map except the Texas panhandle," says the travel guide. "That way . . . lay only madness: the madness of the incessant howling wind (summer and winter); the madness of the unbroken prairie where a man might wander aimlessly until the blistering sun and the windblown dust finally felled him; the madness of icy snow, borne horizontally on the wings of a roaring gale. This was the Texas panhandle."

This was the Okies' escape route.

And in the early nineties, this was the mad track of Timothy McVeigh. Obsessively, he drove to and fro between Kingman, Arizona, where his friends the Fortiers lived, and Herington, Kansas, to visit his pal Terry Nichols.

Here, in this hardscrabble basin, hour after pill-fueled hour, McVeigh envisioned the bombing of the Murrah building. Is it coincidence, I wonder, staring now at cactus, weeds, alkali streaks in the sand, that this parched, dead-flat stretch of the road is also the beginning of the militarized West?

In the thirties, when the Okies sputtered through here, none of what McVeigh would later observe had yet been built: nuclear weapons plants, test sites, Air Force bases.

"Restricted." "Federal Property." "Keep Out."

Initially, the interstate highways that replaced 66 were developed mainly for the military. Dwight D. Eisenhower had returned from fighting in Germany highly impressed by the strategic value of Hitler's autobahn.

In the high plains, and in much of the West, the roads were designed to be emergency runways for fighter planes. A B52 bomber from Oklahoma City's Tinker Air Force Base could land on a long, straight line of I-40, refuel, resupply, and be back in the air in a snap, defending America from the terrible Soviet threat.

Throughout the Cold War, most people who lived in "hot" towns didn't mind the government's presence. Uncle Sam's pockets were deep. But to a migrant, unmoored, lacking direction—to an Army vet who'd finally been rejected by the service, as McVeigh had been—it was easy to believe that the U.S. government was an occupying force, waging war on American soil.

Most farmers, victims of federal price fixing, would agree.

Most ranchers, pinched by federal land regulators, young Ivy Leaguers in big, climate-controlled rooms back east, would agree.

And Native Americans? Workers in the fields? Well. They weren't talking. Or if they were, no one was listening.

Midland, my hometown, lies directly south of Amarillo, south of 66. As a child, watching Roy Orbison on my daddy's brand new Crosley, I wasn't aware of Pantex. I didn't feel the nuclear weight pressing on me from the desiccated plains up north.

But of course the bomb had changed my home.

I know now that most television and computer technology has developed over the years through military research. Satellite tracking. High-frequency radio waves.

Though I wasn't aware of it in 1959, the big-eyed box in my

parents' living room was a poor civilian stepchild of an angry warrior father.

All the while, as Roy wailed "Ooby Dooby," the bomb was sitting just up the road, biding its time. In the hands of fervent Christians. In swales of blowing dust.

Today, with the collapse of Cold War funding (the bomb in hibernation, its messes strewn recklessly across the desert, from Amarillo to Hanford), it's impossible to overstate the sense of betrayal one feels in many parts of the American West.

For example, in Hudspeth County, in far West Texas, the ag-based economy has been severely depressed since the late seventies. The area averages only seven to nine inches of rainfall, yearly.

In the early eighties, the federal government proposed turning the county into a nuclear waste dump, storing 90 percent of the nation's radioactive waste there. The locals were not informed of this decision and only caught on, much later, from newspapers.

Meanwhile, Merco Joint Venture Inc., a private sewage company, purchased a 128,000-acre ranch north of the proposed nuclear site and began disposing sludge there—nearly 225 tons of it a day from industrial sewage plants back east. Merco told the citizens of Hudspeth County it was providing fertilizer for overgrazed rangelands.

In Colorado, men who mined uranium for nuclear weapons, and who developed pulmonary fibrosis as a result, have been waiting for the government to make good on the Radiation Exposure and Compensation Act of 1990, which established one-time payments of up to $100,000 to miners. Over two hundred desperately ill men are waiting for their money, which has been held up indefinitely by congressional budget debates. Some miners have died holding IOUs.

At the edge of the Nevada Test Site, an organization called American Peace Test provides advisory bulletins for protesters: "The Nevada Test Site is a highly radioactive place with many hot spots, dumps, and storage areas . . . There is little that can be done to protect your body from beta and gamma rays which are unseen . . . Cover your face when walking in the wind. Do not eat food dropped on the ground. Don't use bare, dirty hands for eating . . . Depending on [where you are] you will have to deal with ammunition strafing, falling bombs, unexploded bombs on the ground, maneuvering around targets, and stealth bomber[s] . . . Security forces are well-armed and quite capable of shooting if they feel threatened."

Really.

Is it any wonder that many Westerners today, like Southerners after the Civil War, feel they live in a conquered nation?

Is it any wonder that a furious farmer and a disillusioned vet would plan to bomb a government building?

The wonder is, we didn't see it coming.

The miracle is, it doesn't happen every week.

From a speech by Harry Tracy Daugherty, my left-leaning grandfather (1935): "We must stop the destruction of true democracy and the substitution of government by force."

Timothy McVeigh (1993): "The violations of the Constitution by those power-hungry storm troopers of the federal government [must] not succeed again."

Of course, the difference between my grandfather and McVeigh is like the gap between a devout Muslim and a member of al-Qaeda. One revered human life and always sought an equitable solution to conflict; the other crossed an inhuman boundary and equated solutions with murder. But the seeds of their anger are similar.

Michael Fortier (1997): "If you don't consider what happened in Oklahoma, Tim was a good person."

I recall a local television commercial when I was a kid in these parts. A pretty young woman smiled at the camera and said, "If you don't have an oil well, get one!"

See what I mean about betrayal?

From the outskirts of Amarillo, a right turn takes me back to Oklahoma City, on I-40. Cornstalks *scritch* in the fields. High clouds, banked against the blue.

I decide not to call Martha's folks. What would I say to them?

Well, we're apart because—

I'm here because—

I'm really very sorry. I'll miss you.

I know. I know.

Like a bomb.

The Mother Road

1

"Well, you're on your way—over two thousand miles of fascinating highway ahead of you. One of life's biggest thrills is the realization that 'we're on the way,'" says *A Guide Book to Highway 66*, self-published by Jack D. Rittenhouse in 1946. Rittenhouse, then thirty-three, an advertising copywriter from L.A. specializing in oil field equipment, traveled from Chicago to Santa Monica in a 1939 American Bantam coupe with a twenty-two-horsepower engine— no odometer, no radio, no trunk. The car cost $335 new.

He drove from dawn till dusk at an average speed of thirty-five miles per hour, scribbling notes on scenery, gas stations, people, and lodgings on a yellow legal pad.

He printed three thousand copies of the book and sold them for a dollar each at newsstands, cafés, tourist courts. "A trip is no fun if worry sits at the wheel," he said. "So . . . rest assured you're not going to be 'hung up' in some forsaken spot."

In 1997, on what's left of 66 in Oklahoma, forsaken spots predominate.

The road was officially decommissioned on June 27, 1985. The Interstate Highway System bypassed its once-thriving towns, and now several sections of America's "Main Street" have gone to grass and weeds. "Road Closed" signs rattle over rusty guardrails on the prairie.

"I bequeath myself to the dirt to grow from the grass I love/ If you want me again look for me under your boot-soles," Walt Whitman once wrote—a fitting epitaph for the old migrant path.

In 1926, when the highway was born, the country was preoccupied with the Scopes trial of the year before, pitting evolution against the Bible. Sherwood Anderson published his novel *Dark Laughter*, warning of "song[s] killed" by modern machines, and of the death of innocence in factories along the Mississippi River. Literature mattered, then, to a wide range of readers. Ernest Hemingway, Scott Fitzgerald, and H. L. Mencken were celebrities.

That year, in a little-known Latin American country called Nicaragua, U.S. Marines landed in force to protect American business interests there. The world barely took notice.

For Oklahomans, 66 attained its mythic status in the 1930s, when it became the migrant path for poor tenant farmers driven off their land by drought, dust, banks, overplanting, and mechanization. From 1934 to 1938, more than 260 storms blew 300 million acres of topsoil from Texas, Oklahoma, and Kansas. April 14, 1935, "Black Sunday," was the most apocalyptic day of the decade. By midafternoon, a "black roller" swept through the Oklahoma panhandle on an advancing cold front. The Santa Fe mail train running daily between Waynoka and Buffalo passed Selman without stopping because the engineer couldn't see the town.

Mothers wrapped damp dishtowels around their kids' faces to protect them from the particles in the air. By the next morning, the towels had blurred solid red. On kitchen tables, dirt seasoned chicken, corn, and beets.

When I was a child, dust storms often bruised the West Texas sky. A yellow welt. Then darkness. Wheezing wind. I remember the air's bleached smell, the windows filmed like dough dropped in flour. Mama set a vaporizer in my room, but it didn't do much good. I lay in bed all night eating grit.

Woody Guthrie spent "Black Sunday" in Pampa, Texas, directly north of my hometown. He wrote, "So long, it's been good to know yuh—this dusty old dust is getting my home, and I've got to be drifting along."

An estimated 210,000 people migrated from the Midwest to California to escape the Dust Bowl—an echo of the previous century's Trail of Tears, the forced removal of Native American tribes to the Indian Territory—and a corollary to the great black migration from the south's cotton fields, up the Mississippi Delta to Chicago.

Steinbeck wrote: "66 is the path of people in flight, refugees from dust and shrinking land, from the thunder of tractors and shrinking ownership, from the desert's slow northward invasion, from the twisting winds that howl up on out of Texas, from the floods that bring no richness to the land and steal what little richness is there. From all of these the people are in flight, and they come into 66 from the tributary side roads, from the wagon tracks and the rutted country roads. 66 is the mother road, the road of flight."

Within months of reaching Weedpatch, Bakersfield, the San Joaquin Valley, thousands of disillusioned Okies, unable to find work, turned around and came home. Less than sixteen thousand of the actual Dust Bowl refugees remained in California, barely 8 percent . . . still, enough to establish a vital Okie subculture in the southern crook of the state, in the Central Valley, and later, in the Greater Northwest, where people like me are now a modern echo of this hard and twisting journey.

In the summer of '97 I was alone with nothing but highway ahead of me. Timothy McVeigh had been sentenced to death for attacking the American heartland. I returned to Oklahoma and the Mother Road, to see again the grass I loved, to look for America under my boot-soles.

2

Heading west, take a left off Interstate 40, among the jack oak groves. Slow down on the gravel.

This part of Oklahoma—the northeast—is lush, festooned with cedars, pecan trees, stubby pines. The oak leaves are slender and slick: slashes scratched in the air.

Here, in the heart of the Cherokee lands, the soil is apple red from an abundance of oxidized iron, though the true Red Soil Country lies farther west, where the forests leave off.

Nothing graces 66 at this spot except a vacant old hamburger stand, the Top Hat Dairy. Trucks hustle past, heading for Tulsa, swirling up hot, sucking winds. Their bumper stickers say "Jesus Is Lord" and "How's My Driving?"

"The road is good [here] but the shoulders are soggy in wet weather," Jack Rittenhouse wrote in '46. "In the smaller towns, brick streets are often bumpy."

Nowadays, the area's principal attraction is a ninety-foot concrete and steel totem pole built in the forties by a former woodworking teacher named Ed Galloway. It sports a number of faux-Indian animal designs—lizards and birds—colored chalky yellow, maroon, sky blue, and green.

At the top of the pole, a wide, sagging face gazes west, toward the Promised Lands of California, Washington, and Oregon. Painted pastel red, it looks embarrassed to be discovered in its private grove. Overcast skies blacken its eyes, giving it a faint hint of grief.

When I was a boy, my grandfather told me that nearly half of all Americans lived on farms. Now only 2 percent of the population remains there.

In October '93—the year of the first World Trade Center attack—the Census Department stopped counting the number of people who still worked their own land for a living. The figure was "statistically insignificant."

As I travel and read, I begin to see a link between the demise of family farming and the rise of militia movements—and, by extension, global terrorism: in the early seventies, Secretary of Agriculture Earl Butz had told farmers to "get big or get out." Banks urged yeomen of the land to carry larger and larger loans, to trade in their fifty-five-horsepower tractors for two-hundred-horsepower behemoths.

But then grain prices tumbled worldwide. The Federal Reserve raised the cost of borrowing money. Commercial banks announced that they were bailing out of agriculture and called in their notes. By the mid-eighties, farmland values had dropped $146 billion—a figure "equal to the combined assets of IBM, General Electric, Kodak, Proctor and Gamble, Dow Chemical, McDonald's, Upjohn, Weyerhaeuser, and CBS," says journalist Osha Gray Davidson.

Federal subsidies favored the largest producers—"vertically integrated" companies like ConAgra (the nation's leading supplier of pesticides) that control food from farm to store to dinner table.

Six grain monopolies buy all the wheat in the United States these days, as well as most of the wheat in the global marketplace, pitting U.S. farmers against growers in places like Latin America, where a handful of landowners controls everything, paying criminally low wages to workers. In order to compete, farmers in Oklahoma towns like Commerce (Mickey Mantle's birthplace) and Claremore (Will Rogers' hometown) are forced to accept artificially low prices for their products. When their wives need new dresses, or their kids need school supplies, or they need tonight's dinner, there's nowhere to go but down the road to the brand new Wal-Mart, whose profits primarily feed the national chain, leaving only crumbs for the local economy.

The old mom-and-pop businesses, like the hardware store my granddad managed when he wasn't running for elective office, died years ago, when farm prices slipped.

In the Wal-Marts, the frozen turkeys, the instant waffles, and the TV dinners are full of processed sugar, corn, and soy—staples, as ex-farmer Victor Hanson points out, "whose plenitude is underwritten by the government, whose steep profits lie in the processing and merchandising rather than in the growing of the components of those bizarre creations."

Hanson, who lost his grape farm in the unbalanced global economy, insists that long ago—long before America, even, in the rich, fertile soils of Greece and Rome—the social, economic, and political foundations of Western culture were hatched in the countryside. Thomas Jefferson hailed small landowners as the "chosen people of God" and as the "most precious part of a state." But at some point in the twenty-first century, the last family farmer in America will vanish. Most of them are already gone.

If you're one of the few farmers left in Oklahoma, Texas, or Kansas, you might keep a radio on all day in your barn, or in your tractor cab as you circle your dwindling fields.

If you do, you won't hear Will Rogers spinning clever tales to ease your troubles, or reminding you, gently, to forgive your neighbors' faults. Instead, you'll hear G. Gordon Liddy explaining how to shoot somebody in the head with a pistol.

You won't hear Mickey Mantle talking about the love of the game. You'll hear young players who make more money in a day than you'll ever see in your life demanding salary hikes.

You'll hear Rush Limbaugh claiming, "The second violent American revolution is just about—I got my fingers about a quarter of an inch apart—is just about *this* far away. Because . . . people are sick and tired of a bunch of bureaucrats in Washington driving into town and telling them what they can and can't do with their land."

And if you're Terry Lynn Nichols, desperate, leaking money, failing to hold your farm, and here's your old buddy Tim, telling you that the Gordon Liddys have a damn good point—just look around, he says, take a look at the goddamn Wal-Mart—it's easy to hop off your tractor, haul ass into town, buy some extra heating oil and a few bags of ammonium nitrate. It's easy to say, "Yes."

3

West of Claremore, the path of 66, lost beneath a four-lane asphalt road, crosses the lazy Verdigris River. Three steel bridges span the water, one for cars, two for trains. Pecan trees line the highway.

Steinbeck places the Joads near here, southeast of Tulsa. The land is rolling hills and moss, not the Red Soil Country he makes it out to be (he got his geography wrong—he only took one brief car tour through the state, in the summer of '37). Plenty of poor tenant farmers worked the area during the Great Depression, but they weren't Dust Bowlers. The worst winds buffeted Oklahoma's plains west of here, at best a good day's drive away.

East of Catoosa, in a stagnant green pond, a blue plaster whale aims a faded eye at the road. He looks weepy and exhausted. This used to be a swimming hole for kids. Now it's blocked by rusty barbed wire. A sign on a pole choked by finger-fat honeysuckle says, "No Fishing. Don't Ask."

Through a series of canals, the Port of Catoosa, near Tulsa, links Oklahoma with twenty-five thousand miles of inland waterways stretching from the Gulf of Mexico and the Mississippi River to the Great Lakes and the St. Lawrence Seaway. It's an industrial port, forging steel products and mixing fertilizer to be shipped all over the country.

At noon, I ate red beans, rice, cabbage, and fried catfish at a place called Pauline's Buffet, by the port. I remembered Oklahoma catfish fries when I was a kid. My grandfather cooked fish and frogs' legs, which I wouldn't eat (somehow, swallowing the hind parts of a frog sounded much worse than nibbling the body of a fish) until my father tricked me, assuring me I was eating catfish instead. I loved the way it tasted.

My mother's stepfather, Pop, used to stand in his yard skinning squirrels he'd shot in the woods. The meat beneath the skin was marbled, slick, and white, nearly clear like a sheet of Saran Wrap, or a pane of soap before it's blown into a bubble. Sometimes, at family gatherings, he'd offer me and my cousins bites of the sizzling brown meat.

I relished all this in memory, the excitement, the untrammeled joy of lazy plains days, even as I pictured the storage domes at the nearby port, containing thousands of pounds of ammonium nitrate fertilizer ready to be shipped to farmers in Texas, Michigan, and Kansas—many of whom, as Rush Limbaugh will tell you, are mad as hell at Washington.

West of Catoosa, 66 slims to two lanes, passing short cliffs of gray, thick-bedded shale. The soil is getting redder. The road is bounded by cedars, pecan trees, pines, mesquite, and oaks wrapped in sweet honeysuckle. If they'd taken the time to look, the Joads would have seen, here, cornstalks edging rushing white creeks.

On my radio, old-time country music. Voices, fiddles, bass— but in nearly all the tunes, the percussion is muted. Landowners here used to fear the "talking drums" of their African slaves: were strains of rebellion hidden among coded beats?

In time, the owners' worries became a distinct musical style. Drums were labeled primitive instruments of the devil and were downplayed at songfests.

Sometime in the spring or summer of 1937, an ex-slave named Andrew Simms was interviewed by a WPA fieldworker on Route 1, near here, in a town called Sapulpa (the word means "sweet potato" in Creek). He admitted life was still hard in Oklahoma, decades after emancipation. "I didn't see no fighting during the [Civil War]. If they was any Yankee soldiering around the country [here] I don't remember nothing of it," he said. "[To survive], some of the colored folks taken to the voodoo. I don't believe in it. I aims to live by the Bible and leave the rabbit's foot alone!

"Nowadays, I gets me something to eat when I can catch it," he said, sounding like a present-day small farmer. "The trouble is, sometimes I don't catch it."

Past an abandoned Phillips gas station, 66 narrows and curls under a rusty railroad trestle smeared with lovers' graffiti. In tall weeds just off the road I spot the remains of an old motor court: three small housing units made of limestone. From a distance, their walls resemble patchwork quilts, or the stretched skins of diamondback rattlers.

Across the Little Polecat Creek, ochre and slow, in the town of Bristow, man-sized cornstalks circle a football stadium, like skinny, itching fans eager for a game.

Here, on this cool summer afternoon, on this nearly forgotten road in the middle of America, it's easy to believe that the earth is a beautiful garden, and the Lord its kindly old caretaker. No poverty or anger. No Timothy McVeigh.

"Stripped of its green cloak, the silk lies as glossy and abundant as pubic hair," Betty Fussel writes in a book called *The Story of Corn*. The kernels, she says, are "white as a baby's teeth."

Central Oklahoma is rich in what Fussel calls the "sexiness of corn . . . the muck [of] roots stretch[ing] toward the darkness, toward the germinating seeds of life which are sown, as both Christians and Indians knew . . . in blood."

Through oak trees, past dying filling stations and the skeletons of shuttered cafés, the tall silver tollbooths of Turner Turnpike straddle short hills near old wooden bridges, collapsing in clover. Indians in muddy pickups rattle over patches of brick, prickling through decomposing asphalt.

"Mother" is a phantom here, appearing then disappearing in the trees' lushness. Broken old fragments haunt the newer road—an echo, a trace, white as eggs, flaking off into the rich green broom-straw, which is slowly grinding it into dust. Rolls of hay molder in the fields.

East of the town of Wellston, in garish red paint on the side of a barn, an ad for "Meramac Caverns, Stanton, Mo." The barn leans into the trees, as if buckling beneath the weight of its words.

There's not much left of Wellston, a former Kickapoo trading post, though the Cold War left its mark here—the town's middle school snuggles underground, with an earthen roof three feet thick, a fallout shelter in case some crazy fool decides to bomb Oklahoma.

4

West of Oklahoma City, Route 66 evaporates into red, rolling hills and high, yellow grass, as it slopes toward Texas's tumbleweeds. The sky's a dusty orange.

In Clinton, Pop Hicks' Café has been serving greasy fries and thick, runny burgers since 1936. It's now the oldest functioning restaurant on Oklahoma's ghost road. It's owned by a fellow named Howard Nichols, who traveled to California as a kid during the Depression, then hitched back home as a teen.

Along the restaurant's back wall, someone's painted a glacial lake near a needled, snow-capped peak. Deer graze its bushy banks: an idealized version of the Promised Land at the far end of the road.

Locals say Elvis used to stay here on his concert tours, in the Trade Winds Motel. Room 215 of the Trade Winds—the "Elvis Presley Suite"—is a modest shrine, unchanged since the late sixties, though there's nothing to see, really, just a regular old room.

The year I was born, Elvis performed at the Cotton Club in Lubbock, Texas, north of where I lived, inspiring, firsthand, Buddy Holly and Roy Orbison, injecting a little sway into their "country" tales, edging them toward spiky rock 'n' roll.

Billboards west of Clinton advertise fake Indian trading posts pushing Cactus Jelly, "Desert Perfume," kachina dolls. Several signs say, "Unpaid Child Support? Don't Worry. We Collect!"

A rancher herds his cattle using a white Ford pickup, chasing frightened cows across a field.

A young deer leaps a sagging barbed wire fence.

A yellow poster on a phone pole says Merle Haggard is performing tonight in Elk City.

From a rain- and wind-beaten water tower, the painted head of an Indian chief looms above the land, like the covers of the old writing tablets in which I wrote love poems to my cousin Anne, in which I scribbled my very first stories as a child, in which I first wrote the words "Texas," "Oklahoma," and "home."

Hydro is no longer much of a town—more like a chalk outline of a body in the road.

Lucile Hamon's gas station, a square, two-story building meshed with ivy, shades 66. Christmas lights, flecked with khaki-colored dust, wrap two wooden pillars by a pair of empty gas pumps (Conoco—Unleaded). A pecan tree waves at the road, as if to say, *Pass on by, partner, and leave me the hell in peace.*

Lucile, a wiry woman with faded red hair, greets me as I step inside. She wears a black pullover blouse. Her face is skinny and pale. She'd been sitting in the dark until I opened the door; then she pulled a chain near a naked bulb and took her place behind the cash register. The store is all one room. Canned peaches cram the back-wall shelves. Dust covers the front counter like a doily fraying from the center out. Cokes and cans of beer rattle inside a squat old fridge. I buy a Coke. "I never liked selling beer," she croaks suddenly, as if ashamed I've seen the cans. I nod. "What brings you this way?" she says.

I tell her I'm following the old Route 66.

"I been here fifty-six years, longer'n anybody else."

"You've seen a lot of changes, then."

"Oh, Lord." She asks me what I do. When I tell her I'm a writer, she bristles. "Well, you cain't take no notes around here," she says. "I wrote a book, too. Waiting for the UPS strike to finish up so's they can ship me my copies."

"Congratulations," I say. "Your book's about the highway?"

She nods. "Have to buy it, to see."

"Did you ever read Steinbeck?" I ask.

In reply, she calls herself the mother of the Mother Road.

Later, on the Internet, I discovered that her daughter had designed a web page about the filling station. "Lucile . . . has spent nearly all her life on Route 66, serving the public," it says. "I was born in that station . . . I can't begin to tell you how many times we would be missing light bulbs because a guy came in that needed one, or the hamburger I was going to cook for dinner got sold to someone who spotted it on the counter! If you get through Oklahoma on your journey down Historic Route 66, please stop and say hello . . . Your visits are about all that are keeping [Lucile] alive now."

But she doesn't seem much interested in talking today. She eyes her chair, as if eager to nap, and I'm sorry I've disturbed her. Falling pecans trickle down the roof.

As I turn to leave, I tell her, "Good luck with your book, Ms. Hamons. It was a pleasure to meet you."

"When I'm gone," she says quietly, "history's gone."

On the highway just outside her door, a dust devil whirls like an angry child, then collapses at the edge of the bumpy pavement.

5

Three interstate highways converge in Oklahoma City—I-40, I-35, and I-44, which roughly parallels the old Mother Road. On a hilltop overlooking knotty freeways there's a restaurant called the OK County Line. It used to be the Kentucky Club; a notorious speakeasy in the thirties, it was a busy hangout for well-to-do gamblers, bootleggers, and prostitutes. Pretty Boy Floyd used to guzzle gin there and brag about how much smarter he was than the lawmen, like my granddad, who couldn't catch him to save their lives.

Now it's an upscale yuppie place with old memorabilia on its walls—framed fifties-era posters of Ronald Reagan selling cigarettes.

Downtown, at the corner of 23rd and Classen, a curious pie-shaped building still hustles business where the original 66 used to run. It's crowned by a giant, old-fashioned milk bottle—a wooden sculpture, tall as a good-postured child. For decades, the place was a barbecue joint called the Rib Shack: "Let me sweat you up some meat!" The bottle was an ad for Townley Milk.

Now this city-slice is Asian. The Rib Shack has become the Saigon Baguette, a submarine sandwich shop. Nearby, Hondas and Mitsubishi station wagons gleam in the parking lot of the Cao Nguyen Vietnamese Supermarket. Chinese grocery stores, Thai restaurants, Japanese video outlets. The black families who used to live here have picked up and moved northeast, completely out of the area.

Each year, like converging highways, migrating cultures loop around one another more and more in the Heartland, merging, splitting, switching directions.

I remember, from his accounts ledger, an old speech of my grand-dad's dated 1935 and labeled "OKC." I have no idea what he was doing in the city then, or what he was stumping for. But the speech's pleas for racial harmony lead me to assume he was addressing a mixed-race crowd. "Realizing the frailties of humanity," he said, "it gives me real pleasure to know I'm among friends. My friends, it can't be stated often enough: we need each other."

In another convergence—present and past—the thirties seem to have revived in America lately. Last summer, a lengthy drought parched Oklahoma, forcing nearly one-sixth of the state's remaining farmers to foreclose. On the radio, right-wing "patriots" echoed Father Charles Coughlin's Depression-era speeches. In the thirties, Coughlin fed an acid stream of suspicion to an audience of disenchanted farmers from his tiny broadcasting booth in Royal Oaks, Michigan.

Early in 1940, eighteen members of a national paramilitary group called the Christian Front were indicted for planning to bomb public buildings—two years after Coughlin had urged his listeners to form "neighborhood platoons" to protect themselves from the government. Clearly, certain present-day militias are the great-grandchildren of decades-old armed movements.

Even the 1996 presidential campaign had embraced thirties-style populism. The candidates attacked "Big Government." Pat Buchanan railed against worldwide business conspiracies, unfair to U.S. workers. His campaign manager, Larry Pratt, had written a book entitled *Armed People Victorious*, in which he said, "The history of the United States . . . was [always] the history of an armed people with functioning militias . . . It is time that the United States return to reliance on an armed people. There is no acceptable alternative."

On a gentler note, like a 1930s bard, in concerts all across the country, Bruce Springsteen sang of downsized steelworkers, of searching for Tom Joad's ghost.

Steve Earle, a vibrant country singer from south of San Antone, pleaded, "Come back, Woody Guthrie . . . / Tear your eyes from Paradise / And rise again somehow."

This morning, in a greasy Waffle House just off Interstate 40, I sit at the counter enjoying the breakfast crowd.

The clientele is mostly black, middle-aged men in cowboy hats and creaking leather boots. One fellow has just walked in wearing old Army fatigues and house slippers.

Nine waiters and cooks, blacks and Hispanics, scurry behind the counter, never still.

"Two scrambled, for my man Charlie!"

"Charlie, he already *be* scrambled!"

Southern manners and Western informality combine here to create an easy atmosphere I've not experienced anywhere else in the country.

It's no model of ethnic harmony. I don't mean that. I mean people are so loose here, they fully ignore one another's' differences, or absorb them unconsciously—what Ralph Ellison called unity in diversity, the mix of "gestures and elements of style through which we find our definition as Americans . . . the way we walk, talk, and move."

At the moment, no one gives a damn what they look like, or what anyone else looks like, either. It's too hot for vanity.

And we're all really hungry.

"Say, Slick, lookin' *mean*."

"How's them eggs?"

"The usual."

"Hell, sounds good to me."

Outside, on the interstate, a Ryder truck grinds its gears, and I flash on Timothy McVeigh.

This is the city he wanted to attack?

"How'd the Rangers do last night?"

"Sorry sons of bitches, couldn't catch their asses in a net."

"You hear old Mance is retiring?"

"When he *ever* work?"

"Come on over tonight, we'll fry us up some catfish."

I settle back and relish the usual.

My cousin has lost a little weight since I saw her last year. She's pale and tired. She says she's battling high blood pressure.

"I cried when I heard McVeigh's verdict, and again when the jury pronounced the death penalty," Anne says. "I'm not sure why. Relief, I suppose. And sadness over the fact that he's wasted his life."

In general, she says, people who live here don't speak much about the trial. They want to move on with their lives. "I don't go down to the Murrah site anymore. I still have awful dreams about its ruins . . . I just want to put it all behind me now."

The site hasn't changed since I saw it last. I visited it this afternoon, before hooking up with Anne. A snowstorm of teddy bears,

T-shirts, flowers, poems, pictures. A little blonde girl, four or five, paced the street with her mother. She stopped and hugged each bear, pressing her cheek firmly into the fur. A boy, gripping his mother's hand, said, "I'm a'scared there's gonna be a bomb in there."

The Water Resources Building will be torn down soon. The city has approved a memorial design: 168 stone and glass chairs. Each will bear the name of a victim. By day, the chairs will appear to float above the ground on their glass bases; by night, they'll be illuminated from within. "When you see [a vacant] chair, you see the emptiness, the absence," Torrey Butzer, one of the designers, explained.

Fifth Street will be turned into a long reflecting pool, flanked at each end by a large stone gate, solid black, one marked 9:01, the other 9:03. The bombing occurred at 9:02.

Like the Vietnam War Memorial in Washington DC, it will be a monument not to bravery and heroism but to tragedy and loss.

Polly Nichols, a bombing survivor whose jugular was scissored by glass, says the image of lighted chairs reminds her too much of the building's shell in nighttime floodlights, which she observed from her hospital window.

Tina Tomlin, another survivor, says, "The fence and the bombed building over there [the Water Resources Board] is the best memorial. How else to show what an explosion looks like?"

"Whatever," Anne says when I ask what she thinks of the design. Plainly, she can't handle Murrah anymore. She'd rather talk, today, about Balloon Fest '97, a citywide weekend event raising money for hunger relief. Kites, skydiving, karaoke music. The main attraction, this evening, will be the release of over sixty hot air balloons into the warm evening sky. After that, a squadron of Flying Elvises will parachute into the city.

"You want to go see it?" Anne asks eagerly. I see she's nervous, afraid I won't let go of the dark.

I smile. All right, then. No more Murrah. "Sure," I say. "How can we miss it?"

So at sunset we pull off a jammed freeway to watch the balloons go up. They float gracefully into pink-tinged clouds, into the deep purple dome of the evening. Speakers play muzak versions of John Lennon songs. Satiny colors swell in the night. Smooth fabrics—green, yellow, blue, vibrant as neon. One balloon is shaped like a sunfish. Another forms a friendly horse.

They drift like children's wishes (I remember Anne's childhood promise to marry me), or delicate glass lanterns. Fabrics swell like pregnant women.

"Ma, you seen Elvis yet?" a kid asks.

"No, son, be patient."

We all squint into the sky. Black families, white families, Asians, Indians, Latinos.

I look at Anne, recalling afternoons in the park when we were children, our grandfather hugging us tightly in the heat and sweat of the crowd.

My friends, it can't be stated often enough: we need each other.

She turns to me and smiles, and in the time it takes a firefly to signal its presence in the dark, in the time it takes a hero to tumble from the sky, the past returns to the present. We're no longer middle-aged witnesses to tragedies, confusion, heartbreak, and cruelty; we're about to be married; we're about to step bravely into the world.

Weedpatch

Privacy is the least of the promises made by this sad, scorching country. Whatever happens to you here happens wholly in the open.

At the edge of a lettuce field, a tin shack, an old toolshed by the looks of it, has partially collapsed, creating a shaded nest, a promise of relief from the sun. Stepping closer I see its walls are crusts of rust, barely intact. One touch, and scatter. No solace here.

In my pocket I carry a rock the size of an earlobe. The fingers of my right hand are raw from rubbing it, reminding myself of its solidity, sharp as shrapnel, and its weakness. It's a piece of the Alfred P. Murrah building. Somehow, this little crumb of terror has led me here, has taken me from the heart of Oklahoma, where my family had its beginnings, to this site of the Okie diaspora, the end of the Dust Bowl road for many families in the thirties.

All around me, old, abandoned tires line dirt paths skirting patches of lettuce, sinking in brown-water ditches. Bales of rain flooded this place last month. At the end of *The Grapes of Wrath*, John Steinbeck unleashes a storm near here; unmercifully, it lashes what's left of the Joad family and threatens the land: "At first the . . . earth sucked the moisture down and blackened. For two days the earth drank the rain until the earth was full. Then puddles formed, and in the lower places little lakes formed in the fields. The muddy lakes rose higher, and . . . steady rain whipped the shining water."

I've arrived here, today, at the end of another wet cycle; the air feels blistered, almost puckered, like spilled-on paper drying warped. It's strawberry season, but I've beaten most other crops' harvest times.

A smell of onions. A fetid chemical stink, like a sweaty pair of feet.

I return to my rental car, swing down a gravel road to a rectangular, wasp brown building, "Weedpatch Market, Since 1915," and park by a stack of moist potatoes, steaming gently in wrinkled burlap bags.

Inside, the store is dark and cool, mint scented, spacious. Fringed piñatas sway over bins of lemons and limes. I grab a can of Pepsi. In the thirties, say oral histories of the time, Pepsi targeted traveling Okies, with billboards shading Route 66 from Tulsa to Bakersfield, and along the roads to labor camps. Next to liquor and hairy coffee boiled over open fires, Pepsi was the favorite Okie drink.

Ahead of me in the cashier's line, a short Latina, brown as the potato bags outside, thunks a case of beer and six loaves of white bread on the counter. Her kids, five boys—all under twelve, I'm guessing—pound a cracked Pac-Man machine in the corner.

Behind the woman, an old white man, liver spots like pill bugs dusting the backs of his hands, waits to buy a pair of gray socks and a carton of Foster Farms milk.

Wholly open, their lives. Laid bare, flat out, right here in the market.

Back in the car, sitting in the parking lot out of the sun, listening to my cooling engine tick, I sip my Pepsi and finger the Murrah piece. I recall the opening scenes of John Ford's film of *The Grapes of Wrath*. Henry Fonda lopes alone down a highway until he comes to a squatty café called the Cross Roads, shaped exactly like Weedpatch Market. A truck's parked in front, "Oklahoma City" painted on its side. I put the car in gear, move slowly past stagnant, shining water in the road.

In *Grapes*, Steinbeck describes Arvin and Lamont, the towns on either side of Weedpatch, as Okie enclaves, but today, with populations of ten thousand and twelve thousand respectively, they're largely Latino: *mercados* hawking *mariscos*, tacos, *cervezas frias*. Pool halls and Pentecostal churches. I pass an oak-colored man in a frayed straw hat selling rusty stoves in a vacant lot on the outskirts of Lamont. A sign staked among stripped tires and carburetor parts at Sergio's Transmissions announces that someone in the auto shop is also a tax advisor, immigration lawyer, translator, and notary public.

A tall, handsome Sikh in a turban parks his vw bug in front of a brick store called Rapido in downtown Lamont. I can't tell what the place sells. Next to it, the Last Resort Tavern is boarded tight, cobwebbed and peeling.

The local papers are full of flood stories still. In Arvin, a sign for the Senior Center, past No Hill Street off Bear Mountain Road, reminds me of an article I saw this morning in Bakersfield's *Village News*. A home care nurse named Mary Gutierrez was describing the difficulty she'd faced, after recent rains, reaching many of her patients, whose homes were nearly "waterlogged" on "mud roads to nowhere." She had a terminal patient, an Oklahoma transplant who'd lived in Lamont since the thirties, whose "home was nearly at the flood's 'ground zero.'"

"The rain pattered relentlessly down"—Steinbeck—"and the streams broke their banks and spread out over the country."

I pass the Senior Center, a cracker-box building full of old Okies, no doubt, dull in a polleny glaze of dust shimmering against the Tejon Hills south of town.

Pumpjacks, sleek as ponies, nod up and down in weedy brown fields. Oil rigs spread their ribs against the sky. Once, when I was a child and I asked my father what he did for a living, he drove me to the edge of our West Texas town and showed me a place like this. A smell like a thousand angry skunks hovers over rows of oil tanks just off the Weedpatch Highway.

In other fields nearby, Mexican men in clayed cotton shirts check irrigation pipes—arcs of silver water halo their bodies—or claw at the earth with hoes. I see an old man, slumping in glistening spools of lettuce, hug a younger one. The young man appears to be crying. The embrace is rough and brief; other men are yelling at them now. They pick up their hoes and move on down furrowed rows.

The shoulders of the young man in the lettuce field heave as he works. His head's down. Privacy's a privilege, I realize, watching him stab at the dirt, grief a luxury of time that day laborers can't much afford. I reach into my pocket, touch again the Murrah lump.

What little shade there is in these sun-curdled fields, cast by toolsheds, pickups, oil derricks, cuts the ground with authority, a contrast with the light so severe, the darkness looks animal, predatory. The shadows are black or purple or brown, dark gray or blue, depending on the textures of earth they strike. I'm reminded of Woody Guthrie's take on the West, when he'd "crossed the river," as he put it, out of the Dust Bowl and into the Pastures of Plenty: "[The countryside's] got ridges of nine kinds of brown," he wrote, "hills out of six colors of green, ridges five shades of shadow, and stickers the eight tones of hell."

I slip a tape of Woody's songs into the rental car's player, turn down a muddy road called Vineland, and here they are, all around me: the grapes of wrath themselves. Waist-high limbs, wrinkled as paper sacks that wrap a wino's muscatel, thrust from the dirt, sending vines down lengths of silver wire in neatly patterned rows. The grapevines are biblical, somehow, rugged yet stylish in their even lines, like drawings of Holy Land vineyards in Sunday School readers. I imagine migrant Okies, many of them devout Protestants, making this connection, staring in awe at the sacred, rough abundance in which they found themselves.

Farther up the road, I see the entrance to the Arvin Cemetery. I park the car, walk gravel paths past copper plaques in the grass. The first grave I come to belongs to an Okie, John E. Faulkner, a veteran of the First World War, in the Wagoner Supply Company of the 37th Infantry. Born in Oklahoma, 1897; died, Pearl Harbor Day, 1961.

Just yesterday, according to the *Bakersfield Californian,* an Oklahoma exile, a housewife in her eighties, was buried here. Three or four fresh dirt mounds interrupt the smooth green lawn.

Along with kettles, pots and pans, chickens, dogs, and old feather mattresses, many Dust Bowlers hauled bedrock midwestern values over the stubborn Sierra Nevadas. Family, faith, fidelity. "Married 64 Years," says one couple's chalky headstone. "Ever Faithful In Love." Ethel and Van Lee Henderson, "Together Always." Winnie and Lester Minyard, clasping hands before the Lord.

I move on, through tall, slowly waving grass. Latino names weave like braids through rows of Joneses and Smiths. Miguel Salgado. Antonio Castillo, *Abuelito Lindo.* The shared destinies of Northern and Southern America.

A man and a woman in a station wagon turn into the cemetery, leave their car, and make their way to one of the new dirt knolls over by a water fountain under a limp American flag. They glance at me irritably; my unexpected presence has crowded their grief.

The only sounds are crows cawing and the *chh-chh* of water sprinklers in strawberry fields down the road. I rub my eyes, follow the slow putting of a tractor in the distance, and for the first time I see it on the western horizon, the spot I've come here hoping to find. An earth-colored compound. Boxy buildings beneath huddled yellow palms.

In Ford's film, the Joads, desperate, dirty, hungry, pull into a place called Wheat Patch, but in chapter 22 of Steinbeck's novel, it's given its proper name. "It was late when Tom Joad drove along a country road looking for the Weedpatch camp," Steinbeck writes. "There were few lights in the countryside. Only a sky glare . . . showed the direction of Bakersfield. The truck jiggled slowly along and hunting cats left the road ahead of it. At a crossroad there was a little cluster of white wooden buildings."

From here, it appears the buildings are no longer white, but this has to be the place. I know it still exists—the historian Roxanne Dunbar-Ortiz writes about it in her book *Red Dirt: Growing Up Okie*, calling it "not much to see, just a barren, run-down labor camp in the middle of plowed-up cotton fields."

Behind me, the people from the station wagon weep as if their every promise has been broken.

I slip into my car, toss back my head, drain my lukewarm Pepsi. I pop a Merle Haggard tape into the player and head on down to the crossroads.

"A town that loses its children loses its meaning," says a character in Russell Banks's novel *The Sweet Hereafter*, a man who could easily narrate one of Merle's recent sad songs. The book was published in 1991. Maybe it could have been written at an earlier time in our history, but I doubt it. It's about a school bus crash that destroys a community's hopes. Even more, it's a sober view of our national moorings popping loose.

I think of Charlie Manson, in the sixties, humming the Beatles' "Helter Skelter," weaving demented plans in a school bus some-where near here, in the sagebrush wilderness. Desert Storms. Death Valley.

In Banks's book, after the town buries its kids, one of the narra-tors says, "In my lifetime something terrible happened that took our children away from us. I don't know if it was the Vietnam war, or the sexual colonization of kids by industry, or drugs, or TV, or divorce, or what the hell it was; I don't know which are causes and which are effects; but the children are gone, that I know."

I think of these lines whenever I consider the Murrah bombing, and they occur to me now as I approach this harshly real place, where other fictional characters once breathed.

Steinbeck describes a high wire fence surrounding Weedpatch Camp, facing the road, with a wide-gated driveway turning in toward a little house with a light in the window.

Today, the Arvin Farm Labor Center, or Sunset Camp, as it's now called, is still hedged by a wire fence, and the house is there behind an automatic traffic arm blocking the only way in. Metal signs grip the fence, declaring this a "Rural Development Project Financed By Rural Housing Services and USDA." Other signs warn "Keep Out," "Private Property," "No Credit," and "No Tomar Bebidas."

Most of the housing units—there are dozens of them—appear to have been built since the thirties, but still they're old, rough, primitive. Dripping air conditioners squat on several windowsills like fat, naked thieves. On wooden walls, tan paint crusts like clods of dirt. No place for kids to play. "The whole camp buzzed and snorted . . . [with] snores of sleeping people," Steinbeck says. Sixty years later, privacy's still a rare privilege.

Few folks are around—this isn't the valley's peak harvest time. The dangerous trips from San Salvador, Managua, Oaxaca, Michoacán, Puebla, Queretaro, Tijuana will begin in earnest a month or so from now. Still, if I squint my eyes against the glary ground, over by a palm tree, I can imagine its five shades of shadow as a dark woman sitting in a shawl. She clasps a baby's head against the cool, hollow V in her throat. With her free hand she brushes the side of her face, lightly, slowly, as if to shoo a fly, but really to express her enduring bewilderment at this place.

In deeper shadows behind the one-room units I can picture the ragged army Dorothea Lange photographed here during the Great Depression: thin-lipped scarecrows, wrinkles like splinters stitching their palms.

Like a crooked fence post, a timorous man angles toward the sand. He wheezes into a mouth harp, then mutters a little Woody: "Goin' down the road feelin' bad . . ."

I know this place through art, through an indelible national myth, but I'm determined to see it clearly. I switch off Merle.

I step from my car and cross the road, toward the entrance. A tall sign on the fence says, "Housing for migrant farm workers. This center is for residents and visitors of residents only. Others are trespassers and will be prosecuted."

Another, smaller posting says, "Terms of Entrance: Proof of Income, Proof of Migrant Status."

Roxanne Dunbar-Ortiz visited here a few years ago. She said she could "almost imagine a guard tower with armed security officers, like a low-security California prison," and I have that feeling now. Hair prickles on my neck. However distant, my Okie roots stir inside me. As I reach the traffic arm a German shepherd starts to bark. Banging the fence, he paces furiously. A big Mexican man pokes his head through the doorway of the little house in the driveway, sees me, and frowns. I call to him, asking if this is the labor camp John Steinbeck immortalized. *The Grapes of Wrath?* I offer.

He shrugs, steps into the drive. His bulk says, You're not getting in here, amigo. No way.

I try a little Spanish, explaining my curiosity. "No se," he says. "No se no se no se."

He's not about to budge. But just as I'm wondering what to do, I'm drawn by the chain link fence. I remember one exactly like it thousands of miles away—the fence around the Murrah site, hung with toys for all the lost kids—and I feel my shoulders drop. The raw, nervous energy that has spurred me all day dissipates in the space of a breath.

Somehow, though I'm not sure how, I've done what I needed to do, just by coming here.

For three years I've been on a trip—a sometimes dangerous trip, flooding me daily in despair, then hope—with Murrah at one end of the route, smoking and empty. Now, at the other end, Weedpatch Camp, another site of displaced Oklahomans.

At one end, Baylee Almon's broken body; at the other, Tom Joad's plaintive gaze.

It's been a journey both public and private, a sifting of blasted fragments, losses real and imagined, encompassing all the memories of a lifetime. I've been walking up to fences and pressing against them with all my mortal weight.

Which is what I do now. I smile at the Mexican. He doesn't say a word. Then I turn and head down the road, just long enough for the dog to quit barking. I'm not sure what I'm doing, but quietly I approach the camp once more, this time stopping by a corner of the fence out of the Mexican's sight.

The German shepherd loses its mind. It howls and butts the fence. But this time I'm not the object of its anger. I hear a car door slam, rapid Spanish, then engine-whine, gravel-crunch, tires rolling slowly down the road.

I peer around the corner. My rental car is still parked by a cotton field, across the way. By the traffic arm, at the entrance to the camp, a Mexican couple shows a sheaf of papers to the man who'd blocked my path. The fellow with the papers—a boy, really, maybe nineteen—wears a white straw hat, black tennis shoes, and jeans. The girl with him, about his age, hugs a bawling baby to her chest. No bags that I can see. The car that dropped them off is a fine spray of dust in the distance. The guard nods, calms the dog. The couple shuffles up the drive. I keep my eyes on the baby's face until it's hidden in the shadows of the camp.

In the thirties, I recall, agribusiness interests tried aggressively to stop Dorothea Lange's pictures of migrant mothers from making the papers. They tried to ban *The Grapes of Wrath*.

In recent headlines, Alan Greenspan, chair of the Federal Reserve, declares that our nation's economy is strong and that the "American people" are satisfied with their lives.

But no signs lead the way to the Arvin Farm Labor Center on any local roads. It's not on any map, and it's rarely mentioned in the papers.

I gaze into the camp. No flickers of life, no noise, behind its mud brown walls. We hide what we're ashamed of, I think, until we no longer have enough space to keep it tucked away.

Space is at a premium now. The West, the "last frontier," has been fully explored, every highway thoroughly patrolled, so that, lately, America's hidden secrets have been popping into view as regularly as the chorus of a song.

In the early seventies, for example, tons of American bombs turned up in the burning Cambodian countryside, though officially our soldiers were never there.

My baby, she left me this mornin'—

Richard Nixon, declaring "I am not a crook," couldn't account, somehow, for a troubling little gap on one of his White House tapes.

My baby, she left me this mornin'—

In the mid-eighties, Ronald Reagan assured the world that the United States had no presence in Nicaragua; it was simple coincidence that Eugene Hasenfus, a U.S. citizen, was shot down over a Nicaraguan jungle in a cargo plane loaded with M-16 rifles.

My baby, she left me—

In the nineties, our crops are picked by jolly green giants and tiny Keebler elves, and the BATF did nothing wrong in Waco.

My baby, she—

And so the children are gone, "violent on the streets," says Russell Banks, "comatose in the malls, narcotized in front of the TV."

One day, sick of dirty little secrets, one of our children buys a clunker straight out of a Merle Haggard tune and goes cruising the American West, following the old Okie roads. A Desert Storm veteran, he broods about the lies the Army told him. "We were falsely hyped up," he'd say later. "We get there [to Iraq] and find out [the Iraqis] are normal like me and you. [The Army hypes] you to take these people out. They told us we were to defend Kuwait where the people had been raped and slaughtered. War woke me up. War will open your eyes."

He pops into gun shows all across the nation, meeting "patriots" who fuel his anger even further—people like Roger Edwin Moore, who bragged about starting a war against the government for breaking so many promises to its citizens.

Like most Sunday soldiers, Moore was all bluster. His girlfriend back in Arkansas didn't want him "too involved" in violence, he admitted to his friends; otherwise, you bet your ass he'd be on the front lines.

But Timothy McVeigh didn't have a girlfriend. Gun shows weren't just weekend hobbies for him. He'd been trained by the Army to "take people out."

Then one day, reckless shots are exchanged in Ruby Ridge, Idaho.

A church in Waco, Texas, burns to the ground.

And now I find myself on a nearly hidden road, by a notorious old labor camp, with part of a bombed-out building in my pocket.

Like that other child of our country, I'm disillusioned, angry, saddened by layers of lies. I haven't been hyped to kill, as he was. I wasn't trained to rig explosives.

I'm just here to gather pieces for myself, to learn my part in the tragedy.

Two years ago, at what Oklahomans were then calling Ground Zero, when Paul Heath handed me a fragment of the Murrah building, I didn't know I was beginning a trip that would usher me back and forth across the West, along Highway 66, the old Mother Road of the Okies, in a search for lost meanings. But here I am, wholly open, exploring my own Okie echoes, my affinity to families who have long worked the land.

Now I pull the fragment from my pocket. It would be appropriate to bury this tortured stone here, I think, a gesture of mourning and respect for both the present and the past. But I can't part with it. I'll need to feel again the nudge of history now and then. I need to keep it close.

So I lay the piece in the sand for just a moment. Here on the Central Valley floor, where nothing's hidden from the sun, the sand's as brown as an oily old catcher's mitt, the Murrah chip pale as winter flesh.

As so often happens when I need them, lines from a story brace me with their (sometimes) consoling clarity. "I ain't a preacher no more," says Casy, a man of lost faith, early in *The Grapes of Wrath*, when Grampa Joad dies on the road to California. The family requests a few words at the burial. Casy resists at first. Finally, for a minute or two, he subdues his disillusionment.

He bows his head and says, "Heard a fella tell a poem one time, an' he says, 'All that lives is holy.' "

He stumbles, then goes on. "[Now] I wouldn't pray for a ol' fella that's dead . . . He got a job to do, but it's all laid out for 'im an' there's on'y one way to do it. But us, we got a job to do, an' they's a thousan' ways, an' we don't know which one to take."

Around the corner, the German shepherd explodes in vivid howling. I hear a little girl cry.

"Amen," I whisper.

Bakersfield

The longest oil pipeline in the United States runs from Kern County, California, where thousands of hungry Okies decamped in the thirties seeking redemption, to my home desert in West Texas, where, when I was a child, no shelter could spare you from the dust in the air, no meals came without slabs of fatty meat, and the only redemption possible, if you believed the Holy Rollers, was loud, fast, and painful. My Okie parents, who'd followed the smell of oil to Texas's tumbleweed flats, cursed the dust, scarfed the meat, and feared the wrath of God.

That's life in Kern County even now. Though I've never been here before, this is home, as surely as if the All-American Pipeline pumped values, manners, and taste in tons of raw crude through its 1,223-mile artery.

At full production, the pipeline carries three hundred thousand barrels of oil a day. It was built in the mid-eighties at a cost of $1.4 billion and is operated now by a Houston-based company whose biggest storage facility sprawls across the grassy plains of Oklahoma.

Fifty years earlier, another artery linked the folks of Texas, Oklahoma, and California. Route 66 bore tons of tacky bedding, overalls and faded print dresses, jalopies shedding parts like pelts, across the deserts and the mountains, and into the hard-labor towns of the West. Kern County, rich in crops and oil, became Little Oklahoma. By the late thirties, plains migrants had swelled the county's population by over 60 percent.

They dug in, stubbornly, picking cotton, pumping oil, plucking grapes. They built shelters out of strawberry crates, cardboard boxes, old tin cans. They cursed the dust and raised their kids to fear the wrath of God.

That's why, today, walking the back streets of Bakersfield, passing a barbershop and hearing the nasal twangs of fellows being buzz-cut, I'm home, though I'm a first-timer here. There's a lilt of the gospel and the swing of country music in their talk.

An old joke still makes the rounds here: "What are the first words an Okie kid learns? Mama, Papa, and Bakersfield."

A few miles north, moseying down an unpaved block of McCord Street in Oildale, Merle Haggard's childhood home, I glimpse skinny boys in front of rusty trailers. Instantly, I know I'm among the children and grandchildren of Okies. Once, crate and cardboard hovels trembled in the wind here.

I've found where I might have lived if my grandfather hadn't stuck it out in Oklahoma at the height of the Dust Bowl drought; where I might have grown up if my father, an oil man all his life, had been transferred here from Texas.

I've come to the end of the road, the source of the pipeline, three years after the Oklahoma City bombing—another brutal scattering of folks like my own—to see what might have been, and to witness what remains.

"I'll be everywhere," Tom Joad said, "wherever you can look. Wherever there's a fight so hungry people can eat, I'll be there. I'll be in the way guys yell when they're mad. I'll be in the way kids laugh when they're hungry and they know supper's ready."

Lately, I've seen him in dreams standing by the house where I was born, by the banks of the Kern, by the fence around the Murrah site.

Today, in Oildale, in the Happy Acres Trailer Park, a man in jeans and a white T-shirt stands on a wooden stoop in front of his tiny mobile home, scratching his belly. He squints at the haze in the air, a fume of valley dust and refinery steam. He's middle-aged, tired. Querulous and slow. He appears to be confused about something. He drops his gaze, sees me, and nods, both wary and open, noting my strangeness as well as my dim familiarity.

I nod back.

I might be looking at myself.

Later, I stop at a barbershop called "Oakie Ray's," near the Bakersfield airport. Saddles, lanterns, farm tools, and saw blades line the walls of the one-room shop, along with 1930s California license plates, a 1902 Sears catalog cover, and an "Oklahoma Welcomes You" postcard.

Ray, a paunchy, jowly man in a pillowy shirt, is giving a kid a crew cut when I walk in. The child's mother, a bleached blonde, sits in a white plastic chair by the front door.

"Ow!" the boy chirps. "Ow!"

"Sorry, boy," Ray says. "You keep yelling out like that, I'ma jump outta my skin."

"He just got over the chickenpox and he's still got some scabs on his head," the woman says.

"Is *that* what I keep hitting?" Ray runs the electric shears behind the boy's ears.

I relax and settle into my chair. In their talk are the rhythms of home: a bitten-off, aggressive friendliness, a politeness, a competitive humor. "The migrant people, scuttling for work, scrabbling to live, looked always for pleasure, dug for pleasure, manufactured pleasure, and they were hungry for amusement. Sometimes amusement lay in speech," Steinbeck explains in *The Grapes of Wrath*.

"Ow!"

"You keep saying that, I'll sick my dog on you."

"I'd kick him in the *whey*-vos." The boy grins, showing off crooked brown teeth. "That means 'balls.' "

"I *know* what it means," Ray says. "My wife's Spanish. Cojones, eh? You got cojones, boy?"

"Oh Lord, all my boys, they got cojones running out their ears," the woman groans. "This morning, Clint busted his lip on the trampoline—Rusty's riding him like a old horse."

"Least they ain't in no gangs," Ray says.

"That's right. Their old man, he tells them they get mixed up in gangs, if they don't die on the streets, they'll die in the back shed from a whupping."

"Fifteen, sixteen. Rough age. Gotta watch 'em."

"They're into sports."

"*I'm* into sports!" the kid pipes up: the great-grandchild of Winfield Joad.

"*What* sports?" Ray says. "How fast you can grab the TV *ree*-mote?"

"Ol' what's-her-name head back to Oklahoma?" the woman asks now, flipping through a *Car and Driver* magazine.

"Yeah."

"I knew she's wanting to."

"That ol' gal don't know *what* she wants."

"She's a nervous wreck, wudn't she?"

"That fella she's with—"

"*Young* fella."

"Yeah. Real joker."

Petering out, the conversation turns naturally, now, to the weather, and the recent flooding. "Ain't the rain bothers me so much," Ray says. "It's the dadburn wind."

All this time, a teenage boy has been patching a flat bicycle tire for Ray in a weedy yard next to the shop. When he tells Ray he's finished the job, poking his head through a narrow back door, Ray switches off the shears. "Okay, you've worked off your haircut now. But call your daddy and see can you keep your haircut money." I try to remember, and can't, the last time I witnessed this kind of even-up trade among people with only their labor to share.

We all listen to the young man hem and haw on the phone to his father, apparently too scared to come to the point. "Goldurn!" Ray yells over his shoulder into the receiver. "He wants to know, can he keep the money?"

"He said yes," the boy says quietly, hanging up. He disappears again into the yard.

A wide Latina steps sideways through the back door, gripping a raggedy broom. "Spaghetti's ready, Ray, when you get a chancet to get to it."

"Ow!" the kid in the chair shouts one last time, and Ray declares him done.

He turns to me.

"I don't want to keep you from your spaghetti," I say.

"It'll be there. Just let me grab a quick smoke."

I take a seat in the barber chair. A big gold dog chases another pooch past the front door.

"You from Oklahoma?" I ask when Ray snaps the drape across my body.

"Naw, I grew up in the desert here, but I been around these damned ol' Okies so long, I'm one of them now."

"I'm a desert kid myself," I tell him.

"Whereabouts?"

"Midland, Texas."

"Shit. Oildale East."

"Right."

He laughs at a memory of riding his bike in the desert as a child. "When you punctured a tire, you put evaporated milk in it and kept on going. The milk kept it solid, but eventually it ruined the rubber." He seems to be talking to himself more than to me. The electric shears skim the tops of my ears.

He asks me what I do for a living.

"Man, our Oildale boys can't read a lick coming out of school," he says when I tell him I'm a university teacher up in Oregon. "Hell, the other day, I saw three Oildale High boys sitting on the curb. I asked the first one, I said, 'What's three times three?' '156,' he said. I asked the second one, 'What's three times three?' 'Tuesday,' he said. So I turned to the third one. What's three times three?' I asked him. 'Nine.' 'Well now, how'd you arrive at that?' 'Easy,' he said. 'I subtracted 156 from Tuesday.' That's our Oildale boys for you." He trims my sideburns. "These days, all the boys want to do is get the girls pregnant, and the girls, they *want* to get pregnant and get the taxpayers to pay for 'em. Good thing I'm not running the country. If you weren't productive, I'd shoot you. That's how I'd run it." He clicks off the shears and picks up a pair of scissors. "You married?"

"Divorced."

"Shoot yes, I know *that* tune. I thought I's married for thirteen years, first time around. Turns out, I's just in *counseling* thirteen years."

"It's hard work," I agree.

"Worked *me* to the bone."

A young Mexican couple walks in with two long-haired boys, about six and seven, and a baby in a stroller.

"Howdy, girls," Ray says to the boys.

Their father frowns. He looks like any number of guys I went to junior high and high school with in Midland, Mexicans from the "other side of town," whose houses I never saw.

"Be right with you," Ray says. "Y'all from Oildale?"

"Just moved here," says the young mother.

"You *like* it?"

"Better'n where we were."

"Where's that?"

"East Bakersfield."

"God a'mighty. Lotsa gangs there."

"Why we left," the woman says. "Three men was shot on our block and two stabbed, just this year."

"When they robbed our landlord, we decided to move," the young father says, still checking Ray out, wary, but clearly looking for an ally in his new neighborhood. "He was putting in a security light out back, middle of the day. Some guy pulled a pistol on him and shot him for his money. He had three dollars."

We're all quiet. The boys look at their father as if to measure the tone of what he's said. Is he making a joke? "It's even worse up in Fresno," Ray says finally. He slides a soft brush across the back of my neck, then tugs the drape off my legs, spilling curly hair to the floor. "Thanks, *Pro*-fessor."

I hand him twelve bucks. "Sorry about your spaghetti," I say.

He shrugs. "Ought to get yourself out to the raceway while you're in town. Everybody goes out there on the weekends. They put on a good show. Lotsa crashes and stuff."

Afterwards, I drop by a store for a local map and a newspaper (yesterday, Niki Deutchman, the forewoman of the Terry Nichols jury, "criticized the government's case against Nichols, saying too much of the evidence was vague and circumstantial and too little effort was spent pursuing other [bombing] suspects . . . 'I think that the government perhaps really dropped the ball,' Deutchman said").

I set the paper aside and unfold the map. Like a trip to a neighborhood barbershop, even a casual glimpse at a map of Kern County shows why anyone interested in the secrets of America—in the social ferment behind a mess like the Murrah bombing—needs to see this place.

It's not the tourist's California. No pristine beaches, redwoods, or towering bridges. A few days before arriving here I landed in the tourist's California, at the John Wayne Airport in Orange County, south of L.A. Orange County, a stronghold of the John Birch Society, is a consumer's paradise of tanning salons, stretch limos, and malls. America the Prosperous.

In the airport, a larger-than-life statue of the Duke hovers midstride over travelers struggling with their bags. For decades, in the movies, he portrayed men who cleared the path for America's greatness. Standing in his path, though, were the dark-skinned peoples of the likes of Kern County: Yokuts and Yauelamni Indians, Mexican migrants.

In L.A., the self-proclaimed "capital for the twenty-first century," birthplace of the Internet, I toured the brand-new Getty Museum, an architectural marvel of travertine limestone, metal, and glass, with twenty galleries for paintings and a lovely collection of impressionist masterpieces.

The stone for the Getty was quarried in Bagni di Tivoli, near Rome, but the sweat and labor on which the Getty fortune was founded you'll find in Kern County, in the Happy Acres Trailer Park, among drilling rigs and pools of chemical stink.

The most beautiful museum in America rests on the wretched scaffolding of cokers, cat crackers, distillation towers. The twenty-first century may be blooming down the road, but here in Kern County, most people still live in cramped quarters reminiscent of the twentieth century's hardest times.

On a Kern County map, Interstate 40 skirts the old Route 66. Running north/south, Highway 99 cuts Bakersfield in half. To the west, big green patches: "Sundale Country Club," "Stockdale Country Club," "Patriots Park," "Green Acres," "Seven Oaks Golf Club."

White Lane, right down the middle.

East of 99, the streets are called Panama, Casa Loma; the major park is named for Martin Luther King Jr.

The patches here are labeled "Department of Water Resources Waste Treatment Plant," "Mount Vernon Sewer Treatment Plant," and "County of Kern Sewer Farm."

North of the Kern River, fed by snowmelt from the Sierra Nevadas east of town, its banks now scraggly, trampled, yellowed, and denuded (agribusiness tells the water where to go, diverting the snowmelt all over the county and beyond), Oildale is blotted with petroleum tanks, vast refinery compounds.

Near the bottom of the map, south of Bakersfield, Kern County goes nearly blank, with only a few signs of human activity— Aqueduct, Pumping Plant, Oil Field—scattered among the natural landmarks of Bear Mountain, the Tejon Hills, and the Tehachapi Mountains. Only by actually going there will you discover the old labor camp, Weedpatch, and see that what the map doesn't show is a swarm of seasonal laborers.

Nowhere in America are class and race divisions more readily apparent than they are here.

Supplementing the map with the newspaper, I piece together a vivid narrative, a story of contemporary America in miniature. On one side of Bakersfield, affluent whites enjoy the fruits of development, new houses, strip shopping centers, chain stores. Chevron, Arco, and Smith-Barney do their business here, next to the offices of the U.S. Border Patrol. On the other side of town live most of the dark-skinned folks (Latinos make up 25 percent of the population). Their neighborhoods are crumbling. The city dumps its sewage in them. Shootings are a nightly occurrence.

To the north, in Oildale, poor whites, many of them descendants of Depression-era Okies, struggle to keep what little they own as a result of their blue-collar jobs. They live in trailers or box houses tucked among smelly oil derricks, one generation—or one layoff— removed from fieldwork.

This is where Timothy McVeigh would live, if he lived here, hustling from one lousy day job to another, hanging out at gun shows on the weekends.

Good thing I'm not running the country.

And to the south, the poorest of the poor, migrant laborers, cluster in dirt-colored housing units, all but invisible behind chain link fences guarded by nervous German shepherds.

In the thirties, jobless peoples from all parts of the nation believed the riches of Kern County would sweep them into the American Dream: opportunity, social mobility, comfort. Now, when any day despair might take the shape of a bomb blast, the dream's limitations are clear.

"This land," says the California novelist James D. Houston, whose folks were born in Duncan, Oklahoma, "could torture you for years without ever quite killing you."

"Bakersfield's rash of bank robberies continues," said the headlines, the day I arrived here, a dusty traveler looking for traces of home. You'd think Pretty Boy Floyd was on the loose. Three banks had been picked off this month.

Bakersfield's city manager was "gunning for a raise," according to another Old West headline.

"Flat oil prices" was the other big news. The local energy giants, Chevron, Tosco, Texaco, EOTT, Mobil, and Shell, were all hurting because crude was down to $7.25 a barrel (though in a smaller article inside the paper, company spokespeople admitted their profits were still up nearly 40 percent because of "streamlined operating practices"—namely, layoffs).

The paper devotes more space to oil field news than to anything else. Its regular oil columnist, Bill Rintoul, writes in highly technical language that still, somehow, manages to sound as thrilling as a sports event: "[Occidental] spudded in Friday evening to drill its first well . . . The target is the Shallow Oil Zone at the N. 152-36R in the N.E. quarter of Sec. 36, 30S-23E."

Shades of my father's supper talk, in Texas.

The classifieds: "Laborers needed, roustabouts, backhoe operators. Hazardous materials and confined space work."

Pepsi-Cola's huge local manufacturing plant needs production line technicians, floor managers, warehouse loaders.

The Okies brought to California a love of honky-tonk music and rigid Baptist churches. Sin and redemption. That legacy spices the back pages, still: an ad for "George Strait tickets (8th row, make an offer)" borders a box declaring, "Take a wonderful trip to the Holy Land—retrace the steps of Paul."

Of the thirty-eight bookstores listed in the yellow pages here, eighteen of them specialize in Christian material (seven others sell only technical manuals).

"Divorce hurts," said a billboard for a law firm next to my motel, just off Highway 99. I could see it from my window. "When you've taken all you can, call the Divorce Experts."

Over storms of drizzly static on KUZZ, Bakersfield's best-known country music station, Merle sang softly, one dusk, "Tonight, your memory found me much too sober."

Mornings, I ate in a place called Maggie's Café, in Oildale, just around the corner from the Gettin' Hitched Wedding Chapel and Sam's Auto Repair. The restaurant baked in the shade of a billboard: two cowboys chatting on their horses against a red and yellow sunset—a deliberate echo of the old Marlboro cigarette ads.

Said the caption: "I miss my lung, Bob."

Hash browns, biscuits and gravy, chicken-fried steak. Rusty washboards cluttered Maggie's walls.

"Sorry, I served my last biscuits an hour ago," a waitress told a noisy family in a booth as I walked in one day. Her dyed red hair was heavily teased; her body was shaped like a kite, broad in the shoulders, then tapering off, drastically, down to her toes. "My regulars didn't even get none."

One of the boys in the booth had lost his wristwatch in a crack in the cottony seat. "Where's it at?" his mother asked him irritably.

The waitress reached down and found it. "Next time I'm keeping it," she said. "You ain't big enough to fight me for it."

I picked a jelly-stained newspaper off a table, the *Arvin Tiller*, established in 1939 ("Garden in the Sun's Hometown Paper"). An editorial said, "Government in America has become like an overblown fat cow trampling anything that gets in its way."

A man on crutches took a seat with his wife. I overheard him tell the waitress he was a stock car driver at the raceway. Recently, he'd been in a crash. "It'uz a freak accident," he said.

"Them's the worst kind. You look good, though."

In fact, he looked like hell, yellowed, thin, and bruised. "Lost sixteen pounds in four days. Hospital food."

The father of the noisy children said he'd been "out to the race-way on Saturday."

"How's the track?" asked the battered man, perking up.

"Heatin' up, heatin' up."

"That's good," said the driver, plainly proud of his ties to the place, despite its terrible risks for him. His color improved right away, and he eagerly scanned the menu.

"I take a lot of pride in what I am," Merle used to sing.

In frontier towns like Bakersfield, Oildale, and Weedpatch—even in Oklahoma City—where life is hard and most folks don't own much, where the raceway's the biggest draw around for its promise of freedom and speed, pride's at a premium.

A cynic might say pride, like heaven and the assurance of an afterlife, is easy to grant to the poor.

It doesn't cost anything.

It makes families happy and keeps them in line.

If pride is all you have, you cling to it fiercely; you brag about it to noisy families in run-down cafés.

Clearly, some fellows are so proud to be plain-spoken, beer-drinking good ol' boys, they view with suspicion any chance to improve themselves.

So. Sure. The poor can have their pride. Why not?

One day I saw painted on a tan stucco wall at Bakersfield High School a hard-hatted roughneck sneering and gripping a big red wrench. "Driller Pride" said the slogan at his feet.

On the outskirts of Lamont, a sign declares, "Lamont—With Pride and With a Future."

This struck me as an awfully tepid community motto.

Not a *bright* future, necessarily. Nothing bold or special. Just a future—as if to say, Whatever the hell happens, we'll grit our teeth and take it, the way we always have. And by god, we'll do it with pride.

This weekend Merle was in town for a pair of sold-out concerts at Buck Owens's Crystal Palace, a bright red, white, and blue country music mecca in the middle of Bakersfield. "So much has changed here," Merle told a newspaper reporter. "The neighborhood I grew up in was . . . a quiet, elderly, peaceful place but now it's something other than that."

If he'd searched Chester Avenue looking for the Blackboard Café, he'd be flat out of luck. For decades, the Blackboard gave country singers a place to hone their acts. Bill Woods and the Orange Blossom Playboys used to jump-start the place while people tore into chicken-fried steaks. The Playboys have passed beyond memory now.

One afternoon, I ate a bland cheeseburger at a joint called Frosty King, a block from the Blackboard's old spot. That's as close as I could get.

Tall grass nettled with thistles ringed Oildale's Standard Elementary, Merle's first school, the morning I dropped by. "Candy Sale / Winning at Parenting," said a sign out front. "Please Come." Across the street, railroad cars rusted behind a chain link fence, next to a row of oil tanks.

That night, in the Crystal Palace, Merle, now a wealthy elder statesman, a graybeard in glitter, a man who'd like to be honored, he said, by having the Bakersfield airport or a train station named for him, sang nostalgic songs about growing up poor.

Each night, while an older generation of wildcatters and drillers still gathers in the honky-tonks of Oildale to listen to Merle's records, to the grits-and-gravy of pure country music, Bakersfield's teenagers, unaware of the history of their town, its hidden life, cruise sparkling new shopping centers, past Blockbuster video stores, United Artists cineplexes, Pizza Huts. As hip-hop tunes thud incessantly from their state-of-the-art radios, they zip past the old Fox Theater downtown, which used to post a sign in its lobby: "No Niggers or Okies in the Balcony."

An old Bakersfield story: A little boy, passing a dusty field with his dad, sees a bunch of Okies picking cotton. "Look, Daddy," says the boy. "Them things almost look like people when they stand on their legs, don't they?"

Joe McCourn, CPA, born February 12, 1911, in Coalgate, Oklahoma.
    Charles "Chuck" Day, plumber and miner: Ponca City, Oklahoma.
    Bessie Beatrice Weeks, a Sunday School teacher and Kern County resident for over fifty years; born in Oklahoma on August 14, 1917.
    In yesterday's obits, there was even a notice for a Mexican man who'd died in Midland, Texas, and whose relatives all live in Bakersfield. For fifteen years, he worked as a chef in Midland's Petroleum Club, where my father often ate lunch and went to meetings.
    A whole generation, passing quietly into shades within shades within shades.

In a dream I had, my last night in Kern County, I was sitting in a porch swing of an old wooden house, a house similar to my grandparents' Oklahoma home, rocking back and forth. A sloping lawn spread before me; each time I swung high, I could see, beyond the lawn, a vast landscape, changing with each new arc I made. Now a forested valley, then a sunny canyon, now a desert, then a spring-fed meadow. Fireflies and constellations swirled in the sky, now dawn, then dusk. *Where am I?* I thought, the age-old migrant lament. Then: *It doesn't matter. I can take it all inside me.* I opened my mouth for a pleasurable scream.

At that moment I awoke, feeling happy, comforted, expansive. Through my motel window, a big western sun hung in the east. By the road below, an old mattress lay in a ditch, and a glut of cardboard boxes, as if Tom Joad had just clattered by in his truck, spilling junk.

Health Seekers

The world was perfect. It was Paradise. We decided to change it. When we spoiled one spot, we left in search of another Eden. For Americans, this meant moving ever westward. By 1830, farmers in the Mississippi Valley had concluded that no Eden was unpoisoned. The more fertile the ground, it seemed, the higher the chance of unchecked fevers, sallow complexions, pained limbs. Disease was always the snake in the garden.

Perhaps desiccation was the true hallmark of the Promised Land: soils in which no lung-eating elements could flourish, scorching air in which invisible enemies perished. Western emptiness came to be seen as the last chance for a hearty frontier. In the West, it is "most usual to sleep out in the open air . . . for the serene sky . . . affords the most agreeable and wholesome canopy," wrote the consumptive trader Josiah Gregg in a widely circulated book called *Commerce of the Prairies*, published in 1844. "The deleterious attribute of night air and dews, so dangerous in other climates, is but little experienced upon the high plains; on the contrary, the serene evening air seems to affect the health rather favorably."

By the 1870s, health seekers had founded hundreds of new towns west of the Mississippi, both nudged and followed by snake-oil salesmen. "Texas is about as full of quacks as McKinney's Bayou is of ducks," said an editorial in the Galveston *News* in January 1871.

Arguably, a flock of invalids shaped Texas's destiny as much as the Alamo battle. Emigration was spurred by the claims of early boosters such as Stephen F. Austin. "The climate of Texas I deem to be decidedly superior in point of health and salubrity to any portion of north America in the same parallel," he said.

As an asthmatic born in West Texas, I proudly claim my place in the long line of gaspers who made my state.

In the late nineteenth century, tent cities sprang up in Fort Davis, Santa Fe, Roswell. In the Davis Mountains, near the outpost where Robert E. Lee once trained to be a general, a camp formed around a glass and metal structure built by Will Pruett, whose life goal was to "aid sick humanity." He called his device an "Inhalatorium." A patient would stand inside it and breathe concentrated medicinal vapors. Inaccessibility doomed the camp before the treatment could be termed a success or failure. A pair of its rusting walls still droop in the sands where the infirm came to be healed.

In 1914, Texas, Oklahoma, Kansas, New Mexico, Arizona, Nevada, Colorado, Utah, and California joined forces to support the Safroth–Calloway bill in the U.S. Congress, which provided that abandoned military bases in the Southwest be reactivated as federally funded tuberculosis hospitals, to absorb all the indigent consumptives who had "contracted their infection in another state" and were now straining local resources.

This limping pilgrimage continued throughout the twentieth century, accompanied by treasure hunters, railroad magnates, entrepreneurs, electricians, oil workers. In 1999, the *Los Angeles Times* reported that Phoenix had become so swollen with humanity, doctors were coining a new term, "Valley Fever," for illnesses caused by pathogens in the dirt stirred by continuous activity: fatigue, fungus in bones or in the brain. The cost to Arizona topped $20 million.

"Everybody who lives here has a health problem," one citizen said flatly.

It seems the snake had followed each new Adam and Eve to every new garden. He was no longer pretty or seductive. He was just a dusty old rattler, now, on a hot rock in the desert sun. But he still hissed sweetly, "Move on down the road a piece. The next place will be *it.*"

Perhaps, at a certain point, "garden" was no longer an appropriate metaphor for our continent's promise. The land was paved with highways now, offering instant escapes. If we couldn't have Eden anymore, we'd distract ourselves from its loss. In place of southern California's orange groves we'd build a fake mountain and a fairy castle; the masters of this fine new world would be a smiling mouse and a big, goofy dog. The word "orange" in "Orange County" meant nothing now—another distraction.

Along our restless escape paths, eateries—quick and convenient, with golden arches as beckoning as a mother's breasts, play areas to entice our children, and a benign, grinning clown to save us from our sins, our reasons for hitting the road.

Recently, the hidden costs of these spectacles were adroitly cataloged by Eric Schlosser in a book called *Fast Food Nation*: unskilled, underpaid migrant laborers and overworked teenagers; corporate consolidation, weakening local businesses and community ties; the loss of family farms; unsanitary and inhumane slaughterhouse practices.

For three years, searching for Eden along the Okie roads, I moved through this country of instant gratification, feeling, from time to time, my chest grow tighter and tighter, my body slower and slower. Fatigue, I thought. Depression, I thought, fungus on the brain. I moved on.

One evening, waiting for fries in a noisy McDonald's in the San Joaquin Valley, I watched a pretty teenage girl lower a basket of frozen potatoes into hissing hot oil spiced with "animal products." "I will survive," the girl sang softly to herself. Yawning, she pulled frozen beef patties from a box and slapped them onto a greasy metal surface. "I will survive." Behind her, on a yellow wall, a smiling cardboard mouse—a movie promo—grinned and waved at me. "I will survive." A child spilled catsup on his mother's purple stretch pants. She shook him till he cried. I gazed west through a smudged window; in the sky's streaky red light, a man in a straw hat turned his sputtering green tractor and headed for the barn.

Don't Come Back

From an old hobo song, the lyrics of which my grandfather scribbled in one of his notebooks from the thirties:

Clickitty clack, clickitty clack.
Looking back, looking back.
Where you going, where you going?
Where you been, where you been?
Clickitty clack, clickitty clack.
Don't come back. Don't come back.

Yemen

Life can only be understood backwards, but it must be lived forwards: for this reason, of course, it's often difficult to say what we've seen, exactly; to parse the whole story, or to comprehend precisely where we are.

Three months after the United States executed Timothy McVeigh, whom Judge Richard Matsch had called a pure "instrument of death," thousands of people were murdered in coordinated attacks on the World Trade Center and the Pentagon—young men killing mostly other young men, it turned out, though a number of women and children got caught in the maelstrom. These events both overshadowed and revived, like a broken blister, the pain of Oklahoma City.

Within a month, President Bush had declared a global "war on terrorism" and the United States began to bomb Afghanistan. In mid-November 2001, the *Ottawa Citizen* reported, "The terror organization of Osama bin Laden drew up plans to copy the Oklahoma City bomb. A do-it-yourself guide, detailing the components needed to make the bomb and written by a Bosnian recruit to bin Laden's al-Qaeda network, was found among documents and weapons last week in the basement of a Kabul mansion used by the terrorists." It was titled "Explosivija za Oklahomu."

For years, conspiracy theorists had traded rumors on the Internet that Terry Nichols had met with al-Qaeda members in the Philippines several months before the Murrah bombing. And McVeigh was repeatedly invoked in public discussions of U.S. options after the September 11 attacks. "Timothy McVeigh and his collaborators . . . asserted that their ideas of rights and liberty were being violated and that the only recourse was terror . . . Yet, no one suggested that his act had its 'root causes' in an injustice that needed to be rectified to prevent further terrorism," Edward Rothstein wrote in the *New York Times*, chiding those who suggested that America's foreign policy was a prime reason for the hatred behind September 11. McVeigh was cited again by the *News*, a leading Pakistani newspaper, after President Bush announced that captured Middle Eastern terrorists might be tried by secret American military tribunals. "Why was this not done for Timothy McVeigh?" the paper asked, adding that the Bush administration was engaging in blatant racism. The *Times* of London agreed.

Murrah, it seemed, was a touchstone in debates over this latest terrorist attack. Worse, it looked as though the Oklahoma City bombing was just the beginning of a bloody tide.

When I heard on the news that the State Department had identified several Yemeni honey merchants as fronts for Osama bin Laden's network, I recalled a trip I'd made to Yemen in the summer of 1989 with a group of Oregon teachers. One day, in the desert north of the city of Sana'a, we had stopped to buy honey. The beekeepers lived in thatch huts: palm fronds and canvas tenting. Nearby, dozens of tarp-covered boxes—makeshift hives—were stacked. To get to the honey, the men lighted rolled-up burlap sticks and smoked out the bees. In temperatures nearing 115 degrees in direct sunlight, the beekeepers' wives stood absolutely still, covered head to toe in thick black garments.

Quoted in the *Wall Street Journal*, in late October 2001, one honey dealer doubted that Osama bin Laden (whose family hailed from Yemen) lay behind the September 11 attacks—at any rate, he didn't believe the United States could prove it. He vowed to "fight in Afghanistan if local clerics" asked him to.

I thought, again, back to '89, and the withering summer heat: all those angry bees.

1989: before the Gulf War, before the Murrah bombing, the destruction of the World Trade Center, and the war in Afghanistan. Yet the trouble signs—the root causes—were clear: in America's worsening farm crisis, in the tightening of global markets, the spread of poverty (as swift as leaking oil), the Middle East's unabating turmoil. Most of us were too busy fast-forwarding our lives to fully grasp where we were headed.

When I first arrived in Yemen, and met the American ambassador and his staff on the lush green embassy grounds in Sana'a, I wondered what odd personality quirks a person had to have in order to join the American Foreign Service. The economics officer had a Gorbachev-style birthmark above his right eye and a facial twitch centered around his mouth. The AID director twitched too—a rapid gum-chewer, he scanned the grounds to see if anyone was watching him. The head honcho from the Office of Military Cooperation was another twitchy type, a good old boy from Tennessee, with a tight smile as though he could just, with massive effort, hold his jaw in place. The ambassador himself was a smooth character, though he had a funny, froglike look about him—wide eyes and thick, protruding lips. Very thin. Distinguished gray hair.

A Yemeni servant poured us Turkish coffee under a brightly striped canvas tent, which had been erected on the lawn, and passed around trays of hors d'oeuvres—some kind of fish paste on wheat crackers. The sky was cloudy; a light sprinkle had begun.

The air was cool, as were the garden's spiky-leaved, deeply loamy green hues.

Americans visiting Yemen were generally safe, the ambassador assured our group, though later in the day I learned that the embassy was planning to relocate soon near the airport, out of town. "We feel more at ease with our Soviet counterparts in the diplomatic corps than we do with the Arabs," the economics officer admitted to me. "It's not that the Yemenis aren't friendly, but hell, our cultures'll never mesh. I mean, their justice system alone . . ."

His explanation was amended later by the AID director, who told me that the embassy had been attacked eight months ago. No real damage; the lone shell was a dud. "What happened was, this Peace Corps volunteer fell for a Muslim nut, a real anti-American kook," the director said. He smacked his gum loudly and looked very closely at the women in our group. "She let him use her apartment as a base of operations—lived about a block from here."

More expatriate gossip as the party progressed: that very morning, a mortar shell had slammed into an American day care center nearby. None of the children were hurt. A general from the Yemeni army apologized to the American staff. "We were practicing and misfired," he said. I was told that, recently, two young women had been tossed off the downtown post office. They were accused of killing their abusive husbands and were sentenced to death. Their execution was replayed several times in slow motion on Yemeni television.

Despite these stories I was eager to meet the Yemeni people. I felt quite safe on the streets. The black-veiled women stared at me in my casual Western clothes, the men's eyes followed me whenever I entered a café to order bread and tea, but I never sensed hostility from them—just simple curiosity, as strong as my own wonder at their culture.

Most of the women carried tin boxes of household goods on their heads. The men sported curved daggers on elaborate gold belts. The mud-brick buildings in which most families lived—

five or six stories tall, full of farm animals on the first floors—resembled melting candles: sand and wind had erased their definition. There were no streetlights or clearly marked lanes in the village of Rawdah, on Sana'a's outskirts, where our group stayed in an ancient hotel. Trash clouded the streets—plastic bags, torn tennis shoes, cardboard juice containers.

That first night, from my hotel room window, I heard packs of wild dogs howling in the distance, in the direction of the Nahdain, twin mountains called by the locals "Two Breasts," in the hills around the city. The stone windowsill was still radiant with the day's trapped heat. Mosquitoes filled the room; I was jet-lagged and hot, and couldn't sleep. Around five A.M. I was startled by the most arresting sound I've ever heard: the muezzin in a nearby minaret, sounding the call to prayer. The minaret stood less than a hundred yards from the hotel: cinder-block base, square, then circular, thinning at the top, ringed at its peak with metal, bell-shaped loudspeakers. An impassioned male voice rained down on me like the voice of God Himself. Far off, like approaching thunder, or a roar of locusts, other prayers hummed from various minarets. Eerie, echoing voices rising in passion, pleading—horrific and comic (to my Western ear), brutal yet childlike in their calls for attention in the clear desert air. God—or gods—demanding fealty. The chant moved me to my bones. Allah al Akbar—"God is greatest; come to the mosque and pray."

That summer, the Berlin wall hadn't yet fallen. The Cold War was still a hot prospect. At the embassy, the Good Soldier from Tennessee—"I'm a DOD (Department of Defense) guy, so I use a lot of acronyms"—had told me that Uncle Sam had one F-5 fighter plane in Yemen; the Soviets had three MIG-21s. In the week following our meeting I noticed dozens of jets on practice runs, buzzing markets and mosques. MIGs over the minarets. The Americans flew in the mornings, the Russians after lunch: shrieking insect swarms.

"Yeah, it's true, we got a little hardware here," Davy Crockett admitted when I saw him again. "Two or three planes."

"*Only* two or three?" I said.

"Four, maybe. Five. Couple of TOWs."

One day, the gum-chewer showed our group an ag farm that AID had developed north of Sana'a: sleek, new dusty machines. None of the Americans knew how to operate them or train the Yemenis. "*This* is America's foreign policy at work?" one of the teachers asked. "Dump a barrel of cash, *then* figure out what we're doing?"

"We've got to start somewhere," the AID man said.

Later, I learned that none of the foreign service workers could speak more than a few simple sentences in Arabic.

"We *do* have some army business here—we'd like to maintain this country as a moderate member of the Arab camp," the ambassador told us back at the embassy (a wish that exploded, two years later, in the Gulf War). "And let's be honest, we'd like to share in the oil revenues—nothing wrong with that. What's good for us is also good for the Arabs. We both benefit from mutual cooperation."

In the West, where the emphasis is always on looking ahead, we tend to see a lack of the latest equipment, the latest fashions, and the latest goods as *backwards*. Culturally and technologically, Yemen certainly felt to me as if it existed in a previous century. Yet the nation's religious faith, which conferred on most people a serene dignity, seemed to me quite advanced, somehow, despite the social restrictions Islamic law placed on individuals, particularly women. This was a contradiction I never could tease apart. The full story would always elude me.

Nor could I get used to Yemeni farmers' terraced fields, planted on the steepest, wettest mountainsides I had ever seen. Culling crops from these dangerously sloped rows looked to me virtually impossible—especially without the aid of machinery. Was I *really* witnessing a working farm? For all their occasional harshness, Oklahoma's high plains seemed to me a far more civilized place to scratch out a living. Yet one day, as our bus wound up a muddy hairpin road, east of Sana'a, we saw a farmer on a sandstone outcrop, so high he was standing in the midst of a cloud, straddling the top of the planet, raising his wooden staff to tap God's shoulder, it appeared, and I believe everyone on the bus would have given anything to trade places with him, just for a moment—to seize his unparalleled vantage point, the beauty of his world, the composure of his faith and his certainty in his way of life.

The Red Sea isn't red—I was disappointed (a little loss of faith) and didn't want to believe what I saw: gray, muddy waves.

One Saturday, in the port of Hodeida, on Yemen's west coast, we went walking through the evening market. I've never been so hot in my life. Bottle after quart bottle of cold water, and I didn't have to pee all night. The moisture leaked through my pores. In Hodeida's streets the smell of sun-baked fish was overpowering. Vendors spread blankets on narrow walks and covered them with peppers, coffee beans, mountains of yellow cumin, feathery saffron, rice. Water pipes, brass plates, carpets. A severed cow's head in a wheelbarrow. Coastal fashions were much looser than Sana'a's standard dress—cool skirts swayed with the women's bodies. Bright yellow head wraps, blue and red scarves. The swirl of odors and colors made me dizzy. And that relentless heat!—along the streets, men were frying prickly pears and strips of meat in steel drums (boiling grease spattered the passersby); hissing Coleman lanterns and white-hot light bulbs illuminated spices and cloths, shoes, boxes of matches, smoothed sticks for cleaning the teeth.

That night in the hotel, so as not to insult local custom, the men in our group joined a number of Arab men in chewing qat, a faintly narcotic plant; the effect was like chugging a pot of coffee. Our female colleagues weren't allowed to join us and had to return to their rooms.

The following morning, early, the town smelled of olive oil and goat milk. Our hotel overlooked sand hills above shallow clay pits (some kind of gardening system). Seawater; flat, white rocks. Boys laughing, playing on the beaches or walking camels. The animals' necks bulged with ribbed and rubbery bones, like radiator hoses beneath a dirty car hood. For a while, from my window, eager as ever for the full story, I witnessed what I knew, as an outsider, as a male, I should turn my eyes from: women in haiks, faces loosely veiled, carrying baskets of bread, or—in hurried, stolen moments away from their men—washing their bared legs in the sea.

Whether or not the U.S. bombing of Afghanistan struck a long-term blow against terrorism, it was impossible not to be moved by newspaper photographs of Afghani women tearing off their burkas and dancing in Kabul's streets once the repressive, governing Taliban had been forced to retreat.

Back in '89, the women in our group were deeply torn in their responses to Yemeni women, and to the state of women throughout Islamic countries. Many of my comrades reacted fiercely against the veiling, dismissing it as sexist oppression, pure and simple. Others noted that some Yemeni women said they felt immense freedom in their public anonymity and would choose to cover themselves even if they weren't forced to. "Besides," a honey dealer's wife had confessed to one of my colleagues, "I don't *want* to look too closely at all the suffering in the world—pain I don't know how to stop, so why torture myself with it?" She said that, beneath their veils, Yemenis wore lavish makeup, and in private, danced erotically for one another.

No matter how closely you look, my colleague ribbed me later, you can *never* observe the whole story.

Today, as I glance back in order to see ahead more clearly, it strikes me that any definition of "terrorism" that doesn't address gender and childcare is incomplete and useless. In the future, we may reflect on this moment in history and realize that, worldwide, our insufficient attention to the economic and political, as well as sexual and familial, relationships between women and men hampered our efforts to erase global violence.

One afternoon, in one town's marketplace, on Yemen's western coast, some of my companions overheard an impassioned teenaged boy say that women made poor revolutionaries because they refused to give up their menstrual cycles. "If you can't be a star in the sky, be a lamp in the chamber," says an old Arab proverb, on the role of a good wife. All summer, as we traveled, I heard that line in my head, in tandem with a jingle I'd heard the American director of the Office of Military Cooperation singing to himself:

This is my rifle.
This is my gun.
One is for killing.
One is for fun.

Of course, like the Yemeni honey merchant's wife, I don't know how to stop the world's suffering. But I can't help but think it's better to witness as much as you can than to cover your face. Here at the end of 2001, as I think back to 1989, it's hard for me not to summarize what I've observed—in places as varied as Oklahoma, California, Nicaragua, and Yemen—this way: Some people fire guns and plant bombs. Others wait and wail and rock infants in their arms.

That's not the whole story, not by a long shot.

But I swear it's what I've seen.

The Day of the Dead

Molalla, Oregon, named for an Indian tribe with a long history of uprootings and forced isolation, nestles among sprawling asparagus and Christmas tree farms, fields of pumpkins and squash. Mt. Hood, snow-capped, glistening like wax, holds the northwest horizon. About 5 percent of Molalla's population is Latino, most of whom pick fruit. Five years ago, construction began on the Arbor Terrace Apartments, a federally funded housing complex for workers. At the time I read that many local Anglos opposed the place, fearing it would attract hobos, gangs, drugs, and crime. Instead, it's become a blessing and a home to several large, extended families, mostly from Mexico: Mixtecos from Oaxaca, young couples from Michoacán. In the mornings, quiet grandmothers cook in tiny kitchens; kids play ball on the grass, keeping an eye on their younger brothers and sisters.

This afternoon, many of the workers have come together for a Day of the Dead celebration. The ceremonies are open to the general public. Around 3:30, I arrive at the apartments, just as folks are gathering for a Catholic mass. In the boxlike community room, residents have constructed a lavish altar, blooming with bright marigolds, yellow and orange, leaves, fruits, golden brown corn, candles, sketched faces of saints. A portrait of Cesar Chavez curls next to a colorful painting of the Virgin Mary wrapped in red and purple robes.

Someone has placed a plate of bread on the altar, between a pair of skulls, pink and purple, made of papier-mâché. Sweet comal incense freshens the air.

According to Mexican tradition, the souls of the dead return to the earth for a few hours each year—first the *angelitos*, departed children, then the adults. Families, survivors of the dead, offer each spirit food and drink, meals that pleased them most in life. Afterwards, the living relax together and enjoy an elaborate feast.

Now, a pair of Latinos sets a small wooden table in the center of the room, in front of the altar. The table is rickety and old. Paint flakes from its bottom; cobwebs snarl its legs. An Anglo priest places a silver chalice on it. Except for his sunburn, suggesting long days ministering to fieldworkers, he could pass for a banker, conservative in manner and appearance, fastidious and dapper, with a short, stylish haircut. He spreads his hands and, in soothing Spanish, addresses the crowd, a mixture of fieldhands and onlookers like myself. In the middle of the mass he turns to the workers, huddled closely on dusty folding chairs and, up front, on the cold concrete floor. He asks for testimonials.

A large woman in a wrinkled red dress, whose name I later learn is Ricarda Gonzalez, weeps into a handkerchief. In Spanish, she asks everyone to remember her father and brother on this beautiful Dia de los Muertos. She makes the sign of the cross on her chest, lowers her head, and lapses into silence.

In front of me, a young Mexican mother cradles a baby girl. On the floor, a roly-poly bug has caught the child's attention, and she stretches her fingers to it. I reach to touch her and she smiles. We play "hands" throughout the mass.

Across the room from me, a middle-aged man with coarse, dark skin rubs his face. He grips a white straw cowboy hat, which he removed when the priest entered the room. His thumbs have been unnaturally blunted, pared at the tips, sliced, perhaps, by some sort of machinery. He listens gravely to the priest, nodding from time to time, staring at the floor with a thin, quavering smile on his face. His eyes, moist and red, squint with some deep, clear reservoir of pain. Nervously, he rubs his face with his callused right hand.

"Death is not final," says the priest. "It is, in fact, a new beginning." He pours water into the chalice—to signify refreshment, awakening, rebirth—then he circles the room, offering communion.

The man with the blunted fingers whispers, "Amen." Slowly, he brushes his face, clearing it of dust and tears, separations and leaving, the long sorrows of migration.

Lately, I have been thinking of the dead, particularly the lost ones in Oklahoma, New York, Afghanistan. It is difficult to get clear and unambiguous news from the world's trouble spots, but when I travel through Oregon's fruit fields and see migrant workers, I know the war is not over—not in Yemen, Oklahoma, or California, not anywhere that continues to use up landless men and women, like the workers in Molalla.

Not so long ago, a jury returned a guilty verdict in Timothy McVeigh's trial. A Denver radio station hung a sign outside the courthouse: "Honk if you want to fry the killer." Over twenty-four thousand citizens had pounded their horns by the end of the second day: a nation demanding more dead.

"Does he deserve to die? Yes. Should he be executed? No," Reverend George Back told the *Daily Oklahoman*. His church, St. Paul's Episcopal, two blocks north of Murrah, had been scarred in the bombing. "I don't feel any sympathy for [him]. It's hard not to feel he should . . . suffer. But my feelings aren't consistent with my beliefs."

The Reverend John Maycock of Oklahoma City's Tabernacle Baptist Church said, "My personal feeling is that the death penalty has been applied unfairly" in this country, racially speaking, "but divine forgiveness doesn't necessarily mean a person doesn't have to pay for what they've done. I don't see how anyone could ever justify having the death penalty if Timothy McVeigh is convicted of killing 168 people and doesn't get it."

"Killing the guilty is still wrong," Archbishop Charles Chaput, leader of Colorado's Roman Catholics, insisted. "It does not honor the dead. It does not enrich the living. And while it may satisfy society's anger for a while, it cannot ever release [us] from sorrow . . . Only forgiveness can do that."

After the mass, I step into line behind several fieldworkers outside one of the small gray apartment buildings. Lines have formed all over the Arbor Terrace complex. For days, the women here have been preparing sauces and meats for both the living and the dead, and now they'll feed us all.

The spicy aromas of mole, *pozole* and *ponche, champurrado,* and *arroz* swirl with the smell of incense from the altar. Pork and chicken, shrimp, tamales, refried beans. Cinnamon coffee. Calabaza, a squash and corn dessert.

I squeeze with a crowd into a tiny, hot apartment. On a red-tinted television screen, big-time wrestlers grunt and yell. A painting of the Virgin of Guadeloupe tilts above a brown and yellow hound's-tooth couch.

On the kitchen table, a small altar wreathed in orange marigolds. At its base, offerings of bread and rice, candy bars left over from Halloween. Obviously, this family expects an *angelito* with a powerful sweet tooth. Ricarda Gonzalez, the woman who had wept in the mass, dishes us up generous servings of Oaxaca-style chicken mole and rice. A younger woman pours us all steaming hot cinnamon coffee. We take our plates outside and sit beneath a pale canvas tent, where, later, musicians will play long into the night.

We raise our cups and share a delicate communion with the dead, whose appetites, judging from the offerings, are as hearty and robust as ever.

On October 20, 1933, my grandfather, then a deputy sheriff, witnessed an electrocution at the state prison in McAlester, Oklahoma (where Tom Joad was jailed). Two prisoners, Ted Patton, a white man, and Charlie Dumas, black, were sentenced to die that night. My grandfather's papers don't specify their crimes. "I knew that every legal means had been exhausted in trying to save them," he wrote. "I don't know why I went to see it. Perhaps out of curiosity.

"The Negro was the first to die. He walked rather hastily between two guards. He sat down in the chair; two men began strapping his legs while the Executioner was putting the hood cap and mask over his eyes. When the guards had finished and stepped back, the Executioner made a hurried examination of all the straps, then pressed the switch.

"The only movement on the part of the condemned man was the clenching of his fist in a death grip. The current was on for possibly a minute. A slight slump of the body followed. Three physicians made three examinations of the man's heart before he was pronounced dead. Then a sheet was thrown over the body, the straps were undone, and the dead man was carried out."

The procedure was repeated, quietly and efficiently, for Ted Patton.

Three days later, my grandfather responded publicly to an editorial in the *Daily Oklahoman* by Judge P. L. Galloway of Coalgate, who'd also attended the electrocution, and wrote that he'd "enjoyed it very much."

"To watch men die and enjoy it very much, to call it Justice, a man must be imbibing very freely on Oklahoma's Mountain Dew, draining off his reasoning powers, thinking in terms of mob psychology, forgetting that we are taught 'Thou shalt not kill,' " my grandfather said—a sensibility sharply different from Timothy McVeigh's. "If, instead of enjoying human misery and death, we could listen to each other's thoughts, learn each other's heartaches and pains, know the agonies, and comfort each other. Then the world might truly become an enjoyable place."

"I am pleading for my son's life," said Mildred Frazer, Timothy McVeigh's mother, on the final day of the trial's sentencing phase.

McVeigh's father, William, said he still loved his boy.

Charles Tomlin, who lost his son in the bombing, said he felt sorry for McVeigh's folks. "I'm sure they are wondering what went wrong," he said, "just as *we* are wondering what went wrong."

Now, as I sip my coffee, I watch the workers' faces. Some are laughing and happy, pleased to be eating with family and friends. Others are wistful and sad—like the man in the straw hat. Clearly, plenty has gone wrong in his life. Here he is, far from home, bent and blunted by years of blistering chores, remembering his dead.

Many have fallen, all along the migrant road. Here in the valley, too, hardship—anger, exhaustion, grief—has taken a terrible toll. Two summers ago, Oregon's strawberry growers refused to pay pickers a minimum wage of seventeen cents per pound of berries. At the Morehouse Farm, south of Molalla, Mexican workers went on strike. At the time, most Willamette Valley growers were not willing to pay more than twelve cents per pound.

Bartolome Garcia, one of the strikers, said of his fellow laborers, "I think they're wondering what they're doing here in the United States. Many left their families in Mexico with no money. The only reason they're here is to pick strawberries and [earn a living]." Garcia had left his home in Oaxaca and traveled from California to Oregon, along the old Okie paths. "You can work as hard as you can and still make poor wages," he said. "[The owners] don't notice that you work hard. You're faceless, nameless to them. Maybe if the strawberries go bad, they'll notice."

Each June, I've read, about twenty-four thousand migrant workers are needed to harvest strawberries in Oregon. The average
worker picks about eighty pounds in an hour, earning about $600 a
month, full-time. But then, said Garcia, "I have to pay to live in a
labor contractor's camp. I spend about $400 on food each month,
$50 on second-hand clothes to replace the ones I rip in the fields. I
try to save a little to send home to my parents in Oaxaca.

"What's the most important thing in life?" he asked. "Good work.
Living without fear that you'll be thrown out of work for asking
fair wages."

That year, 1995—the year the Murrah building fell, in part from
a small farmer's fury and disillusionment—the Oregon strawberry
crop came in at close to 55 million pounds. Willamette Valley
growers earned $30 million. Eventually, grudgingly, they agreed to
raise workers' wages to thirteen cents a pound.

As the son of Okies, living now in the West, I know I'm somehow
part of this story—that's why I've come here today, to the Arbor
Terrace. Since America was largely founded on family farming,
we're all part of the fieldworkers' story, whether we know it or not.

"All the old [Okie] pickers are gone now, and the spirit of work is
gone too," a "fruit tramp" told Toby Sonneman, a freelance writer,
for a book called *Fruit Fields in My Blood*, published in 1992. One
year, in an Oregon apple orchard, he said, there weren't enough
trees for two separate crews. The foreman flipped a coin. "Tails, the
whites get it," he said. "Heads, [it's] the Mexicans."

After hearing dozens of similar stories, Sonneman observed:
"Workers are no longer valued for their reliability . . . [And as]
orchards have been gobbled up by subdivisions and condomini-
ums . . . small growers with personal relationships to the workers
are forced to sell out, and agribusiness conglomerates take over."

My grandfather saw the future decades ago. "The plight of the
small farmer reminds me of the story of the wonderful milk cow,"

he said in a speech in Oklahoma City in 1935. "A man owned a wonderful milk cow, and he was always bragging about it to his neighbors. He said she was such a wonderful cow, she gave enough milk to feed the man's seven children, she gave enough milk to be turned into butter for the market, she gave enough to feed two calves, she even suckled herself to keep going. Well, like that wonderful milk cow, today's small farmer has worked himself and the members of his family at no salary, he has depleted the fertility of his soil and sold the products of his farm below what it costs to produce them. Lately, he has thrown the farm itself into the jackpot."

And now, sixty years later, like Terry Nichols and Timothy McVeigh, he's finding other uses for his fertilizer. And in places like Molalla, Oregon, *The Grapes of Wrath* continues.

I finish my chicken mole and poke around the Arbor Terrace, which, though cheap, is safe and clean. Kids in Dallas Cowboy T-shirts play freeze-tag on the freshly mowed grass; women wash plates, cups, pots, and pans with Brillo pads and long, green garden hoses.

The man with damaged hands stands by the altar, rubbing his face. Watching him, I think of a poem by Garcia Lorca, whose agrarian, Spanish blood runs through families here:

Out in the world, no one sleeps. No one, no one.
No one sleeps.
There is a corpse in the farthest graveyard
complaining for three years
because of an arid landscape in his knee;
and a boy who was buried this morning cried so much
they had to call the dogs to quiet him.

The man gazes out the window at clouds moving in, low, over the valley, shrouding Mt. Hood in blue mists. Only twice before have I seen a bond of dignity and sadness this powerful, bold, and emphatic: once in Corinto, Nicaragua, sitting with mothers of heroes and martyrs killed in the war, and again last year in Oklahoma City.

I nod hello. He doesn't notice. He's not used to being noticed.

More words come to mind now, the well-known passage James Agee quoted from the Bible for his book about the dispossessed, nearly sixty years ago, while my grandfather was making speeches about small farmers: "Let us now praise famous men. Some there be which have no memorial, who perished, as though they had never been; and are become as though they had never been born."

A cloud snuffs the sun.

"And their children after them . . ."

The tent music ends. The Day of the Dead has drawn to a close.

"But these were merciful men, whose righteousness hath not been forgotten . . . [Let] their bodies [be] . . . buried in peace; [and] their name[s] liveth for evermore."

Invictus

Four days before Timothy McVeigh was supposed to die, researchers at the New York Medical College in Valhalla announced that
the human heart could grow new muscle cells after a heart attack.
This challenged years of medical dogma that heart damage is irre-
versible. As it turns out, the body has much more "recuperative
power" than we thought, said Dr. Valentin Fuster.

   The story appeared in newspapers beside the latest twists in
McVeigh's case. A month and a half before his scheduled execution
in the federal death-house in Terre Haute, Indiana, he accepted
responsibility for the Murrah bombing, as Paul Heath had told me
he would. "It was my choice, and my control, to hit that building
when it was full," he said. "I have the greatest respect for human
life. My decision to take human life at the Murrah building—I did
not do it for personal gain . . . I did it for the larger good." Speaking
through Lou Michel and Dan Herbeck, two *Buffalo News* reporters,

he went on to explain that, if he seemed insensitive, it was because he was a fine, well-disciplined soldier.

He had received basic training at Fort Benning, Georgia, which once housed the U.S. Army School of the Americas, where men such as Panamanian leader Manuel Noriega reportedly learned torture techniques. McVeigh had shot two Iraqis in the Gulf War. One man's head "just disappeared" when he pulled the trigger. "I saw everything above the shoulders disappear, like in a red mist," he recalled. He came to regret Desert Storm, and it seems clear that he returned to the States traumatized, questioning the cause for which he'd been ordered to kill.

The United States was a bully, he felt now, and needed a dose of its own sour balm.

"I think we brought Tim up right," his father told Lou Michel. "This is something that happened when he went in the service, as far as I can see."

McVeigh swore, "Had I known there was an entire day care center [in the Murrah building] it might have given me pause to switch targets." He called the murdered children "collateral damage"—a phrase that would soon gain grisly new currency, as U.S. bombs began to rain on Afghanistan.

No one in Oklahoma City believes he didn't see the day care center. Evidence suggests he cased the building at least four times; as Paul Heath had pointed out to me, the center's windows, covered with children's drawings, were easily visible from the street where McVeigh left the truck-bomb. "I understand what they felt in Oklahoma City," McVeigh said. "I have no sympathy for them."

The details of his plan differed in certain particulars from the prosecution's trial presentation, and from newspaper reports, but his confession contained no major surprises or revelations. He had parked the truck, then run through the alley behind the Y that Dr. Heath and I had strolled together. "It's over," McVeigh said he thought then and relaxed when he heard the blast.

By finally commenting on all this as callously as he did, he obviously meant to increase the collateral damage in Oklahoma and across the nation.

On April 12, 2001, Attorney General John Ashcroft announced that the execution would be broadcast live on closed-circuit television to the more than two hundred survivors and relatives in Oklahoma City who had asked to watch McVeigh die. "The Oklahoma City survivors may be the largest group of crime victims in our history," Ashcroft said, only months before two hijacked planes smashed into the World Trade Center towers. "The Department of Justice must make special provisions to assist [their] needs."

"I'm going to throw it back in their face. I'm going to demand they televise it nationally," McVeigh claimed, insisting on becoming a martyr for the country's disillusioned souls. "I'm going to say, If you want to make a spectacle of it, I'm going to point out exactly what you are doing."

Before McVeigh, the last public execution in the United States had taken place in 1936 in Owensboro, Kentucky, when twenty thousand people turned out to see Rainey Bethea, a black man, hanged for allegedly raping and killing a white woman. The last federal execution was in March 1963, when Victor Harry Feguer was hanged in Iowa for kidnapping and killing a doctor whose drugs he wanted to steal. Witnesses claimed they still had nightmares about Feguer's neck *cracking* when the rope tightened. Fegeur's last words to his executioners were, "I hope you don't have to go through this again, gentlemen."

"The day they take Timothy McVeigh from his cage for the purpose of killing him is not going to bring [my daughter] back," insisted Bud Welch, father of a bombing victim. "It will not bring peace to me or anyone else in America. God simply did not make us that way, to where we are going to get a feel-good from killing another human being."

Meanwhile, in lockup, McVeigh spent his days looking at skin magazines, watching *Star Trek*, *Seinfeld*, and *The Simpsons* on TV.

"Fuck ABC for [forcing me] to make . . . a decision" between watching the movie *The Unforgiven* or the final episode of *Seinfeld*, he complained to reporter Phil Bacharach.

The America that condemned Timothy McVeigh was truly a Land of Opportunity. Hawkers on the eBay Internet site seized the moment to auction "colorful" McVeigh T-shirts commemorating the "final days of America's worst terrorist." Another Internet entrepreneur, who had made his money from online pornography, hoped to merchandise the execution as a live webcast for $1.95 a pop. The major television networks returned to the Heartland, using Oklahoma City as a stage set for their comely news anchors to carry the "message" of the "survivors and the victims"—as if there *were* a unified message.

Special interest groups also got into the act: PETA demanded that McVeigh's final meal be meat-free (McVeigh wrote the organization, saying that since his time was "short," vegans should instead try to convert his prison mate the Unabomber).

As the death date drew nearer, it was clear that McVeigh wasn't really the story (we all *know* the deluded walk among us). The story—as McVeigh's violence had insisted—was America's character, which would be sorely tested, soon, after the attacks in New York and on the Pentagon.

In newspapers, nestled next to the execution countdowns, various snapshots of the country appeared: a young American missionary and her child had just been killed by Peruvian gunners who, aided by CIA contract employees fighting the "War on Drugs," had mistaken them for coca-runners; faced with exposure by eager journalists, former senator and decorated war hero Bob Kerrey admitted he'd led a raid in Vietnam in which he and his men murdered more than a dozen unarmed women and children; an Oklahoma inquiry revealed that an FBI agent may have misidentified or manufactured evidence in over three thousand cases that had led to convictions; thousands of former *braceros* were suing the federal government for wages they had never received; energy suppliers, including Enron, which would soon collapse in the nation's biggest-ever financial scandal, happily fed off of California's electricity crisis; new evidence suggested that hundreds of black voters in Florida had been illegally disenfranchised in the latest presidential election; and questions lingered as to whether George W. Bush was the rightful occupant of the White House.

Then, on May 11, five days before McVeigh was supposed to die, John Ashcroft announced he was delaying the execution, as the FBI had inexplicably failed to turn over more than three thousand pages of evidence to McVeigh's lawyers. Ashcroft said that, under the Constitution, McVeigh's legal team had a right to review the material and possibly ask for a new trial. The FBI's behavior, Ashcroft said, challenged the integrity of the nation's justice system— an integrity that McVeigh, who must have relished this moment, had been ridiculing all along. This was more than a "lapse" or a "scandal," the *New York Times* concurred; it was a "particularly shocking failure."

At the memorial site, Paul Heath told a reporter, "I'm delighted Mr. Ashcroft knows that the Constitution is more important than my feelings." The *Times* pictured him on the verge of tears, tight-lipped, squinting, more fleshy than when I'd met him five years ago—a sad portrait of exhaustion, frustration, unabated grief.

"I think [McVeigh] is sitting in his jail cell laughing. He's saying, 'I've done it one more time,'" said Calvin Moser, who lost much of his hearing in the bombing.

"I have no time for Tim McVeigh," said Moser's wife, Ginny, "but he continues to invade my life." Just three days earlier, she had picked glass from her husband's head—shards embedded in him since the explosion, which had only now risen to the surface of his flesh.

In Terre Haute, K. B. Patel, owner of the Midtown Motel, complained that the delay would cost him a fortune. Reporters would now cancel their reservations, leaving most of his rooms vacant. A tattoo parlor in town that had sold over three hundred T-shirts with a picture of McVeigh and the words "Die! Die! Die!" swiftly printed up a new edition—the same design, but with the word "Cancelled" stamped across the bottom.

McVeigh asked for a stay of execution, to ensure the "integrity" of the justice system. Judge Richard Matsch denied his motion, citing him as an "instrument of death," and the killing was on again. Media crews hurried back to Terre Haute. Stephen Jones, McVeigh's first lawyer, appeared on television, hawking his book, which suggested his client was just a patsy in a broader conspiracy. New T-shirts were printed by the thousands.

The execution facility, a 2,100-square-foot, brick building surrounded by razor wire in a pasture resembling a baseball field, had never been used. It was shaped like a cross; the gurney on which McVeigh would die occupied a small chamber in the center. The media, McVeigh's witnesses, victim witnesses, and prison officials were all segregated in square cubicles, all of whose windows opened onto the final resting place. The "Chemical Room" sat behind the "Execution Room"—all laid out neatly, no different, really, than an efficient office complex beside any freeway in the country. It was a marvel how well America managed its space.

On the weekend before McVeigh was killed, newscasters wondered about the fantasy world he'd lived in. He'd seen himself as an avenger and a patriot, striking a blow for the nation's underdogs. He'd told his friend Michael Fortier that he was like Luke Skywalker, smashing the Evil Empire. How could he have been so deluded? reporters asked. How could he have seen the world as though it were a comic book?

That Saturday, in movie theaters all across the country, people lined up to see the blockbuster *Pearl Harbor,* a special-effects fantasy that turned an old national tragedy into a patriotic carnival ride. In many theaters, just before the previews of coming attractions, the United States Marines ran an ad showing a young man swinging a sword, destroying a computer-generated fire-monster.

A World War Two Memorial design was approved for the Washington mall, which, in the words of architecture critic Herbert Muschamp, was a "shrine to the idea of not knowing or, more precisely, forgetting" the realities of history. "In the United States, public space is rapidly becoming a subsidiary of the entertainment industry," he mused. "It's [becoming] too expensive to police [sidewalks]. Eventually someone will patrol them with surveillance cameras and market the videos on reality pay TV."

And writing in the *New York Times,* Frank Rich noted that presidential photo opportunities had once been used to "dramatize a president's policies," but the new Bush administration was orchestrating them to "disguise" its real agenda. Each one of the president's public appearances was a tightly scripted fantasy. He would show up in Sequoia or the Everglades, touting conservation, when in fact his policies aggressively eroded public lands. He would show up at a Boys and Girls Club, praising them for promoting the "universal concept of loving a neighbor," though his new federal budget eliminated funding for the clubs. He would appear before a sea of police officers, lauding their bravery, while decreasing the number of cops on the streets. His wife, Laura, would kick off the "Campaign for American Libraries" just one week before W. cut the federal outlay for libraries by $39 million. As Rich put it, "It's now reaching the point that a smiling Bush appearance blessing any cause . . . is tantamount to a visit from the angel of death."

Soon, in prosecuting his war on global terrorism, W. would use the phrase "axis of evil" to describe Iraq, Iran, and North Korea.

In this context, the most remarkable thing about Timothy McVeigh was his naiveté. A good citizen, he had absorbed every image the culture pumped into him, just as politicians and entertainers meant him to do. He lived purely, it seems, in the comic book that America was composing about itself.

On Sunday night, hours before the execution, opponents and supporters of the death penalty gathered in separate parks in Terre Haute. They sang, chanted, waved giant puppets of Jesus and Uncle Sam.

"Timothy McVeigh died with his eyes open," CBS reporter Byron Pitts, a media witness, announced shortly after McVeigh was declared dead at 7:14 A.M. Central Time, Monday, June 11, 2001. At 7:10, as he lay strapped to the gurney, sodium thiopental was pumped into his veins. Witnesses said he closed his eyes briefly, swallowed hard twice, then reopened them; they were glassy and moist. A muscle relaxant, pancuronium bromide, was then administered to his body to collapse his diaphragm and lungs. His lips went white, and his skin began to turn yellow. Finally, he was shot full of potassium chloride, to stop his heart.

He had refused to make a final statement, though he had previously released to the press a handwritten copy of William Ernest Henley's famous poem "Invictus," which says, "My head is bloody but unbowed," and "I am the master of my fate. I am the captain of my soul."

The *New York Times* said, "It is a poem favored by teenagers who are rebelling against their parents."

On-site witnesses said he appeared stoic, calm, resolute. Many of the survivors and victims watching the closed-circuit feed in Oklahoma City swore he looked defiant, hate filled, arrogant. The camera's truth is apparently elusive, but no television reporter noted that.

President Bush said, "This morning, the United States of America carried out the severest sentence for the gravest of crimes. The victims of the Oklahoma City bombing have been given not vengeance, but justice." Many from Oklahoma City expressed relief and satisfaction, while acknowledging a sense of emptiness. "We didn't get anything" from his death, said Paul Howell, who had flown from Oklahoma to Terre Haute to witness the killing. I'm "sad, a little depressed, and tired," said Steve Pruitt, who was injured in the explosion. "Oklahoma City was about revenge, and what we did today was revenge. I feel like today we [as a nation] acted like Timothy McVeigh did six years ago."

Television legal experts failed to distinguish "retribution" from "revenge." They claimed, "The system worked" but were unclear about what the "system" hoped to accomplish here. They admitted that, while in prison, McVeigh was no longer a threat to society. They admitted that statistics were inconclusive regarding the death penalty's ability to deter crime. They admitted that executions were not meant to ease the victims' suffering.

On the Fox News Network, a reporter cautioned a former friend of McVeigh's to "be careful" the moment he expressed a touch of sympathy for the bomber. Sympathy was not the official line. "Justice" was the media's mantra, "closure" the keyword. But amid the well-meaning platitudes, Gloria Chipman, whose husband died in Murrah, confessed to an interviewer, "I'm glad [McVeigh is] dead, and I'm sorry to have to say it. I feel like a horrible person. I'm going to have to do a lot of soul-searching" about all the "anger I have felt for another human being." She hoped God would forgive her.

Ironically, downtown Oklahoma City is thriving now, revitalized by tourists at the bombing site. There's even a gift shop selling commemorative items.

The morning of McVeigh's death, as family members gathered on the memorial's lawn, laying flowers on the empty chairs, police detained a man who was writing with chalk on one of the granite walls, "Government is the problem."

"I don't care how you feel about the subject of capital punishment," news anchor Brian Williams told *usa Today*, "the United

States took a life [this morning] . . . Second to declaring war, this is the most important thing we decide to do as a nation. This is what elections are all about. This is what the Supreme Court is all about. This is the whole ball of wax."

Meanwhile, doctors at the New York Medical College were talking about their future research plans. "We want to use what is in the heart to repair the heart," said Dr. Piero Anversa.

On that same page of the paper, Tim McVeigh frowned.

I am the captain of my soul.

I feel like a horrible person.

What is in the heart?

Heartland

Shakespeare writes in *Lear*, "Expose thyself to feel what wretches feel / That thou may'st . . . show the heavens more just."

I believed that's what I'd tried to do in my migrant travels over the years: to Nicaragua's tortured fields, to Yemen, and lately to the Murrah site in Oklahoma City, down Route 66 and into the Pastures of Plenty. To know my country better, I'd forced myself to face America's toughest facts: self-loathing, violence, unspeakable grief, poverty and uprootings, a history of hardships that connects us all on one level or another. These things weren't going away, and they were things I needed to learn. Oklahoma's recent (and ongoing) suffering had personalized them all for my family and me.

And perhaps because I had been prone to depression in the past, I had come to suspect that, if there's any real justice in the world, it lies somewhere beyond the desire for revenge or personal gain, beyond the cruel uses of migrant labor and lethal injections, beyond the wounds we inflict on one another in private. Perhaps *empathy* is the word. Feeling the planet's sadness. Shouldering a share of its burden.

Expose thyself to feel what wretches feel.

But I wasn't quite done. As keenly as I had felt them, the Murrah deaths, the deaths of old Okies like Grampa Joad, the deaths that are still too common in today's fruit fields, up and down the Americas, remained abstractions for me. It took stumbling against my own mortality—there's no undramatic way to say this—to show me how "just" the heavens may or may not be at any given time.

I was about to visit another kind of Heartland.

By the summer of 1999, my ex-wife, from whom I'd been divorced three years, had reacquainted herself with an old college flame of hers and was planning to move to Memphis, Tennessee, to be with him. I had set aside traveling for a while. I had moved in with a wonderful woman named Margie. We'd bought a house together in Corvallis, Oregon, right across the street from where we both taught.

Martha and I wished each other well and promised to stay in touch. We talked about the value of looking ahead.

For days I'd been ferrying book boxes into the new house and feeling short of breath. All my life I've been asthmatic, so I didn't worry much about being winded. But one day, as I was hauling stuff down a flight of stairs, my chest constricted as though a vast hand had squeezed my heart. I had to stop and sit. After about ten minutes, the tightness eased, my breath returned, and I was able to get back to work.

This happened three or four more times during the next three days, but I chalked it up to asthma, extra strain. Once, I had to hold still after crossing the street to the university campus. Once, the pain startled me from sleep.

One Sunday night Margie and I were making love. "I'm sorry. I have to stop," I told her and rolled to the bed's edge. Inside, my chest felt like bread dough, pounded, flattened, squeezed. Stalks of pain spread, like water in a straw, into my jaw and down my right arm. I hugged a pillow and rocked back and forth, trying to find my breath. My head got light, and I thought I might throw up.

Margie rubbed my back. "Should we go see about this?" she said.

I wasn't thinking straight. "Where would we go?" I asked stupidly.

"I'm going to take you to the emergency room."

By the time we left the house, the pain was draining away. I hit a light switch angrily, knowing this would turn out to be nothing, and I'd feel embarrassed in the E.R., wasting the doctors' time.

On the way to the hospital, Margie had to swerve to miss two young deer who had come out of the hills and were strolling, remarkably, through town. She and I looked at each other as though we'd seen an omen, but of what?

Sure enough, the emergency room doctors told me my EKG was normal. I hadn't had a heart attack, or at most I'd only experienced a slight one. Of course not, I thought. I didn't have a family history of coronary trouble. I'd never had high blood pressure or high cholesterol. I ate well. I didn't drink heavily, and I'd never smoked. Naturally, I was too young and healthy to be a candidate for heart disease.

Still, the doctors didn't like my symptoms. They wanted to keep me flat on my back and hooked to a heart monitor. They gave me nitroglycerin pills to dissolve beneath my tongue. The pills began to give me a headache. Minutes turned into hours, and finally, near midnight, a doctor told me I should stay overnight in the hospital; to definitively rule out heart problems, I should have an angiogram. A doctor would insert a catheter into a main artery in my groin, he explained, snake it all the way up to my heart, inject dye into the arteries there, and study the resulting images for any abnormalities.

For the rest of that night and all of the next day I couldn't eat or drink. I wasn't allowed out of bed; the doctors wanted me still and constantly monitored. My angiogram was scheduled for early Monday evening. I was placed in a room with an old man who had apparently been discovered drunk beside a highway. I overheard his conversations with the doctors. He couldn't remember how he'd wound up in the hospital. He had no friends or relatives in the area, nowhere to go. I gathered he'd suffered extensive liver damage. All day he watched Hitler documentaries at high volume on the History Channel. If I wasn't sick and enervated *before* coming to the hospital, I reasoned, I certainly would be before I got out. I was still upset at having to endure this ordeal, certain that time and money were being wasted in a search for nothing serious.

A chaplain entered our room and asked if we needed anything. I told him no. My roommate rasped, "Yeah, I need to find me a Latin American woman. I lived in Costa Rica for a dozen years, and I like 'em down there, you know what I mean, Padre? Where'm I going to find a Latin woman here?"

"I'm afraid I can't help you with that," the chaplain muttered.

Finally, at around 7:30, I was prepped for my angiogram. The nurses shaved my legs. I'd be given a local anesthetic in the groin, and some drugs to relax me, but I'd be conscious throughout the procedure. My doctor was a native Kansan, and he was immensely pleased to learn that I hailed from Texas by way of Oklahoma—he'd found someone familiar with the plains! "Got a joke for you," he said. "A good ol' boy from the high plains finds himself on the campus of Yale University, and he stops to ask a student, 'Where's the library at?' The Yalie looks at him coolly and says, 'I'll tell you, but you must speak to me in proper King's English. We don't end our sentences with prepositions.' The good ol' boy scratches his head then says, 'Well, all right then, where's the library at, asshole?' "

I laughed politely, distracted by the trays of gleaming instruments next to my gurney.

"Good thing you laughed," the doctor said. "That's from the man who'll be in your heart in a minute."

Loud rock music filled the operating room. One of the anesthesiologists asked me if he should turn it off, and I said, "No. I like it." The sound of a steady beat, which I could feel in my body, was reassuring, like Roy Orbison's old boot-thumping tunes.

The anesthesiologist kidded with his colleagues about knocking off early, about what a long day it had been. "So I'm the only thing between you fellows and a case of beer, is that it?" I said. They liked that a lot and were very friendly to me afterwards. They and the doctor seemed fascinated by the fact that I was a college professor. I got the impression they saw older folks, retirees, in here, usually.

"Are you scared?" the music guy asked.

"Hell yes." Earlier, the doctor had told me one of the minor risks of this procedure was stroke.

"Don't be. It's a cinch. It'll be over before you know it."

Despite the local, I felt a diamondlike sting at the very top of my right leg, near my privates. I was starting to feel a little spacy. Almost immediately the doctor said, "We found your problem, Professor." He wheeled my gurney around so I could see a television screen. On it I was able to watch my heart's rather tidy interior. He pointed out to me a narrow stretch of an otherwise fat-looking artery. It was like staring at Route 66 on a map next to the larger interstates. "There, in the left main," he said. "About 80, 85 percent blockage. There's some blockage in a smaller artery, too. You'll need a double bypass."

I couldn't have been more stunned if he had told me my heart was made of cheese. But I could see for myself the trouble.

The funnyman from the plains leaned over and patted me gently on the shoulder. "You're a very lucky guy," he said. "We're going to fix you up."

During the next twelve hours I didn't have the capacity to absorb what was happening to me. I was groggier from the drugs, now, than I had been during the angiogram. Also, I was starving, but as soon as Margie starting hand-feeding me a sandwich (I still wasn't allowed to sit up) I got nauseous. Hitler's hateful voice kept sailing through my head.

The doctor told me, "If we hadn't caught this now, chances are you'd have been in the classroom sometime this fall, and you would have just keeled over. That would have been the end."

He told Margie, "You're the girlfriend? Good thing you broke his heart." I didn't follow his meaning, but somehow Margie understood: he was glad she'd talked me into coming into the emergency room.

Ninety-seven percent of patients undergoing bypass surgery survive it, he assured me. A wonderfully high statistic, but not high enough as far as I was concerned.

Sometime in the middle of the night, a pair of nurses arrived and washed me in cool water, head to toe. Luxurious. Heaven and its angels. I was still groggy enough to think I actually *might* have passed over already.

They shaved off the mustache I'd worn since 1972; the surgeons wanted a clear field for all the tubes they were going to tape to my mouth.

The last thing I remember before waking, post-op, is being wheeled down a chilly hallway. I heard someone tell Margie, "You can get a beeper at the nurses' station. We'll beep you at various points during the surgery, to let you know how he's doing." I looked up at Margie's brave, sweet face: for all I knew, the last thing I'd ever see.

Many times I'd imagined standing inside the Murrah building, just as the walls began to collapse. I'd read and reread the Joads' journey down 66, imagining myself in the back of their old jalopy, like the elders, whose lives would leak away before they could witness the Promised Land.

And once, in Ocotal, Nicaragua, I thought I was going to die, as mortar shells fell in the mountains nearby. When the blasts began, I was peeing in a grungy motel john, staring out the window at a Red Cross ambulance. My ears popped. My bladder blazed. I couldn't stop it. I'm going to die holding my dick, I thought. And: my tax dollars have paid for this.

On the eve of my surgery, a doctor told me my artery damage had probably been building for about twenty years. I thought of my travels: of my shortness of breath in California's Central Valley, outside Weedpatch Camp. I thought of my weariness, my windedness, on a road running past a series of cow barns in Corvallis, where I often went for evening walks. All that time I had been dying.

Which is true of us all, of course. Already, our bodies carry our possible deaths, but most of us go through most of our lives unaware of this until the last minute, broadly speaking. I had gotten a peek at the thing that was going to kill me this year. Throughout my marriage and divorce, my depressions and migrations, death had been living inside me.

These were my thoughts as I rolled down the chilly hospital hallway toward the operating room. The doctors hadn't volunteered details about the surgery. Weeks later, a colleague of mine quipped, "So. Technically, you were dead, right?" and, startled, I began to desire the specifics of what I'd experienced. I started to read and ask questions.

The surgery lasted four hours, I was told. The surgeons split my breastbone, then hooked me to a machine that breathed and pumped blood for me while they stopped my heart. My colleague said the heart is packed in ice during these procedures; all I learned for sure was that my heart was cooled, somehow, to about twenty-eight degrees. Afterwards, it was either warmed back up or shocked into rhythm again ("Ooby Dooby"). (Doctors, I learned, love the passive voice.)

The surgeons rerouted my left mammary artery and "harvested" a saphenous vein from my right leg, suturing it to the aorta, to bypass the blockages.

This kind of surgery has only been performed since 1962. At home later, during my recovery, on a website entitled "Pioneers of

Heart Surgery," I learned that "for most of history, the human heart has been regarded as a forbidden organ too delicate to tamper with." Dwight Harken, a young U.S. Army surgeon in World War II, was one of the first men to try emergency heart procedures. "All of his first subjects died," his profile states flatly.

I woke but didn't wake. I was vaguely aware of Margie's voice—I think it was Margie's voice—saying, "You made it." In the next few days I'd hear this phrase several more times, which made me wonder if the 97 percent survival rate wasn't terribly reassuring to the medical staff, either. They all seemed happily surprised that I'd pulled through.

Now, I had an inkling of what it felt like to be a survivor. Elation. Guilt, as in, *What did I do to bring this on?* The suddenness and unbelievability of it all. Every emotional state the Murrah survivors had told me about.

I was a swimming pool of pain. Pain lapping, swirling, eddying clear through every limb. Huge plastic tubes were taped to my mouth and jammed into my throat. I kept gagging on them, unable to cough. A nurse told me—I barely took it in—"You're not breathing on your own. The machine is breathing for you. The doctors had to collapse your lungs during the surgery. Gradually, as the day goes on, we'll turn the machine down and you'll start breathing for yourself. We'll be very careful, given your asthma."

Now, all I recall of that day is a series of voices shocking me awake each time I tried to sleep. Apparently my breath got too shallow when I began to doze off, so the nurses kept shouting, "Tracy! Wake up! Take a deep breath!" For the next three days, even once I was off the machine, I was afraid to fall asleep. I'd rouse myself just as I was about to rest, still hearing those sudden warning voices. Even now I'm uneasy drifting off, afraid I won't wake again.

Mercifully, after one night in ICU, I was placed in a private room. No more Hitler. I had no appetite and craved only ice chips. But I was on a fluid restriction—doctors feared a buildup in my chest—so my lips and throat stayed parched most of the time. ivs stuck both arms; pacer wires and a fat yellow tube pierced my chest, draining fluid from my body into a plastic container. Two smaller tubes plugged my neck. I felt like Frankenstein's monster.

A friend lent me his Walkman and some headphones, a cd of Carlos Nakai's Native American flute music. Each night my terror of sleep was distracted, if not soothed, by Nakai's soaring southwestern rhythms; I imagined myself floating over purple mesas on a breeze, through the poor, battered lands of the Dust Bowl, which I ached for and loved.

At home, just getting out of bed and walking around a room wore me out. I couldn't shower on my own. Margie had to help me undress, sit inside the shower stall. Then she washed me carefully, gently soaping the incisions in my chest and leg. I worried that I was no longer attractive to her, all sliced up, and she said, "Shhh." Everything I'd once considered private now seemed very public. Since the hospital, my body had felt constantly exposed (those drafty gowns!)—the *inside* of my body felt exposed, along with my weakness, my vulnerability, my finite number of days on this earth.

On my bruised skin, the shower water sped my heart rate some; I could feel the pulse in my shoulder and neck. Stronger than ever, my heart, or so the doctors said, but tracking my pulse was like charting my breaths or my regular swallowing—self-consciousness can turn a natural process into labor. Each heartbeat was a miracle, a gift, but I also feared each one might be my last. Just a few weeks ago, juiced with health, I'd thought dying seemed impossible. Now, *not* dying—I mean, right away—seemed unavoidable.

I fell back in bed, exhausted by the shower.

I watched a lot of videos. I did a lot of reading. *Amazing Heart Facts*:

—Put your hand on your heart. Did you place your hand on the left side of your chest? Many people do, but the heart is actually located almost in the center of the chest, between the lungs. It's tipped slightly so that a part of it sticks out and taps against the left side of the chest, which is what makes it seem as though it is located there.

—Hold out your hand and make a fist. If you're a kid, your heart is about the same size as your fist, and if you're an adult, it's about the same size as two fists.

—Give a tennis ball a good hard squeeze. You're using about the same amount of force your heart uses to pump blood to the body.

—Your heart beats about 100,000 times in one day and 35 million times in a year. During an average lifetime—

but what the hell is an average lifetime, I wondered now—the human heart will beat more than 2.5 billion times.

I read that plans had been made to replace the Alfred P. Murrah building in Oklahoma City with a new federal complex—"among the most daunting architecture commissions in the country," said the *New York Times*. The new building, slated for completion in 2002, will stand just one block from the memorial park now being built on the old Murrah site. "The building is about the future," Carol Ross Barney, the design architect, was quoted as saying. The article concluded, "Her hope is that someday people in Oklahoma City will look at this building and not think of what made it necessary."

One of the worst moments in the hospital occurred when a nurse showed me a video instructing me how my home recovery would go. Six to eight weeks would pass, the narrator suggested, before I could do much of anything. On the screen, doddering old men in house slippers shuffled around grim rooms and seemed inordinately pleased with themselves whenever they managed to fold a pair of socks.

My god, this is what I've become, I thought.

My breath came hard and my head got light. My stomach lurched. The nurse took my blood pressure, fed me calming medications. "Just don't show me any more videos," I told her.

Perhaps with that little lesson in mind, I willed myself quickly into small activities at home and seemed to improve, physically, faster than I'd been led to expect.

Margie walked with me out by the cow barns, just a few yards at first, but each day I gained more strength and went a little farther. I remembered how good I'd felt here in the past, watching ag students from the college feed cattle, a simple but profound act of sustaining life.

The air was warm, now, late in the summer, with evening sun, and smelled of wheat.

One evening the road's covered bridge, about half a mile down, came into view—I'd made it that far. Margie gripped my arm. Breathing was hard. "What do you think?" she asked.

"Let's do it."

Slow, small steps. One tiny breath at a time. But soon I was standing on the bridge's solid wood, over Oak Creek, listening to water lap the stones below. Shadows furrowed dirt in the fields; red-headed nuthatches buzzed golden trees.

"The world was beautiful, just to give us pleasure," Margie said, a quote she remembered from the great Russian storyteller Isaac Babel.

As we walked back up the road I kept repeating Babel's sentence to myself. Swallows dodged hawks in the sky. Cows watched us, casually, with what appeared to be genuine curiosity.

One day Martha came to visit me in the new house, the house I shared with Margie. "You've lost a lot of weight," she said. At first she didn't realize that my mustache was gone, though she'd never seen me without it.

We talked about my recovery, and the shock of it all. We talked about her upcoming move to Memphis and the plans she'd made with her new man. They were going to be married.

Margie left us alone, retreating to her study upstairs.

"I hope you have a happy life," Martha told me.

"I hope you do, too. I'm sorry we had to go through the troubles we did to be sitting here today, wishing each other well."

"I'm sorry, too."

The exchange was like an eerie, off-kilter echo of our wedding vows.

She got up from her chair, walked over, and hugged me gingerly. We both began to cry. The crying was deep and long, not a brief storm, but a small fragment of something large and permanent. I knew, I felt, that—despite her new life—Martha would cry again, many times, for the life she and I had lost together, and so would I, in spite of my good life with Margie. I had been spared so I could feel this sadness, and I was glad.

Nearly a month had passed since Margie and I had tried to make love and my chest pains had stopped us. Now, though I longed for them, I feared her touch, her lips, her sweet skin. I was weak and bruised and sore. My breastbone was broken. My heart was stitched together.

Could it survive a little lovemaking?

Margie moved cautiously above me, her hair tracing my face. Outside our window, a beautiful Rose of Sharon bush was blooming, with bright purple flowers. I tried to relax my shoulders, to concentrate on one breath at a time, and soon I experienced the old sensations that meant I really was alive, that I carried life inside me, restless for release. We kissed. I felt my heart stir, my body twitch. Slowly, more slowly than I'd ever done anything before, I surrendered to whatever was going to take me, pleasure or death, or both. When I opened my eyes, grateful tears moved inside them.

Typed into one of my medical reports (I happened to see it one afternoon in my doctor's office) is the line: "Absence of risk factors."

Which is another way of saying, I suppose, "Anything at all can be a risk. Who knows?"

Back on the path past the cow barns, I told Margie I'd been thinking about the Babel quote.

"What makes it a great line," I said, "is the past tense. 'The world *was* beautiful.'"

"You mean, like it's over?"

"Exactly."

"You *would* say that." She liked to try to tease me if she thought she heard even a drop of depression in my voice.

"No, it's not morbid," I said. "It's wistful. Elegiac. Like the loss of spring."

"I know."

And she *did* know. Together, we'd faced the possibility of the loss of spring, just as we were getting started.

But we were lucky. We knew how wretches felt, but my heart didn't blow up or blow away. Not this time. We'd been given a gift of foresight: we knew—*really* knew, in our bodies, the deepest source of knowledge—that anything could happen, anytime. And would. We knew death was waiting, but not today.

Today we were here together, holding hands, feeling the sadness of the world's pleasures.

PROLOGUE: LIGHT

bright hooves sunk in black nightgrass: Dorianne Laux, "Neon Horses,"
   in *Smoke* (Rochester NY: BOA Editions, 2000), 61.

OOBY DOOBY

let this song be a warning: Merle Haggard, "The Fightin' Side of Me"
   (Nashville: Tree Publishing Company, Inc.—CBS Music Group,
   1969).

hungry eyes: Merle Haggard, "Hungry Eyes" (Nashville: Tree Publishing Company, Inc.—CBS Music Group, 1969).

before there was a [public] Merle; bombs aflying: Iris Dement, "No
   Time To Cry" (Nashville: Songs of Iris [Curb Records], 1993).

We don't smoke marijuana: Merle Haggard and E. Burris, "Okie from
   Muskogee" (Nashville: Tree Publishing Company, Inc.—CBS Music
   Group, 1969).

stop the wrong we're doing: Merle Haggard and Terry Hardesty,

"Winds of Change" (Nashville: Sony/ATV Songs, LLC d/b/c, Tree Publishing Company, Inc./Sierra Mountain Music [ATV], 1996).

ORATORY

Human sentiments and speeches: Edmund Wilson, *The Boys in the Back Room* (San Francisco: Colt Press, 1941), 50.

History erupts and boils: Ralph Ellison, *Juneteenth* (New York: Random House, 1999), 15.

with the development of conscious, articulate citizens; individual's imagination; On the level of conscious culture; search for identity: John F. Callahan, ed., *The Collected Essays of Ralph Ellison* (New York: Modern Library, 1995), 199, 50–51, 197.

accustom[ed] themselves: Edward Bellamy, *Looking Backward* (1888; reprint, New York: Dover, 1996).

NOTHING

I placed a jar in Tennessee: Wallace Stevens, "Anecdote of a Jar," in *The Collected Poems of Wallace Stevens* (New York: Knopf, 1975), 76.

OKIES ON MARS

One minute it was: Ray Bradbury, *The Martian Chronicles* (New York: Bantam, 1967), 1.

Bradbury's Martian Chronicles: Mike Davis, *City of Quartz* (New York: Vintage, 1992), 42.

greatest shortcoming of futurologists: Michael Prowse, *Financial Times* (London), January 6, 2001, first edition, 22.

Sputnik was my lucky star: David Beers, *Blue Sky Dream* (New York: Doubleday, 1996), 17.

HIGH SKIES

It is in the soil of Midland: Nicholas D. Kristof, "Values Grown in the Conservative Soil of West Texas," *New York Times*, May 21, 2000, 1, 20.

desert stillness: Bill Minutaglio, *First Son: George W. Bush and the Bush Family Dynasty* (New York: Times Books, 1999), 39.

Midland struck me as weird: Susan Orlean, "Letter from Texas: A Place Called Midland," *New Yorker*, October 16 and 23, 2000, 128–44.

"nervous" oil men: Larry McMurtry, "A Handful of Roses," in *In a Narrow Grave: Essays on Texas* (New York: Simon & Schuster, 1968), 122.

billowy ocean of land: A. C. Greene, *A Personal Country* (College Station: Texas A&M University Press, 1979), 3, 18.

this gaping land; The highs of the boom years: Buzz Bissinger, *Friday Night Lights: A Town, a Team, and a Dream* (New York: Harper Perennial, 1991), 25, 29.

throws a man face to face with nature: John Howard Griffin, *Land of the High Sky* (Midland TX: First National Bank of Midland, 1959), vii.

From the vantage point of middle age: Jim Auchmutey, "The Boy on the Front Row," *Atlanta Journal and Constitution*, December 8, 2001, 1F.

Midland, impatient with ideas: *New York Times*, May 21, 2000, 20.

EXILED IN LENTS

For background information, I drew on Robert Clark, *River of the West: A Chronicle of the Columbia*; Christina Ernome, *Voices of Portland*; and Manley Maben, *Vanport*.

RILEY

when the world flames a bit; [The gift] . . . seeks: Lewis Hyde, *The Gift* (New York: Vintage, 1983), 20, 24.

Nearly everything I have: John Steinbeck, *East of Eden* (New York: Viking, 1952), dedication page.

RESTITUTION

We had lots of jokes: Laurie Winslow, "Blood Puddles outside Building," *Tulsaworld.com* (February 8, 2000).

government at all levels: Tulsa Race Riot Commission, preliminary report submitted to Governor Frank Keating of Oklahoma on February 7, 2000.

People are going to say: Randly Krehbiel, "Panel Recommends Race Riot Reparations," *Tulsaworld.com* (November 23, 1999).

Kinney, is the world on fire?: Brent Staples, "Unearthing a Riot," *New York Times Magazine*, December 19, 1999, 64; Buck Wolf, "Unearthing Ugly History," *ABCnews.com* (1999).

There was a long tumultuous shouting: Edgar Allan Poe, "The Fall of the House of Usher," in *The Complete Stories of Edgar Allan Poe* (Garden City NY: Doubleday, 1966), 1169.

AFTER MURRAH

One of the most interesting Internet sites on the Oklahoma City bombing, providing compelling evidence of Timothy McVeigh's connection with Elohim City, a right-wing religious compound near Tulsa, Oklahoma, as well as detailed speculations about whether or not government agencies knew of the bombing plot before it occurred, is "The John Doe Times" at *www.constitution.org/okc/jdt*.

a war . . . that we may "have already lost": John Edgar Wideman, "Whose War: The Color of Terror," *Harper's*, March 2002, 37.

I always knew where I came from: Roberta Spear, "Some Voices," in *The Pilgrim among Us* (Wesleyan CT: Wesleyan University Press, 1991).

One tends to persist unquestioningly: Mitchell Smolkin, *Understanding Pain: Interpretations and Philosophy* (Malabar FL: Krieger, 1989), 1.

Pain engulfs: Elaine Scarry, *The Body in Pain* (New York: Oxford University Press, 1985), 56.

The plate glass windows: Andrew Macdonald [William Pierce], *The Turner Diaries* (Washington DC: National Alliance, 1980).

astonishment, reverence [and] wonder: Terrence Des Press, "Terror and the Sublime," in *Writing into the World, Essays 1973–1987* (New York: Viking, 1991), 162.

There is a crime here: John Steinbeck, *The Grapes of Wrath* (New York: Bantam, 1966), 311.

COUSINS

Each year, traumatic brain injury: JAMA: *The Journal of the American Medical Association* 276:5 (1996): 382.

It was a Common Night: Emily Dickinson, "Poem #1100," in *The Complete Poems of Emily Dickinson*, ed. Thomas H. Johnson (Boston: Little, Brown, 1960), 496.

CROSSED OVER

we really don't have to go into all that: Douglas Martin, "Charles Johnson, 76, Proponent of Flat Earth" (obituary), *New York Times*, March 25, 2001, 25.

In March, 1986, the Houston Chronicle: Beverly Lowry, *Crossed Over: A Murder, A Memoir* (New York: Knopf, 1992), 12–13.

man . . . is "burdened": Paul Ricoeur, "Original Sin: A Study in Meaning," in *The Conflict of Interpretations: Essays in Hermeneutics*, ed. Don Ihde (Evanston IL: Northwestern University Press, 1974), 284.

shock is what characterizes: Beatriz Colomina, *Privacy and Publicity: Modern Architecture as Mass Media* (Cambridge: MIT Press, 1994), 72.

IRRECONCILED

Transcripts from the trials of Timothy McVeigh and Terry Nichols were recorded by Paul Zuckerman and are available over the Internet (at various sites, including Court TV and the *Daily Oklahoman*) or from Paul Zuckerman, 1929 Stout Street, P.O. Box 3563, Denver CO 80294.

Where were the greenhouses going: Theodore Roethke, "Big Wind," in *The Collected Poems of Theodore Roethke* (New York: Doubleday, 1961), 41.

THE PASTURES OF PLENTY

Woody Guthrie's song lyrics are quoted from *Pastures of Plenty: A Self-Portrait*, ed. Dave Marsh and Harold Levanthal (New York: Harper Collins, 1990).

I made a little speech: Robert Clark, *River of the West: A Chronicle of the Columbia* (New York: Picador USA, 1997), 277.

The clouds came in; I knowed Purty Boy: John Steinbeck, *The Grapes of Wrath* (New York: Bantam, 1966), 385, 327.

AMARILLO

What's a sonic boom among friends?: My own observations of Amarillo have been supplemented with details from A. G. Mojtabai, *Blessed Assurance* (Boston: Houghton Mifflin, 1986).

As the last echoes: *Fodor's Travel Guide, Texas* (New York: McKay, 1974).

THE MOTHER ROAD

I bequeath myself: Walt Whitman, "Song of Myself" (sec. 52), in *Leaves of Grass* (London: Paddington, 1970), 42.

In 1926, when the highway was born: Michael Wallis, *Route 66: The Mother Road* (New York: St. Martin's, 1990), 2–3.

66 is the path: John Steinbeck, *The Grapes of Wrath* (New York: Bantam, 1966), 103.

equal to the combined assets: Osha Gray Davidson, *Broken Heartland: The Rise of America's Rural Ghetto* (New York: Anchor, 1990), 17.

whose plenitude is underwritten: Victor Hansen, *Fields without Dreams: Defending the Agrarian Idea* (New York: Free Press, 1996), 76.

I didn't see no fighting: T. Lindsay Baker and Julie P. Baker, eds., *The WPA Oklahoma Slave Narratives* (Norman: University of Oklahoma Press, 1991), 381–84.

Stripped of its green cloak: Betty Fussel, *The Story of Corn* (New York: Knopf, 1992), 24–26.

The history of the United States: Larry Pratt, quoted in Kenneth Stern, *A Force upon the Plain* (New York: Simon & Schuster, 1996), 117.

Come back, Woody Guthrie: Steve Earle, "Christmas in Washington" (Nashville: South Nashville Music/WB Music Corp. [ASCAP], 1997).

gestures and elements of style: Ralph Ellison, "Going to the Territory," in *The Collected Essays of Ralph Ellison*, ed. John F. Callahan (New York: Modern Library, 1995), 596.

WEEDPATCH

At first the . . . earth: John Steinbeck, *The Grapes of Wrath* (New York: Bantam, 1966), 385–86.

[The countryside's] got ridges: Robert Clark, *River of the West: A Chronicle of the Columbia* (New York: Picador USA, 1997), 273.

There were few lights; The whole camp buzzed: Steinbeck, *Grapes*, 253, 256.

not much to see: Roxanne Dunbar-Ortiz, *Red Dirt: Growing Up Okie* (London: Verso, 1997), 223.

A town that loses its children; In my lifetime something terrible happened: Russell Banks, *The Sweet Hereafter* (New York: Harper Collins, 1991), 78, 99.

BAKERSFIELD

I'll be everywhere: John Steinbeck, *The Grapes of Wrath* (New York: Bantam, 1966), 572.

The migrant people, scuttling for work: Steinbeck, *Grapes of Wrath*, 1966), 284.

Tonight, your memory found me: Merle Haggard, "The Bottle Let Me Down" (Nashville: Tree Publishing Company, Inc.—CBS Music Group, 1966).

I take a lot of pride: Merle Haggard, "I Take a Lot of Pride in What I Am" (Nashville: Tree Publishing Company, Inc.—CBS Music Group, 1969).

HEALTH SEEKERS

most usual to sleep out in the open air; The climate of Texas: Billy M. Jones, *Health Seekers in the Southwest, 1817–1900* (Norman: University of Oklahoma Press, 1967), 57–62.

Valley Fever: Julie Cart, "Rapidly Growing Phoenix Finds Dust Unsettling," *Los Angeles Times*, September 7, 1999, A1.

Everybody who lives here has a health problem: Julie Cart, "Rapid Growth Leaves Phoenix in the Dust," *Sunday Oregonian*, September 12, 1999, A24.

YEMEN

Explosivija za Oklahomu: Nick Fielding, "Oklahoma Bomb Plans Found in Kabul," *Ottawa Citizen*, November 18, 2001, A7.

Timothy McVeigh and his collaborators: Edward Rothstein, "Exploring the Flaws in the Notion of the 'Root Causes of Terror,'" *New York Times*, November 17, 2001, A17.

Why was this not done for Timothy McVeigh?: Bronwen Maddox, "America Way Out of Order," *Times* (London), November 20, 2001, posted on *www.Lexis-Nexis.com*.

fight in Afghanistan: Yaroslav Trofimov, "At Yemeni Honey Emporium the U.S. Calls a Terrorist Front, Derision and Anger," *Wall Street Journal*, October 26, 2001, A12.

THE DAY OF THE DEAD

Quotes by religious leaders on the death penalty are from various Associated Press reports filed on June 7, 1997. Statements by McVeigh's parents and Charles Tomlin were reported by the Associated Press on June 11, 1997.

I think they're wondering what they're doing: Kate Taylor, "Berry Pickers Want More Money, Respect," *Oregonian* (Portland), June 9, 1995.

Out in the world: Federico Garcia Lorca, "Sleepless City (Brooklyn Bridge Nocturne)" in *Poet in New York*, trans. Greg Simon (New York: Noonday, 1988), 67.

INVICTUS

All McVeigh quotes are from Lou Michel and Dan Herbeck, *American Terrorist: Timothy McVeigh and the Oklahoma City Bombing* (New York: ReganBooks, 2001).

"lapse" or a "scandal": David Johnston, "Citing FBI Lapses, Ashcroft Delays McVeigh Execution," *New York Times*, May 11, 2001, A1.

shrine to the idea of not knowing: Herbert Muschamp, "An Appraisal: New War Memorial Is Shrine to Sentiment," *New York Times*, June 7, 2001, A1.

dramatize a president's policies: Frank Rich, "The Backslap Backlash," *New York Times*, June 9, 2001, A27.

It is a poem: Rick Bragg, "The McVeigh Execution: The Overview," *New York Times*, June 12, 2001, A1.

I don't care how you feel about the subject of capital punishment: Peter Johnson, "McVeigh Story Tough for Media to Cover," *USA Today*, June 12, 2001, 4D.

EPILOGUE: HEARTLAND

Expose thyself to feel what wretches feel: William Shakespeare, "The Tragedy of King Lear," in *The Riverside Shakespeare* (Boston: Houghton Mifflin, 1974), 1255.

among the most daunting architecture commissions: Cheryl Kent, "A Safer Federal Building for Oklahoma City," *New York Times*, August 22, 1999, sec. 2, 34.

SELECTED BIBLIOGRAPHY

Agee, James, and Walker Evans. *Let Us Now Praise Famous Men.*
    Boston: Houghton Mifflin, 1988.

Aho, James A. *The Politics of Righteousness: Idaho Christian Patriot-
    ism.* Seattle: University of Washington Press, 1996.

Bernard, Richard, and Bradly P. Rice, eds. *Sunbelt Cities: Politics and
    Growth since World War II.* Austin: University of Texas Press,
    1983.

Byrd, Bobby, and Susannah Byrd, eds. *The Late Great Mexican Bor-
    der.* El Paso TX: Cinco Puntos, 1996.

Clark, Robert. *River of the West: A Chronicle of the Columbia.* New
    York: Picador USA, 1997.

Cohen, David, ed. *Requiem for the Heartland: The Oklahoma City
    Bombing.* San Francisco: Collins, 1995.

Colomina, Beatriz. *Privacy and Publicity: Modern Architecture as
    Mass Media.* Cambridge: MIT Press, 1994.

Davidson, Osha Gray. *Broken Heartland: The Rise of America's Rural
    Ghetto.* New York: Anchor, 1990.

Dees, Morris. *Gathering Storm: America's Militia Threat.* New York: Harper Collins, 1996.

Dunbar-Ortiz, Roxanne. *Red Dirt: Growing Up Okie.* London: Verso, 1997.

Dyer, Joel. *Harvest of Rage: Why Oklahoma City Is Only the Beginning.* Boulder CO: Westview, 1997.

Callahan, John F., ed. *The Collected Essays of Ralph Ellison.* New York: Modern Library, 1995.

Ernome, Christina. *Voices of Portland.* Portland OR: Neighborhood History Project, 1976.

Evans-Pritchard, Ambrose. *The Secret Life of Bill Clinton: The Unreported Stories.* Washington DC: Regnery, 1997.

Gamboa, Erasmo, and Carolyn M. Buan, eds. *Nosotros: The Hispanic People of Oregon.* Portland: Oregon Council for the Humanities, 1995.

Gregory, James N. *American Exodus: The Dust Bowl Migration and Okie Culture in California.* New York: Oxford University Press, 1981.

Hamm, Mark S. *Apocalypse in Oklahoma: Waco and Ruby Ridge Revenged.* Boston: Northeastern University Press, 1997.

Hansen, Jon. *Oklahoma Rescue.* New York: Ballantine, 1995.

Haslam, Gerald. *The Other California: The Great Central Valley in Life and Letters.* Reno: University of Nevada Press, 1994.

Hodges, Donald C. *Intellectual Foundations of the Nicaraguan Revolution.* Austin: University of Texas Press, 1986.

Hoffman, David. *The Oklahoma City Bombing and the Politics of Terror.* Venice CA: Feral House, 1998.

Houston, James D. *California: Searching for the Golden State.* New York: Knopf, 1982.

Irving, Clive, ed. *In Their Name: Oklahoma City—the Official Commemorative Volume.* New York: Random House, 1995.

Jones, Billy M. *Health Seekers in the Southwest, 1817–1900.* Norman: University of Oklahoma Press, 1967.

Klein, Joe. *Woody Guthrie: A Life.* New York: Knopf, 1980.

Maben, Manley. *Vanport*. Portland: Oregon Historical Society Press, 1984.

Macdonald, Andrew [William Pierce]. *The Turner Diaries*. Washington DC: National Alliance, 1980.

Maharidge, Dale, and Michael Williamson. *And Their Children after Them*. New York: Pantheon, 1990.

——. *Journey to Nowhere: The Saga of the New Underclass*. New York: Hyperion, 1996.

Michel, Lou, and Dan Herbeck. *American Terrorist: Timothy McVeigh and the Oklahoma City Bombing*. New York: ReganBooks, 2001.

Mojtabai, A. G. *Blessed Assurance*. Boston: Houghton Mifflin, 1986.

Morgan, Dan. *Rising in the West*. New York: Knopf, 1992.

Myers, Paul, and Jim Ross, eds. *We Will Never Forget*. Austin TX: Eakins, 1996.

——. *Dear Oklahoma City, Get Well Soon: America's Children Reach Out to the People of Oklahoma*. New York: Walker & Company, 1996.

Padilla, Lana. *By Blood Betrayed: My Life with Terry Nichols and Timothy McVeigh*. New York: HarperPaperbacks, 1995.

Pilkington, Tom, and Craig Clifford, eds. *Range Wars: Heated Debates, Sober Reflections, and Other Assessments of Texas Writing*. Dallas: Southern Methodist University Press, 1989.

Reavis, Dick J. *The Ashes of Waco: An Investigation*. New York: Simon & Schuster, 1995.

Rittenhouse, Jack D. *A Guidebook to Highway 66*. Albuquerque: University of New Mexico Press, 1984.

Sanger, S. I., ed. *Working on the Bomb: An Oral History of World War II Hanford*. Portland OR: Continuing Education Press, 1995.

Schlosser, Eric. *Fast Food Nation*. New York: Houghton Mifflin, 2001.

Serrano, Richard A. *One of Ours: Timothy McVeigh and the Oklahoma City Bombing*. New York: Norton, 1998.

Smallwood, James. *Urban Builder: The Life of Stanley Draper*. Norman: University of Oklahoma Press, 1972.

Sonneman, Toby F. *Fruit Fields in My Blood: Okie Migrants in the West*. Moscow: University of Idaho Press, 1992.

Steinbeck, John. *The Grapes of Wrath*. New York: Bantam, 1966.

——. *The Harvest Gypsies*. Berkeley CA: Heyday Books, 1988.

——. *Working Days: The Journal of* The Grapes of Wrath, *1938–1941*. Ed. Robert Demott. New York: Viking, 1984.

Stern, Kenneth. *A Force upon the Plain: The American Militia Movement and the Politics of Hate*. New York: Simon & Schuster, 1996.

Stickney, Brandon M. *All-American Monster: The Unauthorized Biography of Timothy McVeigh*. Amherst NY: Prometheus, 1996.

Wallis, Michael. *Route 66: The Mother Road*. New York: St. Martin's, 1990.

Walter, Jess. *Every Knee Shall Bow: The Truth and Tragedy of Ruby Ridge and the Randy Weaver Family*. New York: HarperPaperbacks, 1995.

Warren, Donald. *Radio Priest: Charles Coughlin, the Father of Hate Radio*. New York: Free Press, 1996.

Worster, Donald. *Dust Bowl: The Southern Plains in the 1930s*. New York: Oxford University Press, 1979.

Wright, Stuart A., ed. *Armageddon in Waco: Critical Perspectives on the Branch Davidian Conflict*. Chicago: University of Chicago Press, 1995.

Yogi, Stan, ed. *Highway 99: A Literary Journey through California's Great Central Valley*. Berkeley CA: Heyday Books, 1991.